BIG VAPE

BIG VAPE

THE INCENDIARY RISE OF JUUL

JAMIE DUCHARME

HOLT

HENRY HOLT AND COMPANY

NEW YORK

Henry Holt and Company
Publishers since 1866
120 Broadway
New York, New York 10271
www.henryholt.com

Henry Holt® and 🅗 ® are registered trademarks of Macmillan Publishing Group, LLC.

Library of Congress Cataloging-in-Publication Data

Names: Ducharme, Jamie, author.
Title: Big vape : the incendiary rise of Juul / Jamie Ducharme.
Description: First edition. | New York, New York : Henry Holt and
  Company, 2021. | Includes bibliographical references.
Identifiers: LCCN 2021002301 (print) | LCCN 2021002302 (ebook) |
  ISBN 9781250777539 (hardcover) | ISBN 9781250777546 (ebook)
Subjects: MESH: JUUL Labs. | Vaping | Electronic Nicotine Delivery
  Systems—history | Tobacco Industry—history | History, 21st Century |
  United States
Classification: LCC HD9130.5 (print) | LCC HD9130.5 (ebook) |
  NLM WM 295 | DDC 338.1/7371—dc23
LC record available at https://lccn.loc.gov/2021002301
LC ebook record available at https://lccn.loc.gov/2021002302

Our books may be purchased in bulk for promotional, educational, or business use.
Please contact your local bookseller or the Macmillan Corporate and Premium Sales
Department at (800) 221-7945, extension 5442, or by e-mail at
MacmillanSpecialMarkets@macmillan.com.

First Edition 2021

Designed by Omar Chapa

Printed in the United States of America

1 3 5 7 9 10 8 6 4 2

For my parents

CONTENTS

AUTHOR'S NOTE

This book is based on more than sixty interviews with former Juul employees, investors, advisers, and insiders who helped shape the company throughout its evolution, as well as interviews with dozens of doctors, researchers, public health officials, vaping industry insiders and lawmakers. Many of the people I interviewed asked for anonymity, due to fears of retribution, legal action, or professional consequences.

Most of these interviews were completed over the course of 2020, but *Big Vape* is also the culmination of several years of reporting on Juul and the e-cigarette industry for *Time* magazine. My reporting for *Time* brought me inside Juul's San Francisco headquarters and gave me the rare opportunity to interview some of the company's top executives, including founders James Monsees and Adam Bowen and former CEO Kevin Burns. While some material from those interviews is included in these pages, Monsees, Bowen, and Burns did not agree to be re-interviewed for this book.

With very few exceptions, I requested on-the-record interviews with everyone mentioned by name in this book. Some of those people—including former chief marketing officer Richard Mumby, former CEO Tyler Goldman, and former chief administrative officer Ashley Gould—did not agree. Juul representatives were given the chance to comment on every major factual allegation in this book, though they did not always take that opportunity.

In most cases where I directly quote dialogue or communication between people, the quotes were pulled from emails I personally reviewed or were cited in lawsuits, news articles, or government documents. In some cases, quotes are presented as they were remembered by people who heard them directly. This means they may not be verbatim quotes, but I attempted to verify that they capture the speaker's intent.

I also consulted numerous studies, journal articles, governmental and scientific reports, books, videos, social media posts, and news articles, which are cited in the book's endnotes. I owe thanks to the many journalists who have covered this topic over the years; their reporting helped flesh out this narrative.

BIG VAPE

PROLOGUE

"My name is James Monsees," he began, glancing up from his page of notes to look Illinois congressman Raja Krishnamoorthi in the eye. "Adam Bowen and I founded Juul Labs, and I now serve as the chief product officer of that company. I'm really quite grateful for the opportunity to be here today and address you all. From the moment Adam and I began the journey that would lead to the Juul system, we were clear on our goal—to help improve the lives of adult smokers."

Despite the oppressive July heat in Washington, DC, James wore a dark suit and tie. A scruffy beard dotted his chin, and dark circles had settled into caverns under his eyes. His voice was gravelly. He looked and sounded like he hadn't slept much the night before, which he probably hadn't. He was seated at a long table positioned before eleven of the most powerful lawmakers in the United States, his voice echoing through the congressional chamber where he would fight for the reputation of the e-cigarette company he and Adam Bowen had dreamed up almost fifteen years earlier as graduate students who just wanted to quit smoking.

By that day in the summer of 2019, everything had changed. Juul, the device James and Adam had built to help them quit smoking, had helped lots of other people stop, too—by internal company estimates, more than a million people had switched from the cigarettes that were killing them to the supposed safety of Juul's sleek electronic vaporizer, which heated but never burned flavored nicotine e-liquids. After only four years on the market, the device had become one of the most successful consumer products in recent memory. And their company's staff of twenty, who created the Juul vaporizer on a $2 million budget, had ballooned to more than three thousand, all working for a company that had reached a $10 billion valuation faster than any other in history. As James sat in that chamber on Capitol Hill, Juul was a $38 billion empire, worth more than start-ups like Airbnb or SpaceX—and he and his old friend and cofounder, Adam Bowen, had gone from rumpled graduate students to billionaires.

But as with so many Silicon Valley success stories, the road to riches hadn't been smooth. Much of the public health community had turned against Juul, questioning whether its product was in fact safer than smoking—and whether its potential benefit for adults who wanted to stop smoking outweighed the staggering data around youth vaping. By the end of 2019, federal data would show that 27.5 percent of the nation's high school students and 10.5 percent of its middle school students had used e-cigarettes in the past thirty days, with Juul the most commonly cited brand among them. Nearly every day, more news stories suggested that Juul had torn a page from the Big Tobacco playbook and purposely hooked teenage customers for profit—a narrative that had only grown stronger after James and Adam accepted a $12.8 billion investment from Altria, the parent company of brands like Marlboro and Virginia Slims. Now the din had grown loud enough that Congress was investigating how Juul had developed and marketed its products, and James had been forced to salvage what was left of his reputation.

"We never wanted any non-nicotine user, and certainly nobody underage, to ever use Juul products," he continued. "Yet the data clearly shows a significant number of underage Americans are doing so. This is a serious problem. Our company has no higher priority than fighting it."

It wasn't supposed to be this way—cocky, charismatic James reduced to groveling before an unsmiling congressional subcommittee, at least half of whose members seemed already to think him culpable. He and Adam had founded this company to do something good with their lives. They'd wanted to give adult smokers, people like them, a better choice. Somehow, they'd ended up here instead. Or, at least, James had—Adam was conspicuously absent, not just from the congressional hearing but also from the company he'd helped build. By the time things really started to go downhill, he had one foot out the door, leaving James alone to explain away the company's mistakes.

What if they'd designed the product differently, so everyone would stop comparing it to a flash drive? What if they'd swallowed their pride in the beginning and hired some former tobacco executives, people who actually knew how to handle a heavily regulated product, instead of pretending they were just another work-hard, play-hard Silicon Valley start-up? What if they'd taken a different direction for Juul's launch campaign, the one the press loved to compare to old cigarette ads? What if they'd never posted a single photo on Instagram? What if James hadn't been quite so smug during all those interviews, and what if Adam had come out of his shell to explain why he'd made Juul's nicotine formula so strong? What if they'd listened when experts warned them that those educational classroom visits were a bad idea? What if the emphasis on growth hadn't been quite so strong? What if the company said no when Altria came calling? What if Juul hadn't made an enemy of the Food and Drug Administration commissioner Scott Gottlieb? How might things have gone? All those questions were rhetorical now.

James pressed on: "Our incentive is to help [smokers] achieve their goal of transitioning from cigarettes. It is an astonishing business opportunity, no doubt, but it is a historic opportunity for public health," he said, his emphasis heavy on the word *historic*.

"Underage use of our products does not advance that goal," he added, eyes flicking up toward the congressional panel. "It imperils it."

PART I

The Spark

1

James Monsees didn't know what he was doing anymore. Standing outside Stanford University's Design Loft one night in late 2004, a burning cigarette perched between his fingers, the twenty-four-year-old suddenly couldn't square who he was with the smoky mess of paper and tobacco in his hand. Here he was, well on his way to a master's degree from one of the most prestigious product design programs in the country, and yet he was still sucking on a burning tube of tobacco and chemicals, knowing full well it was terrible for his health. It felt primitive. More than that, it felt *dumb*. He looked over at his classmate and smoke-break buddy Adam Bowen, who was puffing away on his own cigarette, and felt only bewilderment. Why were they both still doing this?

Adam couldn't think of a single good reason, either. He'd tried to quit smoking plenty of times before—always cold turkey, never successfully—and yet there he stood, filling his lungs with tar and smoke. "We're relatively smart people," the two marveled, "and we're out here burning sticks." There had to be something better. Why shouldn't they be the ones to create it?

The pair's late-night breakthrough came about two years after Adam enrolled in Stanford's graduate product design program, which taught about a dozen students a year to approach the craft through a unique blend of engineering, business, art, psychology, and sociology. He'd started at Stanford in 2002, four years after graduating from Pomona College with a degree in physics. The quiet, cerebral Tucson, Arizona, native lived up to the small liberal arts college's reputation for attracting the "smartest" students of California's seven linked Claremont Colleges. Anybody who'd known Adam as a kid wouldn't have been surprised to learn that he'd excelled in school and gone on to study product design. He'd spent his childhood drawing detailed renderings of cars and planes—anything with an engine, really. It was a fascination he never grew out of. At Pomona, he took a special interest in researching NASA's so-called Vomit Comet, a reduced-gravity aircraft notorious for making its crew members ill, and he joined the Sigma Xi scientific research honor society.

Adam took a few years off between degrees, but eventually, the pull of the classroom called him to Stanford, where it was immediately clear to peers that he was the real deal. "Adam was obviously a standout from the beginning," says classmate Colter Leys. "He just had an amazing, easy facility for things that other people had a hard time with." He was quiet but easygoing, enigmatic but funny and warm, once you got to know him. Stress seemed to roll off his shoulders—and there was plenty of that at Stanford.

James Monsees arrived at Stanford a year after Adam, but it didn't take long for them to become a duo. "There was a crowd of people who smoked cigarettes, and they were kind of in that crowd together," Leys says. Small talk and brainstorms over cigarette breaks proved enough to help the two men form a bond.

James had always been an improbable smoker. Growing up in St. Louis, Missouri, he was raised by his physician mother to hate cigarettes. Her father had been a heavy smoker, and she'd lost him to lung cancer far too young. James carried that loss with him. But adolescence being what it is, and James being who he was, the temptation to try a cigarette eventually grew too heavy to cast off. He had always been a curious kid, the kind who loved to take things apart and put them back together. As a teenager, when he realized his parents had no intention of buying him a car for his sixteenth birthday, he built himself one instead, filling his parents' garage with spare parts until he could make them run. When he was a young teenager, he decided he wanted to try cigarettes for himself, too. By the time he graduated from St. Louis's tony Whitfield school in 1998 and moved on to Kenyon College in the tiny town of Gambier, Ohio, he was a regular smoker. "I hated cigarettes," James would say later. "Every time I picked one up, I felt conflicted about it." But addiction has a way of drowning out internal conflict.

After graduating from Kenyon in 2002 with dual degrees in physics and studio art, James returned home to St. Louis to try his hand at product design. He worked at a company called Metaphase Design Group, which specialized in ergonomically friendly products. Despite his youth and inexperience, James's talent and charisma were obvious immediately. "James is a very inspiring designer whose interests, abilities and skills are beyond his years," a coworker gushed on James's LinkedIn page, adding that he "possesses an entrepreneurial flair that sparks innovation and discovery." After about a year in the workforce, James decided to explore that flair. He packed his bags and headed west to the manicured lawns and terra-cotta roofs of Stanford's California campus to study product design.

Adam and James did not have the world's most obvious friendship. Adam was studious and low-key, prone to getting lost in thought; James was boisterous and social, always cracking jokes and erupting into his signature loud, barking laugh. Adam listened more than he spoke, while James was happy to fill the silence. Both men still looked like undergrads back then, with shaggy haircuts—Adam's dirty blond, James's brown—but Adam's dark eyes, deep voice, and long, angular face gave him a certain gravity next to bearded, baby-faced James. Or maybe it was more about how he acted than how he looked. Adam was consistently described as "stoic," a word often tossed around in Silicon Valley circles that value drive and hard work. James was harder to put a label on. He had an infectious laugh and a glint in his eye, but both could disappear in an instant.

Still, the pair had enough in common to strike up a friendship. Both were bright and talented, with a clear gift for and lifelong pull toward product design. Both loved solving complex problems and figuring out what makes things tick. Both tended to work in late-night, marathon brainstorming sessions. And, though both had tried to quit smoking before, both were frequently bumming cigarettes and hanging around outside the Design Loft, shooting the breeze and lighting up. It was during one of these smoke breaks, on that winter night in 2004, that Adam and James realized they didn't want to burn sticks anymore. All those years of loving and hating smoking in equal measure had crystallized into one moment of recognition: enough was enough. If they couldn't find a way to quit smoking, they would invent one for themselves.

As existential crises go, theirs was a well-timed one. It was thesis season at Stanford, and a cigarette alternative seemed like a great idea for a project. (Previously, both men were working on projects that involved furniture. Adam was designing a desk that could be folded up without needing to be cleared of its clutter, while James was plugging away at user-adaptable chairs.) After their smoky epiphany outside the design center, the pair began brainstorming and trading emails about how they could design a product for people like them: people who wanted to ditch cigarettes but hadn't had luck with the stale and largely ineffective cessation products currently on the market, like nicotine gums and patches; people who couldn't or didn't want to stop cold turkey; people who didn't want the stigma and risk that came with smoking, but who also didn't want to lose the sensory, social, and ritualistic elements of the habit. "What we realized was this was kind of a false choice, this 'quit or die' mentality," Adam recalled in a 2019 interview. "It wasn't that I really wanted to quit; I just wanted to minimize the harm from smoking."

With about six months left before they had to present their theses, both men began pouring their collective energy into their new idea. They began surveying people on campus about everything they hated, and loved, about smoking. They found that their classmates, like many smokers, were conflicted. In interviews, they told Adam and James that they loved the ritual of smoking, the way it looked, even the elegant way smoke unfurled from the cigarette and the sound of taking a drag. But they hated the smell, the stigma, and the knowledge that the habit could someday kill them. Adam and James began taking apart and rebuilding every tobacco product they could find, searching for a way to get rid of the bad parts of smoking without losing the things people liked.

Pretty soon, Adam and James started talking about their idea at the product design program's Tuesday night workshops, where students could bounce ideas off professors and their classmates. They knew they wanted to create a product that delivered nicotine in a safer way than cigarettes, they knew it would need to be portable and easy to use, and they knew they wanted it to look more interesting than a cigarette, classmate Leys remembers. During a lunchtime brainstorming session with their classmates during which people shouted out ideas and James scribbled the good ones on Post-It Notes and slapped them on the wall, they landed on a name: "Ploom." It had the right ring to it, and it played off the concept of smoking without being too heavy-handed.

Leys says he was intrigued by Ploom's potential health benefits for smokers. Back then, he says, nobody thought too much about the potential downsides of the product—like exposure to new kinds of chemicals or attracting kids—but some of James and Adam's professors were wary of how fast the two were moving. "From an academic point of view, I think it was like, 'Wow, that's cool, but let's try to investigate some of the different options that this could be,'" Leys says. "And I think James and Adam were kind of like, 'Let's drive ahead.'"

They did make at least one concession to their professors' pleas to slow down and do more research. They dug deep into the archive of internal tobacco industry documents made public in part thanks to Stanton Glantz, a tobacco control expert and professor of medicine at the nearby University of California, San Francisco. In 1994, a box full of thousands of confidential tobacco industry documents landed on Glantz's desk, courtesy of an anonymous source identified only as "Mr. Butts." Glantz had heard rumors that other researchers around the country had gotten these documents via an anonymous source, and he'd been hungry to get his hands on them himself. From what he had heard, a paralegal working for the tobacco company Brown and Williamson had begun to grow disturbed over what he was seeing in the company's files. He started sneaking documents home with him at night, copying them, and then returning them the next day. When he had enough compiled, he shared them with "Mr. Butts," who began distributing them to journalists and researchers, including Glantz.

The documents spelled out years of Brown and Williamson's wrong-doings. Company memos, letters, and meeting minutes showed that executives had for years downplayed, or outright lied to the public about, how addictive and dangerous smoking was and had peddled misleading research meant to cast doubt on the idea that cigarettes caused cancer and other health issues. Glantz turned the pages over to UCSF's library for review and publication, hoping that entering the documents into the library's archive would protect them from possible court orders. He and several UCSF colleagues also used the documents to write a book called *The Cigarette Papers*.

In 1998, attorneys general from forty-six U.S. states, five territories, and the District of Columbia reached a landmark settlement with cigarette companies, including Brown and Williamson, Philip Morris, R.J. Reynolds, and Lorillard. Still the largest civil settlement in U.S. court history, it became known as the Tobacco Master Settlement Agreement. The attorneys general involved successfully argued that because smoking-related disease was a major stressor to the public health care system—and one that Big Tobacco companies had downplayed for years—tobacco makers should reimburse states for some of the money they'd poured into these public aid networks. The Big Tobacco companies agreed to pay out billions of dollars a year for the first five years after the settlement, as well as perpetual annual payments calculated depending on inflation and cigarette sales. Manufacturers also agreed to rein in their marketing, most notably by agreeing not to market to children and teenagers. The American Legacy Foundation (now known as the Truth Initiative), one of the nation's leading antismoking groups, was also born from the settlement. And significantly for Adam and James, documents uncovered during litigation were published openly, so the American public could see and understand exactly what Big Tobacco had been up to all those years.

The archive laid out everything—from the way cigarettes were designed and manufactured to how they were sold by advertising executives—and it was all right there, in tobacco executives' own words. Adam and James could study the minutiae of cigarette chemistry to understand what made the product so appealing. Without ever holding a focus group, they could analyze market research about consumer preferences and tastes. They could sift through internal memos to learn how tobacco companies had sold their products to just about any and every demographic—including, as they admitted, teenagers. For two graduate students trying to turn a bright idea into a blockbuster product, the archive was a gold mine. Sure, the documents were full of red flags, ethical dilemmas, and flagrant abuses of public trust—but the information! It was too good to resist. "We had so much information that you wouldn't normally be able to get in most industries," James would say later. "And we were able to catch up, right, to a huge, huge industry in no time. And then we started building prototypes."

They had a good amount of catching up to do: in the race for a "safer" cigarette, they were learning, the tobacco industry had had a sizable head start. Industry executives had been talking out of both sides of their mouths for decades, claiming that smoking was harmless at the same time that they were surreptitiously looking for safer alternatives to it. By the early 1960s, tobacco executives knew that cigarettes caused cancer and other diseases, but they chose to shield their loyal customers from that information. The scientific community had no such reservations. Studies suggesting links between smoking and cancer, respiratory illnesses, and heart disease had been piling up and generating news coverage for some time, and the smoking public was starting to get uneasy. (Their unease was kicked into overdrive in 1964, when the surgeon general released a report that explicitly warned Americans about the dangers of smoking, including cancer.) Tobacco companies introduced filtered cigarettes to calm the masses, pitching them as a "lighter" way to smoke—even though internal testing showed they did little to block the inhalation of cancer-causing toxins.

In the early 1960s, researchers at British American Tobacco (BAT), led by a man named Sir Charles Ellis, thought of a way they could go even further. Ellis's whole idea hinged on avoiding a process called combustion. Combustion happens when a cigarette is lit on fire and the tobacco mixes with the oxygen in the air, producing smoke, ash, and roughly seven thousand chemical by-products, some of which can lead to cancer. If BAT could develop a product that delivered nicotine without all the chemicals and by-products that made people sick, Ellis thought, it could keep many smokers from quitting. Nicotine, he reasoned, was relatively harmless on its own. Yes, it was a mild stimulant, and yes, it was addictive, but it had some benefits, too—like increasing concentration and focus while simultaneously soothing the nerves. Why not get smokers hooked on that alone, instead of on traditional cigarettes? Ellis's project was known internally as "Ariel."

Ellis's team had its first breakthrough in 1962, with a cigarette-within-a-cigarette design. An inner tube of nicotine extract and water was wrapped in a thin layer of aluminum, which separated it from an outer layer of tobacco that smokers would light on fire. As it burned, the outer layer would warm the inner one, and as the internal nicotine extract heated up, it would produce an aerosol that users could inhale. Each puff would bring a burst of nicotine, without all the tar and other nasty by-products in cigarettes. Ellis's fundamental design worked, but it took years of tinkering to get the nicotine extract right. BAT's team worked with what's known as freebase nicotine, a form of nicotine that is quite harsh to consume. It took lots of trial and error for BAT's researchers to figure out that mixing freebase nicotine with an acid could mellow it out and make it much easier to inhale.

Even after that discovery, Ariel never saw store shelves. There was no way to market it. If BAT released its new and innovative product and bragged about how safe it was, the company would be tacitly admitting that its regular cigarettes *weren't* safe. "There was no reason to make it," says tobacco historian and Stanford professor Robert Proctor. Doing so would only rock the boat.

Tobacco companies weren't the only ones who saw promise in a "safer" cigarette. Soon after the 1964 surgeon general's report entitled "Smoking and Health," public health officials began touting the idea known as "harm reduction," the concept of reducing the consequences associated with a risky behavior rather than solely trying to get people to quit that risky behavior. Providing drug users with clean needles is a common example of harm reduction, but the concept has a long history in the tobacco world, too. In the 1960s, health officials recommended pipes, cigars, and chewing tobacco as safer options than cigarettes. Public health leaders also readily accepted and promoted filtered and low-tar cigarettes, not yet realizing that these weren't much better than traditional cigarettes. These recommendations got people thinking that there might be a continuum of risk, with some dangerous products less harmful than others.

By the 1980s, the idea of harm reduction and the appeal of lower-risk products had gotten some traction. British psychiatrist Michael Russell put it well in 1976 when he said that "people smoke for nicotine but they die from the tar." By that, he meant that nicotine wasn't the thing giving smokers cancer or heart disease; it was just keeping them beholden to the toxins that did. A growing body of research was beginning to suggest that smokeless alternatives to cigarettes could eliminate some of those risks. In Sweden, an oral tobacco product called snus started to displace cigarette use in the 1970s. Over the following years, as snus grew more widespread, Sweden's cancer mortality rates fell, which suggested that switching from combustible to noncombustible tobacco had a measurable impact on public health.

It looked like people in the United States might be ready for something similar. The share of U.S. adults who smoked had plummeted from 42 percent in 1964 to 30 percent in 1985, with many people quitting due to health concerns. The U.S. Public Health Service listed lowering smoking rates as one of its fifteen top "healthy people" goals in 1980. Tobacco executives were getting backed deeper and deeper into corners by scientists and lawmakers who by now had no doubt that their products were deadly and addictive. To escape with their businesses intact, tobacco companies needed a holy grail: a cigarette that wouldn't eventually kill off half their customers and that would coax even health-conscious types into picking up or continuing the habit.

R.J. Reynolds, the cigarette company behind brands like Camel and Newport, released its three-hundred-million-dollar baby, the Premier, in 1988. The idea was to heat tobacco instead of burning it, thus eliminating combustion—and, it was hoped, disease. The product looked like a cigarette, but its body was filled with aluminum oxide pellets coated with nicotine and glycerin, rather than loose tobacco. A burning charcoal tip would warm the pellets, releasing a nicotine-rich aerosol that smokers could inhale—thus, in theory, offering a "smoking" experience without many of the health risks associated with traditional cigarettes.

The idea was logical enough, as virtually anything would be less dangerous than the classic combustible cigarette, but the product was awful. According to a 1988 *New York Times* article, test groups "complained, among other things, that the cigarette has an unpleasant smell, that it lacks flavor, that it does not burn down like a normal cigarette and that it is too hot to hold." Many sources floating around the internet quote Reynolds's own then CEO as saying the Premier "tasted like shit." With rave reviews like these, it's no wonder Reynolds pulled the Premier after only a short pilot period. Optimistically, Reynolds began testing a similar product, the Eclipse, in 1994, and sold it in limited quantities nationwide.

Fellow Big Tobacco giant Philip Morris, the company behind brands like Marlboro, also experimented with a heat-not-burn product in the 1990s. Philip Morris's Accord required users to place a cigarette into a device about the size and shape of a tape recorder, which would externally heat the tobacco to produce an aerosol. The end of the cigarette was left sticking out, so users could inhale. But it was difficult to get as much nicotine as smokers were used to, and the taste still wasn't great. "It didn't taste good and no one liked it," sums up one former employee who worked on the project. Like Reynolds's predecessors, the Accord was a flop.

Then, in 2003, a Chinese pharmacist named Hon Lik changed everything. Like many children in China, Hon had grown up watching his father puff through a pack a day. Like his father, he eventually became a heavy smoker, too, but as a pharmacist, he knew the habit was unsustainably bad for his health. He quit with the aid of a nicotine patch, but like Adam Bowen, he realized he missed the ritual of smoking. Unlike a cigarette, a patch "does not create a peak. It's a consistent and slow releasing of nicotine," Hon says. And "as a smoker, you have behavioral customs—you hold a cigarette with your hand and put it in your mouth." The patch didn't compare.

To fill the void, Hon developed the world's first modern e-cigarette, which used a lithium-ion battery to power a heating element that atomized a capsule of nicotine-rich liquid, producing an aerosol. Scientifically speaking, an aerosol is different from a vapor: an aerosol comprises tiny particles suspended in gas, whereas a vapor is the pure gas form of a liquid. Not surprisingly, most people did not care about this distinction and eventually began calling the "smoke" that came out of an e-cigarette "vapor," giving birth to both a new word and a new trend: *vaping*.

With its slim white body and black mouthpiece, Hon's vaping device could easily have been mistaken for a permanent marker, except for the LED light at the tip, which glowed red when a user inhaled. In 2004—shortly after his father was diagnosed with lung cancer—Hon began selling the product in China under the name "Ruyan," which translates to "like smoke." Prior to products like Ruyan, and with the exception of unpopular products like the Accord, smoking was a process that had not fundamentally changed for centuries: dry tobacco, roll it up, light it on fire, inhale. Ruyan felt like a fresh update of that idea, bringing smoking into the increasingly tech-savvy early 2000s. At $208 a pop, the device reportedly earned Hon's company the equivalent of $13 million in 2005 alone. "A lot of consumers were shocked and surprised, in a positive way," Hon says. "They could not believe there was something they could put in their pocket and smoke like a cigarette anytime, anywhere they like."

Early e-cigarettes weren't perfect, but they at least offered a new take on smoking—and this appealed to Adam and James. They realized very early on that people didn't necessary want a "safer" cigarette like the Eclipse or Premier, which usually ended up being a less satisfying and less palatable version of the product they really wanted. Plus, cigarettes had major baggage. People associated them with being dirty, messy, smelly, and toxic. It seemed better to leave all that in the past and give people a product that improved upon the cigarette, rather than a poor approximation of it—a product that would make them forget they had ever craved cigarettes at all. "A new brand, a new company, a trustworthy brand whose goals are aligned with [the] needs of public health, was needed," James later told the *Mercury News* when describing this realization. "Instead of creating safe cigarettes, we created a superior product offering, which keeps some aspects on why people love cigarettes but not any of the ones they don't like." This "superior product offering" was Adam and James's master's thesis project, Ploom.

Standing in a darkened lecture hall in June 2005 with a PowerPoint presentation displayed behind them, James stepped forward to sell his classmates on this idea. "Adam and I were interested in working on designing for social change," James said. "We acknowledged right away that smoking was probably an easy target. There's a lot of people that smoke who are really at odds with themselves. They really enjoy the process of smoking, but at the same time, every cigarette is really self-destructive." Throughout the eighteen-minute thesis presentation, James and Adam laid out their vision for a portable vape pen that would use a liquid fuel source to heat tiny pods of flavored tobacco, producing a nicotine-laced aerosol that users could inhale without harming their health or smelling like smoke. Its design was inspired by a mash-up of the Nespresso coffee pods that were at that time sweeping Europe and the hookahs that were sweeping college campuses. Like a hookah, which uses hot coals to heat tobacco, Ploom would heat tobacco pods without burning them.

"It turns out actually that burning tobacco is the real problem. Nicotine is addictive, clearly, but it's not the nicotine that's really hurting you; it's mostly the combustion that's a problem," James said during the presentation. To support this idea, he pointed to the tobacco industry's search for a safe cigarette, from Ariel all the way up to Accord. (As two product design students, he and Adam didn't have the time, resources, or expertise to conduct clinical research themselves, so they were largely assuming that Ploom would indeed be safer than a cigarette simply by virtue of its being a noncombustible product, though they said they planned to conduct additional research later.) But, James concluded, "there's no design innovation going on in smoking whatsoever, because Big Tobacco's really interested in not shooting themselves in their own foot"—in other words, traditional tobacco companies didn't want to create something that would cannibalize cigarette sales. James and Adams were more than happy to fill that void.

Colter Leys remembers watching the presentation and realizing that Adam and James weren't going to stop until they got it done. "For other people, [thesis season] was a finale. For them, it was a milestone in the middle of a process," he says. "For better or for worse, they were already on their way."

It would have been easy, watching Adam and James's presentation, to think they were designing a smoking-cessation product. But their actual message was subtler than that. Toward the middle of the presentation, James asked the big question, the one that would inform Ploom's ethos as it came into existence: "What if smoking were safe?" he asked. "And, even better, what if smoking were actually not offensive to others?" Health was clearly important to the two men—never mind the fact that they hadn't actually studied Ploom to see if it *was* safer than a cigarette—but to them, "even better" than health was a future in which smoking didn't have to be a dangerous, dirty little secret. If smoking were safer, cleaner, and less annoying for bystanders, it could become cool again. The entire presentation was laced with callbacks to Adam's earlier realization that most smokers don't actually *want* to quit; they just don't want to *die*. "Our goal," Adam told his classmates, "was to basically create a whole new experience for people that retains the positive aspects of smoking, the ritual and everything, but that makes it as healthy and socially acceptable as possible."

Everything came down to that sentence. If you listened carefully, you heard that Ploom wasn't meant to be a smoking-cessation product. It was meant to be the rebirth of the cigarette.

2

AN INDUSTRY IS BORN (2007–2011)

One day during the summer of 2007, Kurt Sonderegger got a cryptic message on LinkedIn. Two guys had reached out to say they were launching an exciting new start-up in San Francisco, with few details offered. Would he like to learn more?

Sonderegger was looking for a change. He'd been living in Los Angeles and working a "cool guy" job at Red Bull for nearly a decade, handling the company's culture marketing and having a blast. But as much as he liked his job, he was itching to try out the start-up life. He'd been talking to some recruiters already, testing the waters and feeling out whether he was ready to try something new. There was a good chance this LinkedIn message would lead to nothing, but Sonderegger happened to be heading up to San Francisco soon anyway. On a lark, he agreed to meet the guys at a hotel in the city on his way through town.

After Sonderegger arrived in the hotel lobby and introduced himself to Adam Bowen and James Monsees, he sat down, reached into his pocket, and tossed his pack of Nat Sherman cigarettes onto the table in front of him. It was a reflexive gesture; he hated sitting with the bulky pack in his pocket, and he removed it out of muscle memory. But as soon as he realized what he'd done, he was embarrassed to have given himself up as a smoker during a job interview with total strangers. "Normally, I would never want someone to know I smoked," Sonderegger says. "But I saw Adam and James's eyes both open up."

If Sonderegger had been a promising recruit before, his being a smoker made him an even better pick for them. They didn't have a working Ploom prototype or a staff or an office yet, but they had a vision for a product that would preserve and elevate the ritual of smoking while, they hoped, eliminating many of the harms. Their words made perfect sense to Sonderegger, a health-conscious California surfer who lived in a constant state of low-grade shame over his Nat Sherman habit. "I was a conflicted smoker," Sonderegger says. "When they said they wanted to preserve the ritual and remove the harm, I was like, 'Wow, if we can make that happen, it's a billion-dollar idea.'"

Taking the job would be a risk. Sonderegger could tell these guys were smart and they had the cachet that comes with a pair of Stanford degrees, but they were young and "a little rumpled around the edges"—they would have looked more at home on a college quad than in a board meeting. There was also an obvious personality clash, apparent even from that first meeting, Sonderegger remembers. With James's smirk and his tendency to crack jokes and Adam's impossible-to-read face, "they're kind of the odd couple," Sonderegger says. But their product sounded like one Sonderegger himself would use and that plenty of other people would use, too. If these guys could do what they had set out to do, he knew it was going to be big. Sonderegger accepted a 50 percent pay cut (with some equity to sweeten the deal), quit his cool-guy job, and packed up for start-up life in Silicon Valley.

He got his first taste of it on day one at Ploom HQ, which at that time was really just a little bit of office space donated to Adam and James by some friends with a slightly more established start-up. Their buddies had asked only that Adam and James brainstorm ideas for their start-up for two hours each week. In exchange, they could have a place to build their own company—literally. "I show up," Sonderegger says, "and they're like, 'We have a truck outside. We have to go buy doors and create the desks.'" He laughs. "There were certainly times I was like, 'Oh my god, what did I get myself into?'"

By the time Sonderegger came on board, two years had passed since

Adam and James's thesis presentation. They'd been a little slow to turn the praise they'd gotten from their Stanford classmates and professors into a real company, realizing just how much work it would take to get Ploom off the ground.

"We had thought this would be easy and fun," Adam later told *Inc.* "We were naïve." After they graduated, the realities of life had set in. Rather than working on Ploom full-time, James had accepted an invitation to become a founding fellow at Stanford's new Hasso Plattner Institute of Design, and Adam was living with friends in a house that sat within an old apple orchard at the edge of Palo Alto. Though they were both working on other things, they kept going back to Ploom, turning the idea over in their minds and talking about how they could make it a reality. They set up a makeshift shop in a tiny room in Adam's house, where they spent long nights building models and making plans. By early 2007, they were ready to take the plunge and do the thing for real. "The first time I told my mom, 'We're going to pursue this tobacco thing,' her immediate reaction was 'Why would you do that? You can do anything you want, just, God, don't go near tobacco,'" James would later remember. His mother's reaction was not uncommon.

In February 2007, Adam sent an email to the Stanford alumni Listserv, announcing an exciting new opportunity to invest. "We're about to launch our product in the high-growth industry of smoking alternatives," he wrote, adding that he expected the category to grow by up to 50 percent while cigarette sales fell by 1 percent each year in the United States. "This [is] an opportunity to greatly improve public health, while building a very profitable business." Investments would be accepted starting at $25,000.

This sort of crowdsourced investing was about as good as two young, unproven entrepreneurs angling to get into the tobacco industry could expect. Many venture capital firms have "vice clauses" that prevent them from investing in controversial categories like tobacco and marijuana. Adam and James learned this harsh reality quickly as they tried to scrape together the money they needed to get Ploom off the ground. As they trolled Silicon Valley's famed Sand Hill Road, home to some of the most prominent investors in the country, even with their pedigreed educations and connections to Stanford professors who were big names in the product design world, James and Adam were initially shown the door by fifty firms. Eventually, they realized it was easier to woo individual investors, who had the freedom to throw their money at any project they wanted. Their first victory came via Ralph Eschenbach at Sand Hill Angels, a collective of independent investors in Mountain View, California.

Fresh out of Stanford and new to the VC scene, James and Adam didn't have the most polished pitch Eschenbach had ever heard, "but they were adept guys, they were bright guys, and they managed to convey the information they needed to get conveyed," he says. They explained that smoking-related disease kills about 500,000 Americans every single year, and they said they'd designed a product they believed could give smokers a better alternative than nicotine gums and patches, which research showed helped only about 7 percent of smokers quit for at least six months. (Never mind that they didn't yet have any studies to back up this point.) They told Eschenbach about their own struggles to quit smoking, about how they'd designed a solution for people just like them. Eschenbach wasn't a smoker himself, but he liked what he was hearing, and he felt in his gut that Adam and James could get it done.

"I look, to start with, [at] are they solving a real problem?" he says. "Is their technology defensible? Is there some magic in there that's going to make it a little trickier [to duplicate]? Lastly, do I think the team can execute on that plan?" Adam and James ticked all the boxes. Taking a chance on two young, unproven guys would be a risk, but Eschenbach knew that if they could do even a fraction of what they were promising, he'd be part of something huge. As Eschenbach says, "That's what early angel investing is about: taking on a risky venture." Sand Hill Angels kicked in about $150,000 of the $500,000 Adam and James needed to get things off the ground.

With one investor on board, it was that much easier to convince the next one: Riaz Valani, an investor at Global Asset Capital with even deeper pockets than Eschenbach. Valani and Eschenbach acted not only as investors, but also advisers who could weigh in on big business decisions and help Adam and James guide the company forward. Valani and Eschenbach met with Adam and James once a month or so, to see how things were going and to offer coaching on whatever obstacles the guys had hit.

Not long after, the cofounders got an investment from Nicholas Pritzker, a member of the dynastic family that owns Hyatt Hotels. The Pritzker family also owned the Conwood chewing tobacco company, before selling it to R.J. Reynolds's parent company for $3.5 billion in 2006. Slowly but surely, Adam and James were scraping together enough money and business experience to make a go of it.

What they didn't have yet was someone with public health or tobacco control expertise who could advise them on the world they were about to disrupt—and, perhaps, to help them determine if their product actually *was* safer than cigarettes. The products were so new that this theory had yet to be borne out by the scientific literature. With this core question—whether the Ploom was, indeed, safer than a cigarette—not yet answered, there would clearly be benefit in partnering with an authoritative voice in the public health world.

The Bay Area is a hotbed of tobacco control and nicotine research, with Stanford and the University of California, San Francisco, both serving as magnets for some of the country's leading scientists and researchers. Around the same time that investment money began coming in, Adam and James embarked on a tour of these experts to look for a partner whose name would carry weight in public health circles.

Stanton Glantz, the UCSF researcher who received the trove of Brown and Williamson documents in the 1990s, was on the list. Adam came by to pick Glantz's brain on the idea of delivering nicotine without fire, describing Ploom's design as a safer alternative to cigarettes. Glantz was intrigued but not sold—he wanted more data to prove that vaping was actually safer than smoking before he put his reputation on the line. "I said, 'Well, this is an interesting idea. Delivering the nicotine aerosol without combustion might be better; we don't know,'" Glantz says. Still, he saw some potential sticking points right away. "I told them, 'The two things I think you really need to worry about are appealing to kids and dual use [of cigarettes and e-cigarettes],'" Glantz says. He thought there was high potential for smokers to use both products simultaneously, instead of switching to e-cigarettes completely, potentially compounding the risks to their health. He also thought an electronic tobacco product would have clear appeal to kids.

"It was cool," Glantz says plainly. He had absolutely no doubt that increasingly tech-savvy young people would want to use it, but he says his worry fell on deaf ears. The Ploom team said, 'Oh, we don't think this will interest kids,'" Glantz remembers. "Back then, maybe they were a little arrogant." (Later, Adam would say he did not recall youth use coming up during the meeting.) Adam left the meeting empty-handed.

Even without a high-profile public health partner, Adam and James pressed forward with their scrappy little start-up, working around the clock to get it off the ground. "I remember having dinner and drinks with these guys, and they were just toiling, grinding, putting in an ungodly number of hours," remembers their Stanford classmate Colter Leys. Most of that work, however, was going toward developing the product itself, and it was clear that they needed someone to handle marketing and branding.

Riaz Valani had been on the guys about this ever since he invested, recognizing that designing a good product was only half the battle. The real challenge would be making an addictive nicotine product socially acceptable in a world conditioned to look down on smoking. He didn't think Adam and James could achieve this on their own, and it's not hard to see why. Their online activity from that first year in business is a time capsule of what it was to be on social media in the early 2000s: everybody was online, but nobody really knew or cared about the ways their digital footprints would live on. The same month that they began searching for investors, February 2007, the cofounders made things official by "recommending" each other on LinkedIn. "Adam gets things done," James wrote of his stoic friend, who, by all accounts, did get things done. "James loves coffee," came the ringing endorsement from Adam. (A sample Adam tweet from around this time: "having a muffin.") Kurt Sonderegger's marketing services were sorely needed—especially because, by the time he was hired in 2007, Ploom had competition.

Patent attorney Mark Weiss grew up in an entrepreneurial family. Weiss's father, also a patent attorney, had taught Mark and his brothers to lock down a good idea when they saw it, because you never knew what could

happen. As an adult, Weiss was always on the lookout for new and exciting products, and he'd learned about Hon Lik's Ruyan e-cigarette through
a business contact shortly after it launched. "I knew instantly it would be a
winner in the U.S. market," Weiss says. "It was obviously a less harmful product, and most smokers I know of always want to quit smoking. It's almost
like someone going to drinking a Diet Coke versus a Coke. It was an obvious
thing."

Weiss's friend happened to have a contact at Hon's company, so he and
Weiss approached the firm about selling the Ruyan in the United States.
The two parties couldn't agree on contract terms or wholesale pricing, and
the negotiations stretched on and on, until Weiss found two other Chinese
companies making virtually identical products that he could get at a lower
price. Weiss formed a business called "Sottera," and by 2007, he was selling e-cigarettes in the United States under the brand name "NJOY." The
product was considered a "cigalike," or an electronic cigarette designed to
mimic the look and feel of the real thing—the thought being that smokers would respond better to something familiar. The first NJOY cigalikes
were basically identical to Ruyan devices: about the width and length of a
traditional cigarette, with a white body, a black mouthpiece, and a glowing
red LED tip. All users had to do was slip in a cartridge of e-liquid and start
inhaling. After a flurry of press in 2008, NJOY did three million dollars in
sales that year and found itself at the forefront of a brand-new category in
the United States.

But, as Weiss soon learned, there were drawbacks to being out front.
In April 2009, the Food and Drug Administration started seizing NJOY's
products at customs and stopping their importation from China, claiming that e-cigarettes were drug-delivery devices and therefore subject to
FDA regulation. "I always thought we'd end up in a lawsuit with the FDA,"
Weiss says. This foresight had prompted him to go on the offensive, finding lawyers who agreed that NJOY's vaporizers were tobacco products, not
drug-delivery devices. When the FDA did indeed step in, Weiss was ready.
NJOY joined a lawsuit against the FDA filed by Smoking Everywhere Inc.,
an e-cigarette company famous for selling its products in mall kiosks. Like

NJOY, Smoking Everywhere argued that e-cigarettes were tobacco products—a distinction that, if proven true, would place their goods out of the FDA's reach.

In early 2009, when NJOY's legal battle against the FDA was getting started, the government body had zero regulatory power over tobacco products. Top FDA officials had been fighting since at least the mid-1990s to regulate tobacco products, but it failed to convince Congress, the courts, and the cigarette industry. The Family Smoking Prevention and Tobacco Control Act, which was signed into law by President Barack Obama in June 2009, right in the middle of the FDA's spat with NJOY, finally ended the battle and gave the FDA the right to oversee tobacco products. The law also allowed the FDA to impose a fresh batch of sales and marketing restrictions on tobacco companies, including banning flavors other than menthol to avoid attracting kids; barring advertisers from making unproven health claims (such as promising that a product was low- or reduced-risk), and forbidding the use of words like *low-tar* and *light* in marketing materials.

Crucially, while the legislation gave the FDA the power to regulate any tobacco product, it had been written with a narrow focus on traditional cigarettes, smokeless tobacco, and loose-leaf tobacco. If the FDA decided to "deem" something else a tobacco product that fit under its regulatory umbrella, it would have to write a whole new rule for regulating that specific product—a document that became known as a "deeming rule." This left tobacco products like cigars and e-cigarettes in a strange limbo. The FDA *could* regulate them someday, but it didn't yet have the full power to do so. "E-cigarettes were these new, weird things. No one had really figured them out," says Eric Lindblom, who at the time worked at the advocacy group Campaign for Tobacco-Free Kids and who would go on to serve in the FDA's Center for Tobacco Products. Given how difficult it had been just to give the FDA power to regulate cigarettes, "nobody wanted to mess with the bill at the late stages to do anything specifically about e-cigarettes," Lindblom says.

Even if nobody in Washington had figured them out yet, by 2009, e-cigarettes were gaining grassroots momentum in the United States. There still weren't many places to buy them domestically, or a ton of brands available, but you could find and order e-cigarettes online from other countries pretty easily. They often weren't very good—the devices didn't work well, or the flavors tasted awful—so early users had to be crafty, finding DIY ways to improve the products by tinkering with their batteries or mixing different e-liquids together. (As vape industry legend goes, a father and son in the United Kingdom started this trend after they modified a flashlight to turn it into a homemade vaping device.) There was a small but passionate community of e-cigarette users who shared tips and tricks, first in chat rooms like the E-Cigarette Forum and then through organized groups like the Consumer Advocates for Smoke-free Alternatives Association (CASAA) and trade shows like Vapefest. They also passed around positive studies, like a Ruyan-sponsored paper from 2008 that found far lower levels of carcinogens in e-cigarettes compared to cigarettes. "People got really passionate really quickly because we had a lot of inveterate smokers," says Julie Woessner, a founding member of CASAA. "I smoked for decades and tried everything to quit, and all of a sudden, here's something. It caught on very quickly with word of mouth."

The global health community didn't necessarily share their enthusiasm. In 2008, the World Health Organization released a statement specifically saying it did not consider e-cigarettes "a legitimate therapy for smokers trying to quit," citing a lack of evidence that the devices actually worked for smoking cessation. By 2009, the FDA was warning consumers that certain e-cigarette ingredients (such as a chemical also used in antifreeze) could be toxic and that the devices could get kids hooked on nicotine. States including New Jersey and countries like Israel, Panama, Brazil, and Saudi Arabia were considering varying degrees of e-cigarette bans and restrictions. But this was all just noise to ex-smokers like Woessner, who had finally found something that helped her ditch cigarettes and wasn't about to let it go. The FDA could dismiss their experiences as anecdotal as much as it wanted. They had still quit smoking.

For these new e-cigarette converts, NJOY's lawsuit against the FDA's seizures was more than a court battle. In their eyes, the FDA's decision could literally mean life or death: a future without cigarettes or a return to smoking.

In the fall of 2010, NJOY's lawyers argued before a federal appeals court panel—which included future Supreme Court justice Brett Kavanaugh—that because e-cigarettes contained tobacco-derived nicotine, they should be considered tobacco products instead of drug-delivery devices. Plenty of people disagreed. Top public health groups, including the Campaign for Tobacco-Free Kids, the American Lung Association, the American Heart Association, and the American Academy of Pediatrics, wrote a joint amicus brief arguing that e-cigarettes should be regulated by the FDA as drug-delivery devices, not tobacco products. But in December 2010, the court ruled in favor of NJOY. If the FDA wanted to regulate e-cigarettes, it would need to get to work on a deeming rule.

"If we [hadn't been] part of the case, the FDA would have been able to just shut everybody down in 2010. [The industry] wouldn't have existed but for us," Weiss says now. Indeed, Weiss's lawsuit bought not just him but also his competitors years and years of valuable time. "There was what turned out to be this totally wrong assumption that by giving [the] FDA all these extraordinary powers over tobacco products, that it would be able to take action," Lindblom says. But it takes time—lots of time—for a bureaucratic beast like the FDA to draft, approve, and implement something like a deeming rule. This delay left open a gaping regulatory loophole for years. Without FDA applications to file and manufacturing standards to meet, all anyone needed to get into the vaping business was an idea and a credit card. The FDA could intervene if a company's products started making people sick, or if companies made unproven health claims about their products' safety or ability to help with smoking cessation, but as long as companies were moderately responsible, they could essentially grow unchecked. There wasn't even a federal law on the books that made it illegal to sell e-cigarettes to minors, although many were implemented at the state level. The FDA's powers were essentially on ice.

Still, Weiss's victory over the FDA was bittersweet. NJOY was hemorrhaging money due to legal costs and the FDA's product seizures. If not for the lawsuit, "we would have dominated the market and really had the money to do a lot of different things," Weiss says. "[The FDA] lost, and there were no repercussions" for it. Weiss had fallen on his sword while trying to save his own company. Yes, he'd won the lawsuit. Yes, he could keep selling e-cigarettes. But he'd also blown through money and time, all while clearing a path for his competitors.

While NJOY was tied up in court, a company called Blu launched with a line of e-cigarettes that essentially looked like combustible cigarettes. They came in a box meant to look like a cigarette pack, and all users had to do was select a nicotine pod in one of five flavors and snap it in. Blu's first production run sold out within weeks. Jason Healy, the Australian entrepreneur and ex-smoker who founded Blu, says he saw an opportunity to introduce a smart, sophisticated brand explicitly marketed for smokers at a time when e-cigarettes were often sold as novelty items at mall kiosks.

"People were marketing it in kind of a cheap, sleazy way," Healy says. "I thought if we come in and aim it at smokers, it could be big." He was right, and Blu quickly became a competitor for NJOY, along with another cigalike maker called Logic. Back then, few people had heard of a little company called Ploom, but that wouldn't be the case for long.

By 2010, almost three years after its founding, Ploom was finally starting to look like a real company, and Adam and James were acting more like real founders. They'd hired a few engineers and designers, and the small but growing team had some office space in an old can factory in San Francisco's industrial Dogpatch neighborhood, which they shared with a Stanford-born company making sophisticated sex toys. It wasn't anything fancy, just a few conference rooms and some desks and filing cabinets arranged around an open floor plan, but it was certainly a step up from squatting in a friend's office space. Adam and James made it theirs, decorating the lime-green walls and the glass conference room doors with Ploom's loopy, cursive logo. Once things were up and running, they even invited a news crew from CBS's now-defunct online magazine *SmartPlanet* in for a tour. James clearly delighted in showing the reporter how "to Ploom," and he spoke grandly about the "new paradigm" his little start-up had created. Adam was a little stiffer, his brown eyes unblinking as he gave a straight delivery of the "pain point" he and James sought to fix: traditional cigarette smoking. The CBS segment was an exciting step for a team that was still so small you could count the number of employees off on your fingers, a team small enough to feel like a group of friends out to change smoking together. "We would have parties at our office once in a while, where we'd move all the desks, put on some music, invite friends and family over," Sonderegger says. "It was pretty cool."

At the time, Adam was Ploom's CEO, and James was its chief operating officer, but those titles were mostly for show. They each had tasks they focused on—Adam's areas were mostly fundraising, flavor development, and everything to do with Ploom's tobacco pods, while James focused on product design, materials, and production—but they were essentially co-running the company, a setup that had its ups and downs. Sonderegger remembers Adam and James disappearing behind closed doors for hours to hash out their disagreements over even small aspects of how to run the business. They seemed to butt heads constantly, and it didn't matter that Adam was technically the CEO. James always wanted to have a say, which meant they were often at an impasse. "Maybe a decision was made, or not," Sonderegger says. "It was a two-headed monster."

There were other challenges to start-up life. Money was always an issue, especially because product development was taking far longer than anyone had bargained for. Adam and James had promised their investors they'd have a working product by the end of 2008, Sonderegger remembers, but the process kept hitting snags. They were still empty-handed more than a year after that target date. "If you ask a designer, 'How long is it going to take?' whatever they say, you multiply it by two or 2.5," Sonderegger says. As Adam and James's team kept pouring money into Ploom without making any back, it was clear they needed to do some more fundraising—somewhere in the neighborhood of a million dollars.

The guys had found an investor who liked the idea of Ploom, but he wasn't ready to hand over a million dollars of his own money. Instead, he organized a pledge fund, a form of fundraising through which lots of people chip in smaller amounts of money to reach a larger goal. The problem was he was having trouble convincing his contacts to get involved.

"They basically said, 'We're not investing in cigarette stuff. That's it. Done,'" recalls a company source. "All of a sudden it fell through, and they were left with no money." The choice was either go under or beg one of the existing investors to give a little more. Adam and James chose to beg—until investor Riaz Valani came through with his own money. The influx of cash helped Adam and James finally complete Ploom's first product: the ModelOne.

The ModelOne looked like a sleek, black fountain pen and vaporized tiny pods of tobacco in flavors like "Café Noir" and "Mint." Expectations were high within the nascent e-cigarette community. In 2010, Sonderegger posted on an e-cigarette message board what could be considered the company's first advertisement. It was simple—just the words "small, dark, and handsome" above an image of the sleek, black ModelOne device—but it did the trick. "We got overloaded with comments and people wanting to try it," Sonderegger remembers. The e-cigarettes widely available at that time were mostly fairly weak cigalikes that came in only a small range of flavors. Devoted vapers like Julie Woessner at CASAA were tired of hacking their own products out of devices they'd ordered from overseas, and the ModelOne seemed like a welcome alternative to all that headache. "The ModelOne—if it had worked—would have sold really well," Sonderegger says.

But as customers were soon to learn, the ModelOne was riddled with problems. For one thing, Adam and James had chosen to power it with butane, a gas often used in cigarette lighters and camping stoves. This meant users had to walk around with cans of butane and deal with manually filling the device's fuel tank themselves. Adam and James liked that the ModelOne didn't look, feel, or function like other e-cigarettes on the market, which they viewed as pedestrian. But Sonderegger could see that butane wasn't the right fuel source, especially when there were plenty of battery-operated, more convenient options available. Nobody wanted to deal with refilling their device using a can of straight butane. Worse, flicking the device on sometimes shocked your fingers, as when you catch a spark on a rogue lighter. The whole thing made the product seem low-tech—which was not a great look given that, at forty dollars, the ModelOne was about four times the price of many e-cigarettes on the market at the time. Finally, and most crucially, Ploom's pods didn't deliver nearly enough nicotine to satisfy smokers. "I used to tape two of them together" to get a stronger hit, Sonderegger says. "James used to give me super stink-eye in the office, because that showed that it wasn't working well enough for me." Ultimately, the ModelOne sold only a few thousand units, and Adam and James begrudgingly admitted that they essentially needed to start from scratch.

Facing an eighteen-month redesign process during which there would be no product for him to market, Sonderegger amicably parted ways with the Ploom team in early 2011. He says the length of the looming redesign process convinced him to leave, but an interview he gave to *Vice* suggests it may have been more complicated than that. "I remember when they hired me, actually, I said that I'd accept the position as long they promised me that they'd never take money from Big Tobacco," Sonderegger told the website in late 2019. It didn't take long to realize that was wishful thinking.

3

REINFORCEMENTS (2011–2013)

James was growing impatient. Start-ups always hit bumps in the road, but Ploom's path had been especially rocky. After years of development, its product wasn't selling. Financing was touch-and-go. And perhaps most serious of all, James was growing increasingly convinced that Adam wasn't the right CEO for the job.

Adam, reserved as he was, didn't seem at home pitching investors or talking to reporters, which was the name of the game for a start-up CEO. He seemed more at home in the lab than in front of a camera. James had always been the more charismatic founder, at least in public. He decided he had to do something.

In early 2011, James started meeting with his investors to figure out a path forward. Everyone seemed to agree on one point: Adam wasn't working out as CEO. He was a brilliant product designer, but he wasn't a born fundraiser, and he just didn't have a mind for finance. He hadn't locked down as many new investors as his financers would have liked, his financial reports were haphazard, and the board was growing increasingly frustrated with the virtually unusable information he was bringing to meetings. By the spring of 2011, James and his investors had come to a joint decision: Adam would handle the technological side of the business, which had always been his strong suit, as well as some administrative tasks, and James would step into the spotlight as CEO. The two-headed monster had officially become one.

Adam accepted the change without much drama—and perhaps even some relief—and investor Ralph Eschenbach swears there were no hard feelings after the swap. But it's hard to say how much was hidden behind Adam's placid demeanor. The mood at the office, at least, seemed to have shifted. There was always an elephant in the room, even if Adam himself didn't acknowledge it. "It gets really tough when it's your baby. It's not just some other person's project. You take it personally," says Kurt Sonderegger, who remained friendly with Adam after leaving the company. "Of course there was some tension there."

With James installed in his new role, he started looking for reinforcements. Riaz Valani and the other investors weren't going to keep pouring money into the company forever, especially if the product barely worked. James and Adam knew they needed investors who could not only offer money but also help with product development. The problem was there were only so many people with the kind of expertise they needed. E-cigarettes were not only a new product, but also a new technology. Pharma companies could have been an option, but they historically hadn't been interested in nicotine products, just like many of the independent investors Adam and James had approached years earlier.

The solution was as clear as it was controversial: people from Big Tobacco, the industry Ploom had been founded to disrupt, would have the answers. Nobody knew more about nicotine chemistry or tobacco product design; and nobody, as Adam and James had learned while doing their grad school research in the Master Settlement Agreement documents, knew more about how to make a product sell. They started putting out feelers, approaching major tobacco brands, including R.J. Reynolds, Imperial, and Philip Morris, in search of the perfect partner.

Their proactive outreach turned out to be unnecessary, though. In 2011, Japan Tobacco International—the international division of Japan Tobacco Inc., the world's fourth-largest tobacco company—offered Ploom a ten-million-dollar investment. A publicly traded company that sold more than

500 billion cigarettes in 2011 had agreed to invest millions of dollars in a shaky start-up that had sold only a few thousand units of its flagship product. What were JTI executives thinking? Perhaps they were just taken with Adam and James's vision. Perhaps, as some industry insiders suggest, they realized they were falling behind other cigarette companies in the race for next-generation products.

Or, perhaps, the problems that had sunk Ploom's ModelOne in the U.S. market were exactly what had caught JTI's eye. Vaping is legal in Japan, but the country forbids the sale of nicotine e-liquids. Because Ploom ran on tobacco pods rather than e-liquids, it may have represented one of Japan Tobacco's best chances of getting in on the growing cigarette alternatives market in its home country. And ten million dollars mattered very little to a company like JTI, even though it was life-changing for Adam and James.

But it's probably an oversimplification to say that Adam and James took the deal only for money, or even as a last-ditch resort. They had pitched Ploom as a product that could disrupt Big Tobacco, but not because they hated Big Tobacco. In fact, both men *liked* smoking—a lot. In interviews, James has called cigarettes "the most successful consumer product of all time," and he has waxed poetic about the "magic and luxury of the tobacco category." Ploom wasn't born from hatred of cigarettes or of Big Tobacco; it was born from a desire not to die and to create a cool (and profitable) new product that could help other people continue to consume nicotine without dying. Adam and James's message had always been about giving smokers an alternative product they could feel better about using, rather than convincing them to quit using tobacco or nicotine outright. If a Big Tobacco company wanted to help them do it, so what? Says a source close to the company, "There was a belief that [JTI had] accepted the mission and realized [that] the future was ultimately in these alternatives."

Plus, JTI was making all kinds of appealing promises. While James and Adam kept running day-to-day operations and guiding the business forward, JTI pledged to help with the global sales and distribution of Ploom products. "They had promised to do [something] like Apple stores for the products, with walk-in demonstrations," says a source with knowledge of the deal. From the way they were talking, it sounded like JTI was going to make Ploom a household name. A source with knowledge of the founders' thinking says they accepted JTI's offer in part because, "unlike the other [tobacco] companies, they were willing to do a minority investment" rather than a full sale. But some former employees wondered if, someday, JTI would acquire Ploom outright, taking their technology global and making the two Stanford grads Silicon Valley success stories before they turned forty.

With a boost from JTI, Ploom released its second product in 2012. It was called Pax, and it vaporized loose-leaf tobacco—at least, theoretically. The $250 device was considerably sleeker than the ModelOne, with a design that *Inc.* magazine likened to a "stubby iPhone." The Pax had a metallic body, a retractable mouthpiece, and a subtle graphic logo that looked like a cross between a flower and an *X*. It was also much easier to deal with than the ModelOne. Users would fill a small reservoir with loose-leaf tobacco, then wait thirty seconds for the internal battery to heat and vaporize the tobacco before they started to inhale. No butane required.

The device was explicitly marketed for use with tobacco, but company executives were well aware that it could work with marijuana, too, and that many customers were using it in this way. Many potential investors over the years had asked if Ploom vaporizers worked with marijuana, so they knew that the curiosity and interest were out there. The company didn't explicitly encourage this off-label usage, but it didn't exactly discourage it, either— much to investor Japan Tobacco's chagrin, company sources remember. JTI had no interest in jumping into the marijuana market—or inviting the kind of scrutiny that this could bring. But JTI's was a minority opinion. Sure, most customers were using Pax to vaporize weed, not tobacco, but at least they were buying the device—and in the increasingly crowded e-cigarette market, that was success enough.

After NJOY won its lawsuit against the FDA in 2010 and cleared a path for other makers to launch e-cigarette products almost without restriction, a flood of new vaping devices and thousands of flavored e-liquids hit the market, many made by entrepreneurial types launching small businesses. For the most part, they were making "open-system" devices: vape pens that users could refill over and over again with different e-liquids. "For a very long time, the open-system, small mom-and-pop players completely dominated the market," says Rob Crossley, CEO of the e-liquid company Cosmic Fog Vapors. Specialty vape shops selling these devices—along with every e-liquid flavor under the sun, from "Cookies and Cream" to "Unicorn Poop" (aka rainbow sherbet)—were starting to open in cities across the country.

As open-system devices became more popular, the biggest vaping enthusiasts perfected the art of modifying (or "modding") them to fit their exact specifications. Vapers had been doing this out of necessity since the very earliest days of e-cigarettes, but modding was increasingly becoming a hobby of its own. People began to geek out over building their own heating coils and vaping devices, either totally from scratch or by combining parts made by different e-cigarette manufacturers to get a bespoke device. Users also began tinkering with the battery power and wattage on their devices, tricking them out so they could vaporize more liquid at once and blow fat clouds of vapor into the air.

"Your traditional smokers who didn't care about any of this stuff, a lot of them were using older equipment," like simpler cigalike models, says Kurt Sonderegger, Ploom's original marketing director. But the new guard was building a vibrant subculture out of mod vaping, holding cloud-blowing contests and vape festivals and flooding message boards with tips on getting the biggest hit or building the best device. America's view of the vaping industry became "these obnoxious guys just blowing huge clouds," Sonderegger says.

Pax did not fit into that world. It came with no tweaking or modding required, and it looked sleek and sexy. Customers, bloggers, and journalists immediately noticed the difference. Beyond the iPhone comparison, the Pax won nicknames like "the Lambo of vaporizers" (from *The Verge*) and was deemed (by the site *Social Underground*) "sleek enough to fit in a three-piece suit." Ploom leaned into those implications of luxury. Up until this point, vaping had not been considered "cool," at least not in mainstream circles. Outside the mod vaping world, vaporizers were often seen, at best, as a techy novelty and, at worst, as the butt of a joke. ("I get made fun of by smokers," lamented one e-cigarette user on the online E-Cigarette Forum, and "I get made fun of by non-smokers.") But the modern, slender Pax fit in perfectly with the tastes of twenty- and thirty-something Millennials. It was easy to envision someone holding an iPhone in one hand and a Pax in the other. And maybe there was something appealing and rebellious about turning a product designed for use with tired old tobacco into the hippest new way to consume marijuana.

Pax's release in 2012 coincided with a new movement to take marijuana use mainstream. A majority of likely U.S. voters that year said they supported the idea of legalizing marijuana and regulating it similarly to tobacco or alcohol. Colorado and Washington both legalized recreational use of the drug in 2012, joining a group of about a dozen states that had already approved pot for medicinal use. Customers in Ploom's home state of California, where medical marijuana had already been legal for more than a decade, were also more than ready for a device like Pax. People who liked to get high but didn't necessarily jibe with traditional stoner culture, or who had legitimate medical marijuana prescriptions and wanted a subtle way to use the drug, clicked with a device like Pax.

Capitalizing on the moment, Adam and James hired a marketing team that could make Pax a vaporizer for trendsetters. Sarah Richardson, who joined Ploom as its marketing director in 2012, after nearly a decade in alcohol marketing, did the best she could with what was still a fairly limited budget. Often using grand arguments about changing the world and saving lives, she was able to convince publications to run advertisements on the cheap. But even better than cheap was free, and that's where social media came into the picture. Because e-cigarette companies were not yet regulated, and were not covered by marketing limitations from the Tobacco Master Settlement Agreement, they were free to do almost whatever they pleased online, as long as they didn't make any health claims that would upset the FDA.

Richardson and her team created the handle "@paxvapor" and started posting on Instagram in 2012, blasting out a mixture of staff photos, blurry concert pictures, San Francisco cityscapes, and stylized product shots. There were Pax vaporizers next to sweating glasses of beer and heaping platters of nachos, held aloft in Times Square, clutched in dark-manicured nails, and propped against laptops streaming the *Anchorman 2* trailer; and the Pax was referred to in hashtags like #PaxOnTheTown and

#LadiesWhoPax. The company also sponsored music festivals and concerts, and it looked for influential people and famous Pax fans, like actor Donald Glover and rapper Big Boi, who could help them get the buzz going. The company was building not just a brand but a lifestyle. Pax wasn't a dirty, smelly traditional cigarette, but it wasn't a clunky, dorky e-cigarette, either. In Pax's world, using tobacco could be aspirational again. Sleek, safer, and socially acceptable enough, the Pax was a device that people could feel good about using.

James and Adam were also trying to make nicotine seem at home in the progressive San Francisco lifestyle. They hammed it up in interviews, making a show of vaping in front of reporters and using shock value as a public relations strategy. "Unlike most of his valley peers, [James Monsees] enjoys describing himself as a tobacco executive," read one *Bloomberg* story from 2013, which went on to recount a dinner party at which James was "booed" for his line of work before he went on to explain that he was making cigarette alternatives. "Eventually, they applauded," James told the reporter.

The pair also tried to chip away at the stigma around nicotine. "People need to question their biases against tobacco," Adam said in the same *Bloomberg* article, his frustration almost leaping off the page—his point being that there was nothing wrong with using nicotine if people could do it in a safer way, without combustion. (The article did not grapple much with the big question of whether vaping was indeed safter than smoking.) The founders were doing their best to normalize nicotine by coaxing Americans to view it more like other habit-forming substances that were seen as fairly benign, like caffeine, alcohol, and, increasingly, marijuana. "I consume a lot of nicotine and drink a lot of coffee. This enables me to sleep less and work more," James breezily told entrepreneurial site IdeaMensch when asked about his productivity hack. In the same article, he said Ploom's products were for "people who want to enjoy tobacco but [who] don't self-identify with—or don't necessarily want to be associated with—cigarettes." It wasn't *exactly* describing Ploom's products as recreational, but it came awfully close.

Now that James was CEO, he was running a little wild in the press. He had a tendency to be too clever for his own good, drifting away from the core message—combustible cigarettes are bad, so we're making something better—and toward something harder to tie up in a neat sound bite. In an interview with the Millennial news video channel 20to30, James pointed out that Ploom was "not an activist company," and he emphasized that if people "don't like what we're making better than cigarettes, then have a cigarette, that's fine." It was a jarring comment from someone who'd built a brand on the idea of making smoking obsolete, but it got to the heart of what he and Adam had always thought. They weren't smoking-cessation evangelists; they were just guys trying to give people a newer, hipper, and (they hoped) healthier way to "smoke," and they were using Big Tobacco's money to do it. James explained JTI's investment away in the 20to30 interview, too. "Our fear was that it would be advantageous for [tobacco] companies just to not to have us around one way or the other—buy us out, put us out of business, wrap us up in court, who knows," he said. "We were at least able to find one [JTI] who was pretty well aware of what it takes to be innovative."

By 2013, in part thanks to JTI's investment, the Pax device was really starting to blow up. A former employee with knowledge of the company's sales says it was never difficult to convince head shops to stock Pax products, and most sold out once they did. Dispensaries were a harder sell back then, as most were used to stocking only marijuana flowers and edibles, but it didn't matter. It was beginning to feel like everybody in San Francisco had a Pax vaporizer. In the darkness at concerts, the former Ploom employee remembers, a sea of illuminated Pax logos would appear where once there had been the flames from lighters.

By this point, Ploom was established enough to move into a Mission District office space all its own. Its offices were right below those of the Burning Man music festival staff, and in interviews, company executives liked to joke that the Burning Man crew made Ploom look conservative by contrast, which was no easy feat. Employees who worked at Ploom at the time lovingly describe the atmosphere as a tech start-up/frat house. Most of the growing staff, which was approaching forty people, were Millennials in their twenties or thirties. They may have been attracted by the mission of giving smokers a safer alternative, but the vibe at Ploom wasn't so different from that of any other Silicon Valley tech start-up. People would skateboard back and forth across the office's concrete floors and shoot each other with foam Nerf darts, and the company organized group outings to cocktail bars and the Lagunitas Brewing Company. One former staffer remembers "Icing" a coworker (i.e., tricking him into chugging a Smirnoff Ice) on his birthday. "It was a great, strong culture," the employee remembers. "That's how I met all the people who became my friends in [San Francisco]." Other Ploom staffers remember the vibrant social fabric at the office, with bonds so tight that Ploomers were sometimes asked to be in one another's weddings. An undercurrent of anticipation buzzed beneath everything, a constant feeling that something big was just around the corner.

Adam and James were always down to join the party. With the company as small as it was, the cofounders behaved more like part of the gang than C-suite executives. They installed a pool table in the middle of the Mission District office and often stayed after hours to drink beer and shoot pool. They came to company happy hours and were pleased to chat during their many early mornings and late nights at the office. Ploom employees remember Adam and James as approachable, friendly guys who involved themselves in nearly every aspect of the business and got to know their hires well enough to throw them going-away parties. "They still, to this day, have been the most involved CEOs and leadership I've dealt with," one former staffer remembers.

But a close eye could see that the two founders didn't necessarily treat each other with the same fondness. "They were definitely not buddy-buddy," one former employee remembers. Another early hire remembers hearing about the two founders running into each other on the street and not saying a single word to each other. They got along fine at work, and there was no public awkwardness around the company pool table, but their Stanford-era friendship had certainly cooled, congealing into something more like what one would see in an old married couple who knew each other's quirks but bickered constantly. "You spend so much time with people in this environment that is sometimes stressful, and that brings out everything," says the founders' old Stanford friend Colter Leys. And though Adam wasn't the type to say so out in the open, a leadership swap is never easy on the ego—or on the relationship. "When two people found an endeavor and one of them is the CEO," says a former employee, "the relationship almost always fractures."

While Pax was taking off, Ploom also launched the redesigned version of its first product, dubbed the ModelTwo. It got some positive reviews from bloggers and the trade press, and it was clearly better than the first version. It was battery-powered and generally less buggy, which was a huge step in the right direction, but it still wasn't landing right with customers.

ModelTwo didn't fit seamlessly into the vaping marketplace. There were the hard-core vapers who built or modified their own devices and talked about them on e-cigarette message boards, and then there was the growing segment of people who couldn't be bothered to make their own coils or research wattage, people who wanted something cheap and simple, something they could buy at the convenience store just like they used to buy cigarettes. Increasingly, the second group's needs were being met by the same companies that had once sold them cigarettes.

Smoking rates in the United States were continuing to tumble, dropping to a record-low 17.8 percent of American adults in 2013. Cigarette sales, logically enough, continued falling, too. They'd begun to drop off in the United States starting in the 1980s—and when e-cigarettes started taking off around 2012, it seemed only to accelerate that decline.

Independent vaping companies had proven that e-cigarettes could be successful, and now Big Tobacco wanted in. In 2012, Lorillard acquired e-cigarette company Blu. "They were looking for someone who had established as a brand," says Blu founder Jason Healy. "They wanted to get in early."

This turned out to be a smart play, because the United States' top-two tobacco companies, R.J. Reynolds and Altria (the parent company of Marlboro maker Philip Morris USA), were quick to jump on the bandwagon. In 2013, R.J. Reynolds introduced its own line of rechargeable e-cigarettes, called Vuse. They looked like silver pens, and their cartridges drew on a new type of e-liquid, one that used a nicotine salt (a mixture of nicotine and acid that wasn't as harsh to inhale as freebase nicotine). That same year, Altria piloted its own brand of e-cigarettes, MarkTen, which looked similar to the Vuse. With multimillion-dollar advertising budgets and existing relationships with distributors, these Big Tobacco–backed brands quickly began taking root in the fast-growing convenience store market.

Ploom's ModelTwo was trying, unsuccessfully, to straddle two worlds. If convenience stores wanted to sell simple, mass-market e-cigarettes, they could turn to the cigarette companies whose products they'd been stocking for decades. Meanwhile, specialty vape shops were selling mostly open-system devices, e-liquids, and the materials that hard-core vapers needed to build their own equipment. Ploom's ModelTwo fell into a no-man's-land. It was too techy for old-school tobacco shops, too weak for hard-core vapers, and too complicated for gas stations and convenience stores. "You're cold-calling someone working behind the counter at a gas station, and you're trying to explain vaporization and this brand-new technology," remembers a former employee with knowledge of Ploom's sales process. Such conversations were often challenging.

Adam and James knew that if Ploom were to survive, it would have to adapt. James was working with an outside design firm on a new device prototype that he hoped could compete with the slew of big-budget devices entering the convenience store market, and Adam was going back to square one in terms of nicotine delivery. Ploom's tobacco pods simply didn't deliver enough nicotine—and Adam should have known this better than almost anyone, because he was still, secretly, smoking traditional cigarettes. He would ploom all day long and still find himself with nicotine cravings.

A nicotine salt, like that R.J Reynolds had used in its Vuse e-cigarette, seemed like a promising solution. In those days, most e-cigarette liquids used freebase nicotine, which is incredibly harsh to inhale. Because "e-juice" companies could use only a small amount before their formulas became almost unusably strong, most e-cigarette liquids tasted fine but didn't satisfy hard-core smokers. As both an inventor and a smoker, Adam knew that the best way to beat a cigarette was to mimic one. Nicotine salts seemed the way to do that.

Adam apparently went looking for inspiration in old tobacco industry documents, just as he had while in graduate school. In one of his searches, he came across the work of Thomas Perfetti, a longtime R.J. Reynolds scientist.

Perfetti had done some of his best-known work in the 1970s, when he was in his twenties. He was fascinated by how nicotine acted as a naturally occurring insecticide for tobacco plants. A volatile substance, nicotine evaporates easily—but tobacco plants somehow kept nicotine stable on the surface of their leaves. Perfetti wanted to know how they did this. The answer, he found, traced back to the acids found in the tobacco plant, which neutralized and stabilized the plant's nicotine to prevent it from evaporating. He began experimenting with acids that might mimic those naturally found in the tobacco plant, mixing them with freebase nicotine to make nicotine salts. Perfetti eventually wrote a seventeen-page memo detailing how to make nicotine salts using more than a dozen different types of acid. This research became very useful to Adam Bowen a few decades later.

After retiring from Reynolds, Perfetti had opened a tobacco consulting business in North Carolina, advising clients on everything from tobacco smoke chemistry to the production of flavorings. One day, out of the blue, Adam called him with some questions. He was having trouble with the Ploom device's ignition, and he also had some questions about nicotine aerosol and flavored nicotine—essentially, he needed to know how to make Ploom's next product more satisfying to customers. Perfetti was glad to talk these things through with the young inventor; he even turned down offers to become a paid consultant for years because he didn't mind doing it for free. Soon, Adam would call whenever he needed guidance on Ploom's products—in particular, how he might harness nicotine salts to help those products deliver the same hit of nicotine as a combustible cigarette.

With the ModelTwo still selling poorly, Adam was devoting more and more of his time and energy to this research. In the summer of 2013, he brought on a talented chemist named Chenyue Xing to help. She had years of experience in the pharmaceutical industry and had recently been working on developing inhalable medications. Her experience, and her personal values, seemed like a natural fit for the company. Although she'd never been a smoker herself, Chenyue liked the idea of a product that could help smokers switch to something less dangerous. "I do want to have an alternative product for people without [their] having . . . to stick at a very-high-nicotine intake level," she says. With Chenyue's help, Adam kept working toward a nicotine salt formula whose nicotine content and delivery—the way it came with just enough burn and a little hit to the back of the throat without becoming too harsh to handle—would rival those of a traditional cigarette.

Once they had a few formulas mixed up, Adam recruited Gal Cohen, who was running Ploom's science division, and Ari Atkins, an R&D engineer, to start "buzz-testing" them. The process was just what it sounds like: in the Ploom office, Adam, Cohen, and Atkins would inhale the different nicotine salt mixtures to see how strong a buzz they got from each one. (Xing opted out, as she'd never been a smoker.) They'd puff on various formulations and then rate them based on their potency and the rush they produced. It was clear from these tests that Adam's nicotine salt mixtures were stronger— much stronger—than anything he'd been able to achieve with Ploom's earlier products. Sometimes, according to later Reuters reporting, they were so strong they'd send testers to the bathroom nauseated and shaking.

Buzz testing was hardly the pinnacle of careful science, though it wasn't unheard-of for product designers to act as their own test subjects, especially when money was tight. Even still, some company insiders had issues with the testing process.

"Buzz testing," according to one source, is "the wrong starting point" for testing a highly addictive product. In the case of the e-cigarette, to limit a product's potential for abuse, you'd ideally want to deliver only as much nicotine as it took to satisfy a smoker—not what would come with a heady buzz. "You shouldn't be starting with what is most likely to make someone's head ring," the source says. And while it was one thing for a founder to test a product on himself, the situation got ethically stickier when other employees were brought into the mix.

In those days, though, the company—and indeed the whole vaping industry—was still small and scrappy and somewhat lawless, operating without much of a rule book. E-cigarettes weren't regulated by the FDA. Federal officials weren't going to be double-checking anyone's lab procedures. Even many career scientists still didn't know what to make of e-cigarettes, unsure whether products like Ploom's were safer than cigarettes.

It was a logical conclusion to think so, because just about anything is safer than a combustible cigarette, but James and Adam didn't have a single authoritative, long-term, human study that could prove that using a Ploom device was safer than smoking. They could fall back on emerging research that suggested that e-cigarettes, as a category, were less dangerous than traditional cigarettes. But even that literature wasn't conclusive, and it also wasn't based on the specific devices Ploom was making. Their company's entire foundation came down to an educated guess, one that Adam and James believed in passionately—so passionately, in fact, that they now felt ready to expand the product line with a device they hoped would disrupt the public's idea of what an e-cigarette could be.

4

One day in 2014, James came into the office with big news. "This," he said holding up what looked like a flash drive, "is going to be the new Juul."

In his hand was the latest prototype of the device he and Adam hoped would destroy combustible cigarettes, the device they'd been working on for months and were banking on to succeed in ways Ploom never had. It was tiny—small enough to fit in the palm of one's hand—and its rectangular body, which would come in subdued colors like slate gray and black, did look just like a flash drive; you could even charge it in a computer's USB port. At its top was an opening where users snapped in a pod filled with nicotine salt e-liquid—which the company would be calling "JuulSalts" and which they planned to release in flavors like "Mint" and "Fruit." A clear, diamond-shaped window between the device's body and its mouthpiece let users see how much liquid they had left. There were no buttons or switches. To activate the device, a user needed only to inhale. A tiny light on the front glowed green when the device was charged and red when the Juul's battery was almost out of juice. And in a fun but pointless twist, the device flashed in rainbow colors if you waved it around. The only branding on the whole thing was the name, "Juul," engraved in small capital letters at the bottom of the vaporizer.

"Part of the company went, 'Ugh,'" remembers Paul Moraes, who had joined the team in 2014 to run the company's supply chain. This little thing, about half an inch across and three and a half inches long, was supposed to be the future not just of the company but of the entire tobacco industry? "It wasn't what we expected," Moraes adds. "It just looked like a little box. It just didn't look appealing to certain people."

Moraes's concerns were both aesthetic and functional. He thought the design too plain, but more important, he doubted his team could ever get it to work the way James and Adam wanted. Many of the vaping products on the market at that time were considerably larger than the Juul prototype. Moraes had trouble imagining finding batteries and other materials small enough to fit the Juul prototype, let alone buying those materials at a price that would let the company turn a profit. The company's engineers were also working on a temperature-control system that would prevent the device from overheating the nicotine e-liquid in each pod—a necessary precaution, as devices that ran too hot could produce excessive amounts of dangerous by-products like formaldehyde. It was crucial to get that system right, but it seemed difficult to do it in such a slim device.

Others within the company questioned the wisdom of creating a tiny device at a time when the biggest vaping fans favored large, high-powered devices that produced huge clouds of vapor. Maybe no one wanted a sleek little device that produced a delicate wisp of vapor, even if it did have a kick that could rival that of any cigarette. Maybe they just wanted something that would look flashy and let them exhale huge clouds of vapor.

Still, despite these concerns, "James was adamant that the size was not going to change, the pod wasn't going to change," Moraes remembers. James had a vision for the product. He wanted it to be so small and subtle that smokers could slip it into their pocket or purse undetected and steal outside for nicotine hits throughout the day. And though the company's founders did plenty of disagreeing, Adam had James's back on this one. So, Moraes had two options: figure it out or get out.

Trying to be the voice of reason was not unfamiliar to Moraes.

When he started at Ploom in 2014, Moraes immediately saw his role. Yes, he was there to clean up the supply chain—but he was also there to be one of the "adults there for supervision . . . trying to bring a little bit of structure," Moraes says. The company still felt very young, and there weren't nearly as many processes and procedures in place as he would have expected for a company making a product that came with a lot of liability.

A consultant who worked with the company at the time remembers struggling to get James and Adam to listen when he told them they needed to whip things into shape. He urged the founders to set up a formal system for users to report health problems if their devices malfunctioned or if they had a bad reaction to the product. He told them to look into hiring a nurse who could triage these complaints and direct people to medical care if necessary. "They didn't implement any of this stuff" until later on, the consultant remembers. "Adam and James were strong believers in self, that they were creating blockbuster products. They don't want to believe anything that is not congruent to their worldview."

James was so set on his small, sleek Juul prototype—which had been nicknamed "Splinter," after the rat who teaches martial arts in *Teenage Mutant Ninja Turtles*—that it sometimes felt like he was losing sight of reason. It took Moraes's team tens of thousands of hours of labor to get James's design actually to work. And even when he and his team finally found a way to squeeze all the necessary components into the device, there were still issues. Chief among them: the pods leaked. Sometimes, when a user pulled too hard on the device's mouthpiece, e-juice would spill out and get on their tongue. Internally at the company, this was known as JIM, for "juice in mouth," and Ploom employees were very familiar with it. Internal testing hadn't stopped with the buzz testing of the nicotine salt formula. It wasn't unusual for the company's engineers or scientists to tap coworkers on the shoulder and ask them to try out whatever they were working on, which meant many employees had firsthand brushes with JIM.

"[The juice] was foul to get in your mouth and on your tongue," says one former employee who was often recruited as an informal tester. It was also a buzz kill, a reminder that the company's freewheeling atmosphere maybe didn't lend itself quite as well to safety. "Even while I was there, I had an inkling [of], 'Am I the guinea pig on a new thing?'" the employee muses. "Am I being smart, in the third-person perspective, living this right now?"

Leakage aside, Adam's team was making real headway on the JuulSalts mixture. By mid-2014, they were ready to go beyond buzz testing and run an actual study on the potency of their nicotine salt formulas, which consisted of nicotine, acid, flavorings, and propylene glycol, a chemical often added to foods to improve their texture and shelf stability.

Adam's team chose to do its testing in New Zealand, at a research center commonly used by tobacco companies. They recruited twenty-four current smokers willing to test various nicotine salt formulations, as well as a Pall Mall cigarette for comparison. But before the formal study got under way, Adam, science director Gal Cohen, and R&D engineer Ari Atkins once again volunteered themselves for what was essentially a test run—a "Phase Zero" study.

After hitting various nicotine salt formulations and dragging on Pall Malls, they measured the amount of nicotine that had been pumped throughout their bodies. Their test results showed that, after a few minutes of puffing at thirty-second intervals, several of their nicotine salt mixtures produced maximal blood nicotine concentrations approaching that of a Pall Mall cigarette. It was hard to extrapolate much from a study so small, especially since there's huge variation in how people use and respond to nicotine, but the data suggested a nicotine salt formula could indeed rival the feel and effect of a regular cigarette. For some users, when using certain e-cigarette devices, a benzoic acid salt that was 4 percent nicotine by weight actually produced a maximal blood nicotine concentration even higher than that of a Pall Mall.

These were exactly the kind of results Adam had wanted. His goal all along had been to create an e-cigarette that mimicked a combustible cigarette. Surely no one would be tempted to go back to traditional cigarettes if they were getting all the nicotine they wanted from this new, supposedly safer device. But when the company began testing the Juul device and its nicotine salt in consumer focus groups, they got some surprising results.

A representative from Ploom's market research group emailed Chelsea Kania, the company's brand manager, in late September 2014. She had some good news and some bad news from the Juul focus groups. "The younger group is open to trying something new and liked [Juul] for being smart, new, techy, etc.," she wrote in an email later included in a consolidated legal complaint filed as part of multi-district litigation alleging that Juul deceitfully marketed its products and created a public nuisance by addicting people to nicotine. (Juul largely denied the claims and argued that the FDA, not the court system, has jurisdiction over e-cigarette marketing and sales. A federal judge disagreed but dismissed racketeering claims from the consolidated complaint; as of January 2021, the litigation was still proceeding.) In what was surely music to the PR team's ears, one tester wrote that Juul "might manage to make smoking cool again," according to the complaint.

The email also contained a gut punch for Adam, though. "The qualitative findings suggested this product isn't going to fit as well with customers who are looking to cut back on the cigarette intake," the market researcher wrote, according to the complaint. The next day, she sent another email elaborating on why. "The delivery was almost too much for some smokers, especially those used to regular e-cigarettes," she wrote. "When they approached the product like they would a Blu or other inexpensive e-cig, they were floored by the delivery and didn't really know how to control it." Though some testers did say they liked the formula, several said the product was "too much for me" or "too strong," at least after they'd taken their first few puffs. They might get the hang of it over time, but the first inhale was heady.

Chenyue Xing, Adam's co-chemist, was uneasy with reviews like these, she later told Reuters. Adam wanted to make a strong nicotine salt because it would match the experience smokers were used to, and thus help them quit cigarettes. This made sense, but the focus group's responses seemed to suggest he could do that with a slightly less potent formula, which seemed like a good thing.

A high nicotine content was worrisome not only from an addiction standpoint, but also because it could make people sick (or at least jittery). Traditional cigarettes have a built-in Off switch in that they burn out. Smokers have to consciously decide to pull out another and light it, and even that small amount of active participation forces them to decide if they truly want more. An electronic product shortens that easy off-ramp. Juul's e-juice pods were designed to last two hundred puffs and to deliver about as much nicotine as an entire pack of cigarettes, all in one convenient package. Eventually, the device's battery would run out its charge or the e-juice would run dry, but Xing could imagine people accidentally ripping through an entire pod without realizing they'd just dosed themselves with as much nicotine as they'd get from a whole pack of cigarettes—and worse, becoming dependent on that level of consumption. She and Adam had specifically set out to make a smooth formula, one that wouldn't irritate the throat or cause discomfort. And when all you had to do was inhale, using the device was almost *too* easy.

"You hope that they get what they want, and they stop," she told Reuters. "We didn't want to introduce a new product with a stronger addictive power." The company explored the idea of a dosage control feature, but it was never implemented.

Despite the mixed results from the focus group, the patent application for JuulSalts, which was filed in October 2014, specifically hyped the mixture's strength. "It has been unexpectedly discovered herein that certain nicotine liquid formulations provide satisfaction in an individual superior to that of free base nicotine, and more comparable to the satisfaction in an individual smoking a traditional cigarette," the application read. The Ploom team had also stumbled upon the "surprising and unexpected" finding that some of their nicotine formulas caused users' heart rates to skyrocket higher and faster than they would after they'd smoked a traditional cigarette, the application added. To support those claims, the application cited data from the studies in New Zealand, which showed certain nicotine salts could lead to a higher blood nicotine concentration than a traditional cigarette after about five minutes of periodic puffing.

From an intellectual property standpoint, it was valuable to demonstrate that Juul's nicotine salt formulas could exceed a cigarette's maximal nicotine concentration, as it would be difficult for other e-liquid makers to match that result. Many e-cigarette liquids, especially those that used freebase nicotine, were fairly weak. To make one that not only rivaled, but exceeded, a cigarette's nicotine delivery was a coup for founders trying to set themselves apart from the rest of a growing industry. But a result like that also clearly opened the door to criticism. Traditional cigarettes are considered one of the most addictive substances on the planet. Introducing a product that could deliver even *more* nicotine would surely raise some eyebrows.

The Juul product that ultimately hit the market was similar, but not identical, to the one described in that patent application, and company representatives said its nicotine delivery did not exceed that of a cigarette—but in news coverage and lawsuits down the line, Juul would never quite shake the perception that it had beat the cigarette at its own addictive game.

Gal Cohen, Ploom's scientific director, had something he wanted to show his old friend David Abrams. Abrams, a professor of social and behavioral sciences at New York University and a former bigwig at the National Institutes of Health, was one of the tobacco control community's biggest names and a primary supporter of alternative nicotine products like e-cigarettes. Gal finally had a prototype of the Juul device and JuulSalts, and he was eager to show off his company's latest innovation to Abrams and his colleagues. From the moment they saw the data, Abrams says, it was clear the product was a game changer. Nicotine salt wasn't anything new; the research underlying it had been around for decades, and e-cigarettes like R.J. Reynolds's Vuse already used it. But Abrams could plainly see from Cohen's data that Juul had a better mixture with its benzoic acid salt, one with a very solid balance of flavor, nicotine delivery, and strength. Everyone in the room at NYU "looked at me, and said, 'Wow, here's the ticket,'" Abrams remembers. Everyone thought, "'They've done it.'"

Many people in the public health world would not have reacted as Abrams did. Tobacco harm reduction is a uniquely volatile topic for the normally civil researchers in public health. For a long time, the tobacco control community was united around one common purpose: getting smokers to quit cigarettes. Everyone could rally around that shared goal, even if there were different ways of approaching the problem. "There was a kind of unity of purpose, but underneath the surface, there were different motivations," says Clive Bates, who previously ran the United Kingdom's Action on Smoking and Health and is now a proponent of e-cigarettes. Bates says some people were laser-focused on reducing chronic disease associated with smoking; others were concerned with getting cigarettes out of public places to reduce bystanders' exposure to secondhand smoke; others were driven by a hatred for Big Tobacco; and still others had a more moralistic view, seeking to stamp out any addictive substance use. For a while, these various subgroups were able to coexist more or less harmoniously, because they all wanted the same end point: no more cigarettes. But as noncombustible alternatives like e-cigarettes became more popular, the waters got murkier.

By 2014, most researchers agreed that e-cigarettes exposed users to fewer of the toxins and carcinogens of traditional cigarettes, theoretically reducing their risk of developing cancer and other smoking-related diseases if they switched completely. But almost everything else about the products was up for debate.

"These products came on the market as consumer products, not as devices or drugs that were regulated by the FDA in any way," says Dr. Nancy Rigotti, director of the Tobacco Research and Treatment Center at Massachusetts General Hospital. "The usual body of evidence that we would have to look at efficacy and safety were not available." The products were so new that there weren't long-term studies on them, which meant nobody really knew how e-cigarette liquids would affect the human body over the course of years.

"I don't know what the long-term effect, for instance, of inhaling heated propylene glycol is," says Thomas Glynn, a lecturer at Stanford University who formerly directed research at the National Cancer Institute's Smoking, Tobacco, and Cancer Program and later held high-profile jobs at the American Cancer Society. It was hard to imagine vaping turning out to be more dangerous than smoking, Glynn says, "But it's a little bit of 'Why take a chance?'" There also wasn't a scientific consensus on whether e-cigarettes actually helped smokers quit—some research found that they did, while other papers suggested many smokers didn't find them a satisfying replacement. Other research found that many smokers didn't fully switch at all, instead alternating between vaping and smoking, which likely reduced or eliminated many of the benefits associated with vaping in the first place.

As the science evolved, dividing lines were drawn between those who supported tobacco harm reduction and those who took a more prohibitionist stance on nicotine and tobacco. The harm-reduction camp admitted that e-cigarettes were not risk-free and should not be used by anyone who didn't already smoke (and, ideally, only temporarily by those trying to quit), but they viewed them as a valuable lesser of two evils. They thought their lower carcinogen levels, compared to traditional cigarettes, meant they could help reduce deaths from smoking-related disease. And they pointed to studies on toxin and carcinogen levels—and plenty of stories from ex-smokers who had successfully quit—to bolster their points.

For those who believed in harm reduction, it was totally reasonable to switch smokers from cigarettes to a noncombustible product that mimicked a cigarette, as Adam was trying to do with Juul's potent nicotine salt formula. As Adam and James realized in grad school, plenty of smokers can't or won't quit smoking using products like nicotine gum, because nicotine dependency is only half the battle. Smokers are just as accustomed to the motions involved in smoking, the ritual, the kick that accompanies a drag off a cigarette, the buzz of nicotine and the little spark at the back of the throat. Translating that sensory experience to a safer delivery method made sense. If smokers could get the experience they wanted in a way that didn't kill them, they would have every motivation to switch.

There was even a public health argument for creating an e-liquid as potent as Juul's. First and foremost, it kept smokers satisfied—at least, once they got used to the feel of inhaling the product's vapor instead of smoke. Second, because there are chemicals in and by-products produced while heating any e-liquid, you want to use as little of the liquid as you can to minimize exposure to these potential toxins, says Dr. Neal Benowitz, a professor of medicine at the University of California, San Francisco, and one of the nation's leading experts on nicotine pharmacology. If you could get all the nicotine you craved from just a few puffs, versus dragging on a vape all day, that would cut down on your exposure to chemicals and by-products. Juul's highly potent nicotine salt formula did exactly that. It still probably wasn't something you should use for the rest of your life, but it could be a helpful crutch in the short term.

But while the product's potency might have been a positive thing for experienced smokers who were using e-cigarettes to switch, it meant that non-smokers experimenting with e-cigarettes could be exposed to high amounts of addictive nicotine—and that was a major concern for scientists who opposed vaping. Most of these scientists agreed that e-cigarettes weren't as risky as traditional cigarettes in terms of exposure to carcinogens and toxins, but they still thought them a bad idea. In their view, the better solution was to get smokers off nicotine completely, rather than keeping them addicted to a product that might be safer but still wasn't totally safe. "In terms of the health risks, we also need to consider the other ingredients that are in the products: the flavorings, other toxicants that can be generated," says Maciej Goniewicz, an e-cigarette researcher from Roswell Park Comprehensive Cancer Center. Perhaps e-cigarettes produced fewer of the known carcinogens of traditional cigarettes, but that didn't mean they weren't generating health risks of their own, ones that might not come to light for years or decades. And even at that time, there was at least one major problem associated with vaping.

Just as UCSF professor Stanton Glantz had predicted when he met with Adam before Ploom launched, teenagers were quickly drawn to the vaping products that preceded Juul, especially e-liquids that came in appealing flavors—of which there were now thousands, everything from "Pink Lemonade" and "Cotton Candy" to "Banana Cream Pie." In the federally run National Youth Tobacco Survey, more than 13 percent of high school students in 2014 said they had used an e-cigarette in the past thirty days, up from just 4.5 percent the year before. Perhaps even more notable, only 9.2 percent of teenagers reported smoking that year, which meant that e-cigarettes were now more popular among high schoolers than traditional cigarettes. Suddenly, teachers had to be on the lookout for clouds of fruity vapor in addition to the telltale odor of cigarette smoke.

Some researchers argued that the surge in youth vaping actually had a positive side, given that it suggested that teen smokers were using e-cigarettes instead of smoking, or to quit smoking, traditional cigarettes. But many public health advocates didn't see it that way. In a worst-case scenario, experts feared that the e-cigarette boom would prime teenagers for nicotine addiction and make them more apt to start smoking regular cigarettes, erasing decades of public health progress.

"Kids who become addicted to one substance are more likely to try other substances," says Benowitz, the nicotine researcher from UCSF. "It's hard to say which comes first, but there's a very high concordance between vaping nicotine and vaping THC, smoking cigarettes and smoking marijuana." Studies show that nicotine use can affect the way adolescents' brains develop, potentially disrupting the maturation of systems that control attention and decision-making. Some research also suggests that children's still-developing brains are more likely to become dependent on nicotine than adult brains are.

For these reasons, the popularity of teen vaping was a major concern for many in public health. "It is critical that comprehensive tobacco control and prevention strategies for youths should address all tobacco products and not just cigarettes," the CDC wrote in a report about the 2014 National Youth Tobacco Survey results. Groups such as the Campaign for Tobacco-Free Kids were less diplomatic, often blasting the vaping industry in the press and accusing it of pandering to children with its tasty flavors. Vaping is "a

Wild West marketplace with irresponsible marketing and no control over the product," a CTFK spokesperson told *USA Today* in 2014.

Lawmakers, too, were worried about e-cigarettes and the way they were being marketed. The companies that beat Ploom's products to market, like NJOY and Blu, were not known for their restrained sales pitches. In Manhattan, NJOY purchased a flashy Times Square billboard and threw a launch party for one of its products at the scene-y Jane Hotel. Perhaps more galling to many in public health, given the long-standing ban on televised cigarette commercials, the company advertised during the 2014 Super Bowl with a spot that showed a man swapping his friend's cigarettes for NJOY's e-cigs. Blu was also a prolific advertiser, often showing attractive celebrities in its ads and boasting that its products could help vapers circumvent smoking bans. It even created a social networking platform just for vapers.

The companies' advertising drew enough backlash that a Senate committee questioned their respective CEOs during a hearing held in June 2014. Senators berated executives from the two companies for their youth-friendly marketing, for tweets bragging about celebrities using their products, and for their products' kid-friendly flavors, like "Chocolate Treat" and "Cherry Crush." "I don't know how you go to sleep at night," chided West Virginia senator Jay Rockefeller. "I don't know what gets you to work in the morning except the color green of dollars."

Lawmakers' concerns were only deepened by the fact that the FDA still hadn't finalized its policy for regulating e-cigarettes. By 2014, several years had passed since the FDA gained the power to regulate e-cigarettes, and yet the government body still hadn't made it official by publishing a deeming rule. Eric Lindblom, who at the time worked in the FDA's Center for Tobacco Products, says part of the delay had nothing to do with e-cigarettes.

Not too long after the FDA gained the ability to regulate tobacco products in 2009, the agency decided to issue a deeming rule that covered cigars and hookahs as well as e-cigarettes, to get it all out of the way in one fell swoop. This proved problematic, because the cigar industry was lobbying hard for exclusions, arguing to the Obama administration that premium cigars should be exempted from the FDA's regulations. Those conversations, and the political considerations they raised, kept delaying the process. The FDA could have written a deeming rule just for e-cigarettes, but its leadership chose to wait and do it all at once—a decision that made Lindblom very nervous. "It was sort of horrifying," he says. He remembers thinking, "'If Obama loses, it's all over for us.'"

Of course, Obama didn't lose in 2012, and the FDA finally issued proposed regulations for e-cigarettes and other tobacco products in April 2014. Even though it was just a draft, the document inspired a fresh round of lobbying on the part of cigar companies, but now vaping companies were in the fray, too. Chaos erupted when the e-cigarette industry and its customers saw that the FDA was considering a total ban on flavored nicotine e-liquids. The FDA pointed to research that suggested that flavoring agents could be dangerous when inhaled and highlighted survey data that showed that many underage users vaped because the liquids came in appealing flavors. Clearing flavors from the market seemed like a prudent way to reverse what was already shaping up to be a worrying new trend among young people. The agency proposed approving only menthol- and tobacco-flavored e-liquids, which mirrored what was currently available in combustible cigarettes.

During the draft rule's 120-day public comment period, the FDA received 135,000 responses. Some were from public health officials applauding the proposal, but many were from vaping advocates deriding it. Vape shops and e-liquid makers argued that they would go out of business if they couldn't sell and produce, respectively, the thousands of flavored products currently on the market. Vaping advocates also stressed that for many adult smokers, having access to palatable flavored products could mean the difference between sticking with cigarettes and switching to a less harmful vaping product. They cited survey data that showed that adults, not just teenagers, preferred flavored e-liquids, and often drew on their own personal experiences. "I seriously feel my stomach turn when I smell cigarette smoke now, and Tobacco e-juice is even worse," wrote a forty-two-year-old commenter who'd used e-cigarettes to quit a decades-long smoking habit. "But do you know what I love? Pineapple Cheesecake e-juice."

The outcry put the FDA in a tough spot, Lindblom says. The Center for Tobacco Products had to go through every single comment and use them to weigh the pros and cons of the proposed rule. Trickier, the Obama administration was nervous about upsetting the powerful tobacco industry and the lawmakers who supported it, especially if banning flavors would really put vape shops out of business. "There was a big concern about not hurting the economy because of the big recession Obama [had] inherited when he first came into office," Lindblom says. Concerns like these made it very difficult for the FDA to push the rule through. "There's a clearance process," says Mitch Zeller, the director of the FDA's Center for Tobacco Products. "When it comes to rule making, first we need to get it out of the FDA, then we have to get it out of the Department [of Health and Human Services], and then ultimately it needs to be cleared by the White House following interdepartmental review." All that would take time and political maneuvering.

Some elected officials, like Illinois's Dick Durbin, weren't sympathetic to those challenges. Durbin, who, as a teen, had seen his father die of lung cancer, made a name for himself standing up to Big Tobacco companies. Indeed, after winning a seat in the House of Representatives in 1982, he started working on antismoking legislation, starting with a smoking ban on commercial flights shorter than two hours. Durbin was one of the first lawmakers to sponsor legislation that aimed to give the FDA the right to regulate cigarettes, laying the groundwork for the bill that eventually passed in 2009. He was also one of the most influential voices calling for a perjury investigation after several tobacco executives lied under oath during a 1994 congressional hearing by claiming that nicotine was not addictive. In 2010, the Campaign for Tobacco-Free Kids gave Durbin its Champion Award.

Durbin was uneasy as he watched the e-cigarette industry's growth far outpace its regulation. E-cigarettes were now in just about every convenience store. Celebrities like Lindsay Lohan, Bruno Mars, and Katy Perry used them publicly; NJOY had enough money to run a TV commercial during the Super Bowl; and the *Oxford English Dictionary* went on to make *vape* the word of the year for 2014. E-cigarettes clearly weren't going away. "When I took a look at this vaping and e-cigarette situation, I thought, 'There are too many parallels [to Big Tobacco] here,'" Durbin says. "As kids gave up tobacco cigarettes, [tobacco companies] needed a replacement. E-cigarettes would be the way to do it." Just before the FDA's proposed deeming rule came out in 2014, Durbin and a group of other senators sent the first of what would be many letters to the White House, citing concerns about youth e-cigarette addiction and urging the Obama administration to hurry up and implement regulations for e-cigarettes. Vaping companies "really had an open stage for the longest time," Durbin says. "There was ample opportunity for [the] FDA and the federal government to step in with this product. I don't know if it was neglect or what, but it didn't happen, and they started building their market share."

Durbin couldn't have known it yet, but companies like Ploom were just getting started.

5

THE COOL KID (NOVEMBER 2014–MAY 2015)

There was a new kid in town, and his name was Richard Mumby. Mumby was nothing like the stereotypical Silicon Valley tech bro. In a start-up world dominated by hoodies and flip-flops, he was stylish and suave, with well-coiffed, wavy brown hair. He'd gotten an MBA from Dartmouth and then worked in consulting and finance before moving over to the New York City start-up world. He worked first in marketing for the buzzy luxury flash sale site Gilt, which pioneered the idea of exclusive, limited-time sales on designer clothes; and then at Bonobos, a Millennial-focused men's fashion brand beloved on social media. He also started his own marketing firm.

Mumby joined Ploom as a consultant toward the end of 2014 and quickly developed a fan club within the company. He was smart and polished and well put together—perhaps a refreshing change of pace from Adam and James's rumpled, Stanford buddies vibe. "He was very, very well thought of," remembers supply chain head Paul Moraes. "He was super smart, super friendly, and definitely the day he walked in the door he had a strategy." The company was already on the right path, picking up traction on social media and at music festivals and events, but Mumby wanted to slow down and focus on basics, like clearly defining employees' roles and putting together a strategic growth plan for the marketing department beyond haphazardly posting things on social media. A solid foundation could help establish Pax's products as the vaping devices to beat, those that would clearly stand out from the pack. "There's a lot of stigma in the vaporizer space," Mumby later told the fashion website Racked. "It's cluttered and confusing and there's opportunity for a premium brand to help redefine the category altogether."

With that kind of ambitious strategy, the "adults in the room" at Ploom saw big things for Mumby at the company. "He took the whole concept of what we were doing and just expanded it by six degrees in each direction," Paul Moraes says. Some executives even thought Mumby had a future as Ploom's president, a company source remembers. It made some sense: Mumby seemed like the yin to CEO James's yang. James could play the part of the brilliant and irreverent founder who was perhaps a bit too opinionated and confident for his own good, and Mumby, with his master's degree from Dartmouth and his toothpaste commercial–white smile, could balance him out with the kind of polish and poise the business needed to grow.

Mumby never became Ploom's president, but it almost felt like he assumed the role naturally. It didn't take long for Mumby to become the head of a little clique within the marketing department and, indeed, across the whole company, according to some former employees. If Ploom had been a high school, Mumby would have been the homecoming king and his friends the adoring cheerleaders. He had so much latitude to do what he wanted that some employees (mistakenly) wondered whether he was a major stockholder or held some other sway over the leadership team. Any idea he had seemed to get green-lit.

Mumby also had quite a bit of responsibility within the company. Shortly after he joined Ploom, he began coordinating the launch campaign for the new Juul device. The company was working with a Canadian advertising agency called Cult Collective, and in December 2014 Mumby and some members of the marketing team traveled to Calgary to hear Cult's vision for the future of Juul.

"JUUL is the kind of transformation that only a tech company can bring about," the Cult team wrote in its pitch presentation, which was later included in a legal complaint filed by the Massachusetts attorney general, which Juul heavily disputed in court filings of its own and which is moving toward a trial date in 2023. "Short of trying one, the best way to point out the dramatic difference that the technology in JUUL can bestow, and the dated idiocy of analog cigarettes and existing vapor products, is by illustrating the other intelligent evolutions that smarter thinking and technology have provided mankind." As the pitch pointed out, making this comparison would be "childishly easy," given the rate of technological innovation over the past few decades.

According to the presentation, Cult planned to run ads with big photos of laughably outdated consumer products of the not-so-distant past in the foreground: boom boxes, joysticks, chunky old cell phones. In the bottom corner, they'd add a photo of a Juul device and the slogan "Everything changes, eventually. Juul: The evolution of smoking." By showcasing these outdated pieces of equipment, Cult wanted to make the point that traditional cigarettes, too, were passé and low-tech. Juul, by contrast, would be seen as the hip smoking alterative for the digital era, the product that would make smokers stop and wonder why they were still sucking on "a tube of dead leaves" as they fired off texts and called Ubers on their iPhones.

Richard Mumby was not impressed. "It was very, 'It's not your daddy's cigarette,'" says a source involved with the launch campaign. "You know, super corny." There were other problems, too. It seemed like bad judgment to include images of potentially kid-friendly gaming devices, even if they were outdated. And some people within the company felt their ads didn't do enough to actually show off the sleek Juul product. At that time, many e-cigarettes were not visually appealing. As with Pax before it, Juul's sophisticated look and design were some of its best selling points, and it seemed foolish not to highlight that—especially since many smokers, who hadn't had luck with older, less refined products, would need extra coaxing to try another vapor product. Mumby decided to bring in backup.

He called Steven Baillie, a fellow Bonobos alum with whom Mumby had recently worked on another project. He was a New York City–based art director and photographer who billed himself as a "creative director/troublemaker," and he'd worked at big publications like *GQ* and at *T: The New York Times Style Magazine*. Baillie knew how to make a product look desirable. His aesthetic looked to be sex, sex, and more sex, his portfolio filled with photos of women in provocative poses wearing lingerie or nothing at all.

The portfolio matched Baillie's playboy reputation in the fashion industry. One photography website dubbed him "the Purveyor," thanks to his willingness to scout new models in exotic corners of the globe. And in 2006, Baillie was the subject of a wild *GQ* story called "The Mail-Order Bride," in which the then-thirty-eight-year-old Baillie traveled to South America to find a bride through a service that matches low-income Colombian women with paying Americans. The article cast Baillie as a foul-mouthed, hard-partying New York City bachelor, a portrayal to which Baillie later objected.

Mumby asked Baillie to come up with some new concepts for the Juul launch campaign and to work with the Cult team to get them done. Baillie knew what to do right away. A few years earlier, he'd pitched a campaign for the Gap in which he'd layered an interlocking, multicolored triangle pattern over images of happy, carefree models—the point of the triangles being to symbolize different people and ideas coming together. Gap didn't run with the campaign, but he and Mumby had used something similar during their prior freelance work together, and Baillie thought it could work for Juul, too. The triangles played nicely off the look of the diamond-shaped window on the Juul device and the colorful caps that denoted the flavor of each pod: Crème Brûlée, Tobacco, Mint, or Fruit. The shapes looked lively and effervescent on the page, their arrangement subconsciously calling to mind vaporization.

Mumby loved it. It was eye-catching and dynamic, and it celebrated Juul's sophisticated look. As an added bonus, it would play well on social media. It seemed like the perfect way to make Juul the coveted vaporizer among young adults and influencers, who could in turn make Juul a phenomenon online. "They call it a 'trendsetter dynamic,'" explains a source involved in the launch campaign. "They would get certain things in certain people's hands" and wait for it to take off.

In January 2015, Baillie presented Mumby with a mood board expanding on his idea, which he called "the Vapors." The mood board, which Baillie captioned "Objects that are exposed to intense heat," looked like a manifestation of his own portfolio: high-fashion models, black leather jackets, Juuls hanging out of red-lipsticked mouths, Juuls superimposed on photos of celebrities like Rihanna and Jake Gyllenhaal, and of course, those colorful triangles left over from the Gap pitch. Mumby signed off and sent Baillie out to Calgary to work with Cult Collective on getting the campaign produced.

The whole process was a whirlwind. Within days of Mumby's approval, he and Baillie began planning the photo shoot that would underpin Juul's launch campaign, which they had named "Vaporized." The photos would appear in Juul ads online, on social media, in stores, and, biggest of all, on a billboard standing multiple stories high above Manhattan's iconic Times Square. The company didn't want to use a celebrity spokesperson, as e-cigarette companies like Blu had done. The idea was to cast people who looked like "New York trendsetters who embody the JUUL brand and speak to millennial consumers seeking a stylish and simple new way to enjoy nicotine with the latest vapor technology," according to an internal marketing document later included in a legal complaint filed by the California attorney general. (Juul largely denied the attorney general's claims and, as of January 2021, the case was moving toward a trial date in 2022.) To guide the casting, Baillie put together another mood board inspired by street-style photography, full of photos of various influencer types—trendy chefs, singers, deejays, photographers, and designers in their twenties or thirties, all fashionably dressed and conventionally attractive and with just enough edge to make them sexy.

In 2015, the oldest Millennials were in their midthirties, while the youngest were nineteen. Smoking was far more common among adults older than twenty-five. But the thinking was that by making Juul attractive to twenty- and thirty-somethings, the older adults would come next—sort of like how Facebook started on college campuses before it attracted parents and grandparents. Of course, there was also the very real possibility of things going in the other direction: of hip twenty-somethings starting a trend among *teenagers* desperate to look and act like hip twenty-somethings, rather than among older adults.

Despite this risk, the idea of marketing to "cool kids" like the models and deejays and actors from Baillie's mood board became the company's religion. As the Vaporized campaign was coming together, communications director Sarah Richardson circulated a document outlining the company's PR priorities—a document that later appeared in the consolidated complaint associated with multi-district litigation against Juul. A "key need," the document read, was to "'own the early adopter'/'cool kid' equity as we build out volume." (A company source clarified that "cool kids" was supposed to refer to the target demographic of twenty-five-to-thirty-four-year-olds.)

Outside the hard-core vaping community, which was growing larger but remained fairly fringe, e-cigarettes were still seen as pretty "douche-y," the marketing document read. A 2013 *Wall Street Journal* article dubbed them "vice's lame new devices," and Business Insider opined the same year that it was "hard to feel like James Dean while sucking on a plastic glow stick." They were also not seen as a good way to quit smoking, even for those who tried. Studies and anecdotal reports alike suggested many smokers didn't like the e-cigarettes available to them. Changing these perceptions—that e-cigarettes were low-tech and unlikely to work—were high priorities for the team marketing Juul, just as they had been when they launched the Pax vaporizer a few years earlier.

With its sleek design and lifestyle-oriented, Millennial-friendly marketing, the Pax device had upended stereotypes about both stoner and vaping culture. Richardson's team apparently wanted the media to see that by giving customers a far more sophisticated product than either the novelty gadgets supposed to look like cigarettes or the clunky, inconvenient tank vapes beloved by serious e-cigarette fans, Juul was doing the same thing for vaping nicotine. Juul was an effective e-cigarette people didn't have to be embarrassed about using in public, which meant it was one they would actually use. When the company pitched journalists, according to the marketing document included in the complaint, its message would be that "Juul singlehandedly made e-cigarettes cool."

Baillie and Mumby's Vaporized photo shoot helped achieve that aesthetic. "I remember seeing the other models and thinking, 'Wow, they're so much cooler than me,'" says Nicole Winge, one of the models. Otherwise, she says the shoot felt pretty normal. It was just a bustle of models in and out of hair and makeup, posing however photographer Marley Kate told them to: slinging their arms around each other, jumping up and down, flirting with the camera, dancing, playing with their hair—of course, with a Juul in hand. Most of the models, like Winge, were in their late twenties or early thirties. She didn't think too hard about being styled in short shorts and a crop top for one shot, both because she was in her late twenties at the time, a mature adult, and because, as a model, "your job is kind of not to ask questions," she says.

Winge remembers seeing executives on set, overseeing the whole thing, but she says they didn't interact with the models much. She didn't find out until years later that some of the company's top executives were allegedly concerned by how young she looked in photos from that day.

With the FDA still working on its regulations for e-cigarettes, vaping companies didn't have to follow the same stringent anti-youth-marketing provisions as cigarette companies. But since e-cigarettes were only legally available to people age eighteen and older in most states, if a company's ads looked like they blatantly appealed to kids, this could still open them up to unwanted scrutiny from lawyers, regulators, journalists, and public health advocates. The company had confirmed that all of the Vaporized models were at least twenty-five, to avoid appealing to youth. Even so, there were concerns about some of the photos from the Vaporized campaign, according to emails cited in the multi-district litigation complaint.

In one shot, Winge was dressed in a blue-and-white-striped T-shirt, her brown bob tucked behind one ear and red plastic sunglasses atop her head, with a Juul between her teeth. Some people on staff worried the pose could be perceived as too suggestive, one source remembers. But the legal complaint suggests there may have been other concerns, too. "There was some commentary at the youthfulness of these models" at a board meeting that spring, as Kania wrote in an email included in the multi-district litigation complaint, though she added that nobody disliked the images. No one said anything to Winge on set, and her photos appeared in the campaign anyway. But when Winge showed the photos to a friend years later, "She goes, 'Oh you look so young there,'" the model remembers. "That was the first thing out of her mouth."

While Mumby and Baillie were busy with the launch campaign, Adam and James were back at the bargaining table with Japan Tobacco International.

The Ploom ModelOne and ModelTwo had never really taken off in the United States. The devices weren't strong enough to satisfy longtime smokers, and consumers couldn't quite wrap their heads around the idea of vaporizing little cups of real tobacco when most products on the market ran on liquid nicotine. But despite the disappointing sales numbers in the United States, JTI executives seemed confident the products would be a hit overseas, where people were more accustomed to heat-not-burn tobacco products like Ploom. For ten million dollars, exactly the amount JTI had invested in Ploom years earlier, JTI offered to sell back its equity in the company in exchange for the ModelOne and ModelTwo patents and the Ploom brand name.

The offer was a little surprising, company insiders remember. Adam and James "didn't feel that JTI had done anything remotely close to what their commitment was supposed to be," says a former employee. There had never been any Apple-inspired Ploom stores, an idea the tobacco giant had floated around in the beginning, or much support for the product's marketing and sales. A big part of the problem, company sources say, was that JTI didn't want to touch the Pax device with a ten-foot pole.

"JTI did not want to be associated with a company that was starting to get into the cannabis market," recalls investor Ralph Eschenbach. As it became clearer that people were almost exclusively using Pax devices to vaporize cannabis, sources say JTI started pulling back from its relationship with Ploom, apparently uninterested in risking the stigma and controversy that could follow a marijuana product at that time. ("Our company strategy is to offer a wide choice of tobacco and nicotine products which are specifically targeted at adult smokers," a JTI spokesperson said in a statement. "Cannabis does not fall in this range and as such we have no plans to enter this business.") But, apparently, they'd never given up hope on Ploom's first devices.

The deal seemed like a smart one for everyone involved. If it sold off its equity, JTI could stop associating itself with a company in the cannabis space while getting the Ploom name and patents for, as Eschenbach says, "effectively no dollars." Meanwhile, Adam and James would get back the equity they'd given JTI, which they hoped would turn out to be worth far more than ten million dollars as the company grew. They'd be free to focus all their energy and resources on the Pax and Juul devices, while also getting out of a partnership that hadn't worked out as they'd planned—or been great for employee morale, for that matter. Many employees didn't think about JTI much, but for others, the name stirred up some cognitive dissonance. "Despite feeling like we were an innovative San Francisco vaporization technology company, the truth was we had an affiliation with Big Tobacco," one former employee remembers. It was uncomfortable, especially for young, mission-driven staffers who liked to think they worked at a technology start-up rather than a tobacco company. Taking back JTI's stake in the company seemed like the right move all around.

The JTI deal closed in February 2015. Ploom renamed itself "Pax Labs," after its star product, and offloaded its early product line on JTI.

Meanwhile, the rebranded company was getting closer and closer to launching the Juul device. The Vaporized ads were fun, bright, and eye-catching. They made the Juul look like an object of desire, something cool young (and not-so-young) adults would want to use. It was easy to imagine the campaign taking off on social media. But some people on staff questioned whether that was the right move. It felt like the marketing team was trying to capture the same lightning in a bottle that it had for Pax while ignoring that Juul was a fundamentally different product.

Since the launch of the first Pax device, in 2012, marijuana had been legalized in some capacity (medical or recreational) in dozens of states across the country, and by 2015, the majority of Americans said they supported legal use of the drug. Pax's team had capitalized on this sentiment and marketed the device as a sophisticated, luxurious product that adults could use recreationally but responsibly. They rarely ran into issues with underage use—with the device priced at $250 a pop, few teenagers could afford one—and many of Pax's best customers were older adults who used the device to consume medical marijuana. The marketing team could therefore sell Pax as a cool lifestyle product with relative confidence that they weren't hooking teenagers, and they did their job well.

But Juul was supposed to be different. It had been designed specifically as a cigarette alternative for adult smokers, not as a recreational product in any capacity. For two years, Adam had been laser-focused on creating a product that would emulate the experience of smoking a cigarette, while James had worked on a physical design subtle and convenient enough to replace cigarettes in smokers' pockets. If the goal was to give adult smokers a better option, these approaches had merit. But if Juuls weren't sold in exactly the right way, that vision could easily get lost. With the right branding, the company probably could have convinced people that its nicotine salt was carefully designed to give smokers an experience that rivaled smoking a cigarette and that its discreet design was perfect for the office worker tired of carrying around a clunky tank vape. But the lifestyle-oriented marketing that made Pax a trendy accessory wasn't necessarily going to convey that message with the nuance this task required. Perhaps the Vaporized campaign would make the Juul look better than other e-cigarettes, but it also made it look like any other covetable tech product—one that smokers and nonsmokers alike might want to try.

Plus, while there were definitely Millennials who smoked, the stereotypical American smoker was a middle-aged adult from a fairly low socioeconomic class, and often a person of color. As the Silicon Valley–born "Apple of e-cigarettes," Juul already had a pretty high barrier to entry with this crowd. In its prelaunch focus groups, the team had learned that young people seemed more open to trying Juul than older adults. Why make the sell to older smokers even harder by coming out with a social-media-friendly launch campaign chock-full of twenty-somethings in ripped jeans posing next to colorful triangles?

"I know they weren't going for kids," says a former employee who was on the marketing team at the time. "But they were going for influencers, and at that point, you can start splitting hairs. Is an influencer who's twenty-one a kid? Yeah, they are." Worse, a twenty-one-year-old influencer is very likely influencing people considerably younger than that. Juul's ads may not have been made with kids in mind—indeed, the company has strongly and repeatedly said they were not—but they certainly appealed to people who held a lot of sway with teenagers.

It was also hard to ignore that, when placed by side by side, the Vaporized ads bore more than a passing resemblance to old advertisements for cigarette brands like Kool, Lucky Strike, and Parliament. Given how widely criticized tobacco companies were for advertising to teenagers—which Adam and James surely learned about when they studied tobacco industry history in graduate school—it probably would have been wise to avoid any chance of comparison, even if the resemblance was coincidental and the campaign's intent innocent. A company source says members of the marketing team did, indeed, study old cigarette ads in an effort not to duplicate them—but when placed side by side, it's hard to deny the similarities. Some stills from the Vaporized shoot echo cigarette ads right down to the models' styling and poses.

With other e-cigarette companies already drawing scrutiny from lawmakers and public health officials, it was a risky time to take any chances. Senators had already blasted NJOY and Blu for their allegedly kid-friendly marketing, and the problem had only gotten worse since that 2014 hearing. In the year before Juul's launch, the percentage of high school students who reported vaping in the past thirty days rose from 13.4 to 16 percent.

In March 2015, before Juul was officially unveiled to the world, a group of senators wrote to officials at the Department of Health and Human Services begging them to speed up the FDA's still-unfinished plans to regulate the e-cigarette industry. "E-cigarette makers are dedicating extensive resources to reaching young people through social media, sponsorship of youth-oriented events, and television and radio advertisements that reach substantial youth audiences. Children are responding to this outreach while regulation on the federal level awaits final action," the senators wrote. It was a dangerous time for any e-cigarette company to make moves that could spark extra scrutiny.

During an executive meeting held not long before Juul's launch, Paul Moraes remembers voicing concerns about how the Vaporized ad campaign might be perceived. Immediately, he says, at least three other people nodded in agreement. "It didn't take someone with a PhD to say, 'Hey, guys, follow the logical conclusion of where this is going to go,'" Moraes remembers.

Another former executive had no memory of such a meeting—but there were other warning signs. A couple of months before Juul officially launched, Chelsea Kania, Pax's brand manager, wrote to her contacts at Cult Collective, which was involved in buying placement for Juul ads, with some hesitations. Juul ads were apparently appearing, or set to appear, on a website called YoungHollywood, which had an audience of primarily twelve-to-thirty-four-year-olds. That seemed to Kania a strange choice. Though ad buyers don't always control where a spot will appear—they're often served to individuals based on their browsing habits, rather than purchased via a specific website—Kania seemed to want to quash the appearance of advertising on YoungHollywood. "Weighing the % [of visitors] who could actually afford JUUL against the risk we'd run being flagged for advertising on that site—I don't think we should do it," she wrote, according to documents included in multi-district litigation against Juul.

James, too, seemed to be aware of the risks that could come from marketing Juul wrong. Moraes remembers hearing James, in a passionate conversation in the office, stressing that Juul was for adult smokers and that the company needed to act like it. He made variations on this comment often, Moraes says, always emphasizing that Juul had been created to give adult smokers a better alternative. But "with the start-up culture, nobody was really paying attention," says a source involved in the launch campaign. Adam and James saw the campaign before it was released and didn't voice any issues with it, a source involved in the launch remembers, but they were not intimately involved its production.

The whole thing moved so fast, too. Models were cast and photos were taken less than a month after Baillie came on as a consultant. Even if people had concerns, there wasn't much time to litigate them. The company was also fairly small then, and it didn't have the budget or time to scrap the Vaporized campaign and start from scratch, even if anyone had wanted to. Plus, as Moraes remembers, "Marketing at that time was the golden child."

"I never saw a single proposal by marketing ever be pushed back on," Moraes says. Mumby "was kind of running the company at that time," says a former employee on the sales team. That may have been an overstatement, but he certainly did have authority over projects like the Juul launch campaign; after all, he was the marketing expert.

Still, it's too simple to pin all of Pax's decisions on Richard Mumby. Though he may have acted like it, he was not the company's president or CEO. Though he was deeply trusted, he did not have carte blanche. Whether they worked on it directly or not, it seems likely that every executive and board member at Pax had at least a vague understanding of what the Vaporized campaign would look like.

Every high-ranking employee knew that Juul's nicotine salt could be highly addictive because it had been specifically formulated to rival the nicotine in cigarettes. With virtually any amount of critical thinking, surely they could have come to a healthy understanding of the risks: a potent nicotine product, marketed in a way that made it look fun and desirable, could fall into the wrong hands at least some of the time. Paul Moraes says he warned his colleagues about this possibility, and James seemed aware of how Juul needed to be sold. Did other executives truly see no problems with the campaign? Did things simply move too fast to change course? Did Pax's executives think they could avoid the pitfalls that could come with a flashy launch campign? Or were those possibilities seen as the cost of doing business, the price to be paid for building a successful brand?

PART II

Catching Flame

6

Juul vaporizers were everywhere. Stacks of the slim devices littered every surface, lying there free for the taking—which people were doing happily, grabbing them and exhaling plumes of sweet-swelling vapor into the air. This was the first thing that Emch, a New York City musician from the band Subatomic Sound System, noticed when he walked into the Juul launch party in June 2015.

The second thing he noticed was how much money Pax had poured into the party. By that point, Emch had known people from the Pax marketing team for a few years—they'd been thinking of sponsoring a small music festival he put on every year, but it never came to pass. When he first met the Pax team, they seemed like a fun if ragtag group that worked for a growing start-up. But this party gave off a different vibe entirely. It was slick and polished, obviously put together by people with a very good sense of what a fashionable party in New York City should look like.

"I was pretty shocked when I went to the Juul launch, with how different it had become," Emch says.

The party was at Jack Studios, a giant industrial loft space in

Manhattan's artsy Chelsea neighborhood. The space was often used for fashion photo shoots and had striking views of the illuminated city skyline with the Hudson River below. For the Juul launch, Pax's team had splashed colorful Vaporized branding all over the sleek, white space. While red and blue spotlights punched colorful holes in the sultry dimness, guests could pose for photos in front of the same multicolored triangles that appeared in the Vaporized ad campaign. "It reminded me of going to a fashion event or an art gallery opening," Emch says. "It was a very slick, high-end event. They were targeting a younger, affluent crowd."

Emch was right: Pax clearly had gone all out. Drinks were flowing from the open bar, and every guest left with plenty of Juul swag—on top of the free vaporizers they could grab by the handful if they wanted to. The events team hired buzzy deejays Phantogram and May Kwok, and *Top Chef* winner Ilan Hall handled catering. Marley Kate, the same photographer who'd shot the Vaporized campaign, was there taking photos of guests, which were then projected onto the loft's walls as live art. The best shots even had a chance at appearing on the company's Times Square billboard the following week.

The goal of the party was simple. Juul needed cool New York City socialites to be seen using the device, pulling on Juul vaporizers as frequently as they did the cocktails passed around from the open bar. The company had specifically chosen to launch Juul first in New York City, then in Los Angeles, two trendsetting cities full of influencers and journalists—not to mention Pax's beloved "cool kids," who, according to a company marketing document circulated in May 2015, could build buzz. Building a strong social media presence for Juul seemed to be pivotal to the company's launch strategy.

Pax had spent much of its marketing budget on advertisements that appeared in convenience stores and other retail spaces, as well as on the Times Square billboard and a print ad that appeared in *Vice*, part of the self-styled "#1 youth media company in the world." Just inside the cover, *Vice*'s readers could find a picture of a sleek Juul device right next to an image of a young woman with a high ponytail, a letterman jacket, and a crop top, a trail of vapor creeping from her seductively pursed lips.

But social media marketing was valuable too, in no small part because it was free. "Social media was part of every business and it was a way to extend the reach of limited dollars," says a source involved with the launch. If influencers were seen using the Juul, their followers would want to try it. And once their followers tried it, they would post about it and tell their friends. It was a classic social media marketing strategy, one used by plenty of start-ups before and after Juul—but unlike with most start-ups, this one hinged on selling an age-restricted and highly addictive nicotine product on platforms used heavily by teenagers.

To get the word of mouth flowing, Sarah Richardson, who was now Pax's director of corporate communications, hired Grit Creative Group, a creative marketing agency that called itself "an authority on Millennial culture," to secure at least twenty influencer guests for the Juul launch party. After that, a network of nearly three hundred New York and Los Angeles influencers would be gifted free Juul products over the coming weeks. On the list for free products were movie star Leonardo DiCaprio, who was often photographed vaping, and model Bella Hadid. At the time Juul launched, Hadid had almost a million Instagram followers—and, at nineteen, was only barely able to legally purchase an e-cigarette in most states.

Giving launch party guests the chance to pose for a professional photographer, and potentially appear on a Times Square billboard, was also a brilliant viral marketing move. Back in 2015, Instagram wasn't quite the ubiquitous cultural presence it would soon become, but Emch still remembers plenty of people taking selfies and posing for the camera all night.

"It was a little bit [of being] seen to be seen," he remembers. After the party, social media was awash in photos of young, attractive people holding drinks and puffing on Juuls, their photos tagged with the hashtags

#Vaporized and #LightsCameraVapor. Juul's official accounts posted some photos, too.

"Having way too much fun at the #JUUL launch party," read one tweet from Juul's handle, right above a photo of five fashionably dressed young women pouting at the camera. As one employee wrote afterward in an email to COO Scott Dunlap, which was later included in multi-district litigation against Juul, "The party was a resounding success (at least in my mind) in terms of winning over the cool kids."

Juul didn't stop at one great party. It set off around the country on a six-month "sampling tour." The tour took different forms in different areas. Outside major cities like New York and Los Angeles, Pax sent samplers to retail chains and convenience stores where its future customers would, they hoped, buy Juul devices. According to documents later included in a pending lawsuit filed by the attorney general of Pennsylvania, which Juul heavily disputed and is set for trial in 2022, company representatives, usually dressed in brightly colored Juul T-shirts, would stop shoppers as they approached the counter and offer them a free sample. Once the customer had taken a hit from the sample device, the company rep would give them the rest of the e-juice pod and encourage them to buy their own Juul device.

It was a curious tactic for a brand that claimed to be interested in selling its products only to current smokers looking to switch. Only 15 percent of American adults were current smokers in 2015, but by picking out convenience store shoppers at random, Juul's samplers were almost certainly putting potent nicotine pods in the hands of people who didn't already smoke.

The sampling campaign was even more aggressive in big cities like New York City and Los Angeles. In urban areas, Juul-branded shipping containers popped up at concerts, clubs, and rooftop bars, beckoning people inside with bright colors and the promise of free product. The cargo containers featured a lounge area, an "animated gif booth" where people could pose for the camera, and a flavor bar where guests could sample vapes in Juul's four flavors. Juul's flavor selection was pretty tame compared to that offered by other companies, with their Unicorn Poop and Gummy Bear varieties: to start, people could buy Juul pods only in Tobacco, Mint, Fruit, or Crème Brûlée.

As the year continued, Juul broadened its sampling tour to Las Vegas, the Hamptons, and Miami. At each event, according to a pending legal complaint filed by the New York attorney general which Juul largely disputed, a staff of company representatives—often attractive young women told to follow a dress code of skinny jeans and high-top sneakers or booties—handed out thousands of free hits of addictive nicotine.

It was clear that people liked what they saw. People were responding well to Juul's products and, even better, posting about them online. And to keep word of mouth spreading, that summer Sarah Richardson signed a second contract with the marketing firm Grit, to ensure that "social buzzmakers" with at least thirty thousand social media followers each would attend, and post about, these events.

Not everyone was thrilled with these results. Indeed, the social media posts coming in after sampling events made some executives uneasy. "I would catch myself saying, 'Wow, they look really young,'" former COO Scott Dunlap told the *New York Times*. "But you don't really know. It's social media after all, where everyone is their younger, idealized selves. All you know is that you are seeing the early signs of a viral brand taking off."

There were encouraging posts, too. Despite some of the feedback from prelaunch focus groups that suggested the product was too strong even for smokers, Juul's e-liquids seemed to be landing well with people looking for alternative ways to consume nicotine. Alex Clark, a former smoker who is now the CEO of the pro-vaping Consumer Advocates for Smoke-free Alternatives Association, says he was impressed as soon as he tried a Juul in 2015. "I was sort of pleasantly surprised that I was getting a more intense nicotine hit than what I was accustomed to" with other e-cigarettes, he remembers. "[It] immediately was like, okay, this is going to be a game-changer." His feelings were echoed by others online: "@juulvapor is the best, most satisfying #ecig I've ever tried. Great product! Only $50 too!" one seemingly adult customer tweeted only a few days after the product launched. "Juul has won me over in just a week," one blogger wrote on the site Engadget, marveling that after fourteen years of smoking, Juul had helped him drop from twenty to thirty cigarettes a day to just eleven over five days. Even the mainstream press was noticing. A *Wired* profile proclaimed Juul possibly "the first great e-cig."

In a case study later posted on its website, ad agency Cult Collective bragged, "We created ridiculous enthusiasm for the hashtag #Vaporized." Less brag-worthy was the reality that young adults, and people even younger than that, seemed to be in large part driving this trend. Says longtime Campaign for Tobacco-Free Kids president Matt Myers, "They figured out a sleek design to appeal to the coolest kids at a time when cigarette smoking was something that the cool kids didn't do."

These realities didn't sit well with much of the Pax executive team. Paul Moraes, the company's supply chain VP, remembers sitting in an executive meeting shortly after Juul was released, when a younger employee brought up concerns about Juul appealing to teenagers. "To a person, we were horrified. We knew, and we vocalized, that day that this is a problem," he says. "Juul knew from day one that children smoking Juuls was a disaster. There's no doubt about that."

Indeed, shortly after the product launched, the company got a very public warning: an *Ad Age* article in which a spokesperson from the Campaign for Tobacco-Free Kids voiced concerns about Juul's marketing appealing to kids. "We're seeing more and more irresponsible marketing of unregulated products such as e-cigarettes," a CTFK spokesman told *Ad Age*. "We are concerned any time a new product or new advertising campaign goes public regarding cigarettes and tobacco and their addictive nicotine."

The story was a wake-up call. When the *Ad Age* article came out, "We were like, 'Oh my god, that's terrible,'" says a source involved in the launch campaign. Company executives didn't want their products to appeal to kids, or even to be perceived as appealing to kids. Vaporized had only been in the world for a short time, but already, executives were realizing it could sink the company before it swam.

In July 2015, just a month after Juul officially launched, Pax investor Alexander Asseily began to get very vocal about his concerns, according to documents included in a legal complaint filed by the Hawaii attorney general, which Juul later filed a motion to dismiss. (The judge had not ruled on that motion as of January 2021.) Pulling CEO James Monsees aside, he said that if the company kept marketing in ways that could be seen as targeting kids, Pax was going to get lumped in with Big Tobacco, an industry infamous for targeting young people with its marketing. To make sure this message was getting through, he followed up with an impassioned email to board members Nick Pritzker and Riaz Valani, according to the complaint. "Our fears around tobacco/nicotine are not going away," Asseily wrote. "We will continue to have plenty of agitation if we don't come to terms with the fact that these substances are almost irretrievably connected to the shittiest companies and practices in the history of business." If people thought Juul was marketing to teenagers, the comparisons to Big Tobacco companies were bound to come next. That could tarnish the company's reputation before it even got off the ground.

"The trouble with just 'doing what others do' is that we'll end up[,] as Nick [Pritzker] rightly points out[,] in the same ethical barrel as them, something none of us want[s] no matter the payoff (I think)," Asseily wrote. He continued: "It's not about faking it—it's about doing it correctly . . . which could mean not doing a lot of things we thought we would do[,] like putting young people in our poster ads or drafting in the wake of big players in the market."

Shortly after this email, Asseily began brainstorming with Mumby, who was now the company's chief marketing officer, about what the company could do differently. They kicked around ideas such as a program through which smokers could turn in their cigarette packs or subpar vaping products in exchange for discounts on Juul products. It would "send the only message that's needed," Asseily wrote in an email to members of the leadership team. "Juul is a superior alternative to conventional smoking and mediocre vaping products."

That particular idea never got off the ground, but it was clear something had to change. Mumby began working on a replacement for the campaign he had only just launched, one that people within the company hoped would have no appeal to—or even the perception of an appeal to—kids. He and his team began working on a new concept with a more muted color scheme, one that focused on shots of the product itself rather than on models. Some of the Vaporized ads were pulled immediately, even before the new spots were ready.

While this was happening, however, the wheels were already in motion. Juul was beginning to spread, slowly but surely, on social media and online.

If parents had known what Juul was back then, they probably would have been appalled. But the device was so new, and looked so much like a flash drive, that they might not have known their children could see advertisements for a highly addictive e-cigarette on Instagram and online. If they did realize Juul was an e-cigarette, they certainly wouldn't have known how much nicotine it contained. That particular ingredient was disclosed only at the very bottom of the ad, in print so tiny you had to squint to read it. Besides, the eye was drawn to other words. "JUUL," the ads read in huge block letters. "VAPORIZED."

E-commerce presented other problems. When Juul launched, the company partnered with a third-party provider, Veratad, to help manage age-gating on its website. To pass Veratad's system and buy a Juul, customers had to enter personal information on Juul's website such as their name, age, and address. From there, Veratad would consult its database and try to match that information to a person of legal purchasing age— eighteen in most states, or older in a few with stricter laws. If Veratad found a match, the sale went through. If not, the customer could enter his or her social security number. If that still didn't work, they could upload a photo of their driver's license for a Pax employee to review manually.

This whole process was more art than science. One former customer service rep who performed these driver's license reviews remembers some being "obviously fake." Others were marginal, so the team would have to do a little digging before they decided whether to pass the sale. "Every once in a while, you'd do extra work to look at somebody's email address, or you might find their Facebook and it might just plainly state they were seventeen or something," the employee recalls. In these cases, Pax's customer service team could manually cancel the order. "Sometimes we would err on that side," the former employee says, "but only if we were pretty dang confident."

Still, even with the Veratad system in place and Pax employees reviewing licenses, young people were finding ways to buy Juul vaporizers. If a teenager could get her hands on a parent's ID and credit card, she could sometimes enter the information online and pass the system. And there were glitches—sometimes, if a user's exact birth date didn't match the information in Veratad's database but the birth year did, the sale would go through anyway. Or, if a father and son shared a name and address, the son could sometimes pass if the system mistook him for his father. An adult would have to sign for the delivery when it arrived, no matter who placed it online, but that part was out of Pax's hands.

Devices were also getting shipped to college campuses, where some students are of age and others aren't. Sometimes somebody would buy so many devices that they almost definitely meant to resell them, perhaps to underage users, which was a red flag but hard to do much about without hard-and-fast purchasing limits. Before too long, Juul products also began showing up frequently on resale websites like eBay, where it was much easier for teenagers to buy them without going through age verification.

Shortly after the Juul device launched, staff members started fielding calls and emails from people who were clearly underage asking where they could buy the products. Other times, angry parents would call up demanding to have charges on their cards reversed after they'd learned what their child had managed to buy online. Age verification was suddenly a much bigger part of customer service representatives' jobs than it had been for the Pax device.

Matthew Myers, who advised state attorneys general when they sued Big Tobacco in the 1990s and who then became CTFK's president, watched uneasily as all this unfolded. When he saw Juul's ads, all he could think of were old cigarette ads. These newer ads ticked all the same boxes: young, fun models selling sex, sophistication, and a good time. Even some of the models' styling and poses looked eerily similar to old promotions for popular cigarette brands—which Adam and James should have known, as they'd studied those ads while putting together their thesis project for Ploom. "As somebody who's worked in this field and looked at cigarette industry behavior too long," Myers says, "the instant reaction is: Juul is replicating the 1950s and 1960s playbook from the cigarette companies." Pax executives may have *said* Juul was for adult smokers only, but to Myers, their actions didn't match their words.

Myers wasn't alone in his concern. A few months after Juul launched, comedian Stephen Colbert lambasted e-cigarette ads on his talk show, giving a special shout-out to Juul's Vaporized campaign. After showing a clip of models dancing on the Vaporized set next to the brand's signature colorful triangles, Colbert joked, "Something about inhaling poison steam just makes me want to dance in a way that doesn't require much lung strength." He added, "It's not just ads featuring hip young triangles that appeal to the youths. So do vape flavors like cotton candy, Gummi Bear, and Skittles." (Never mind that Juul didn't actually sell vapes in these flavors.)

Juul's Vaporized campaign came out in the midst of a spirited debate in the public health world. There was still nothing close to consensus over whether e-cigarettes were overall a good or bad thing for public health. In 2015, the World Health Organization warned that such products might damage the lungs and heart and could possibly even cause cancer via prolonged exposure to some of their ingredients. Meanwhile, that year Public Health England, an agency within the United Kingdom's Department of Health and Social Care, declared in a highly publicized report that, thanks to their lower levels of carcinogens and harmful chemicals, e-cigarettes were 95 percent safer than combustible cigarettes. It was difficult figuring out whom to believe.

There were dozens upon dozens of studies to support both sides of the debate, but the antivaping crowd had at least one serious leg up: they could always bring the conversation back to Big Tobacco, especially as Pax and other companies made dubious marketing decisions like the Vaporized campaign. By the time Juul launched, Big Tobacco's fingerprints were all over the vaping industry via e-cigarette brands that predated Juul, like Vuse, MarkTen, and Blu. Many people in the tobacco control community were, for obvious reasons, highly suspicious of anything Big Tobacco did—including investing heavily in noncombustible products. For influential groups like the Campaign for Tobacco-Free Kids, and for the many scientists who worked with them, it would have been a political grenade to back vaping companies after years of fighting Big Tobacco—especially because billionaire public health advocate Michael Bloomberg, who was deeply committed to stamping out tobacco use of all kinds, backed CTFK financially. To people like Matt Myers, who saw in Juul's Vaporized campaign nothing but echoes of cigarette advertising, the e-cigarette experiment felt like history repeating itself. All Myers and his colleagues needed to do was remind people that Big Tobacco had lied to the public and targeted children for decades, and suggest that e-cigarette companies were following in their footsteps, and right or not, e-cigarettes suddenly came out looking a bit more sinister.

No matter how deeply scientists believed in tobacco harm reduction, there was little they could do to defend themselves when e-cigarette brands were lumped in with Big Tobacco. "When we push back against it [and support e-cigarettes], we sound like we're defending the tobacco industry," laments Raymond Niaura, a tobacco dependence and treatment expert at NYU who supports the use of e-cigarettes. There were not many scientists willing to put that kind of black mark on their reputation. With plenty of non-scientific incentives for researchers to distance themselves from vaping, smokers had few advocates in the vaping debate. "We're sending smokers down the tubes," says NYU's David Abrams. "Anything you do to diminish the harm reduction alternative is helping to kill smokers."

Flashy, allegedly kid-friendly marketing only added another strike. Even researchers who thought e-cigarettes could be useful for smokers weren't eager to cozy up to a company drawing comparisons to Big Tobacco. Shortly after Juul launched, a few Pax employees came to pitch Dr. Steve Schroeder, who directs the Smoking Cessation Leadership Center at the University of California, San Francisco, on their new product, he remembers. Schroeder thought it had promise—it delivered a high dose of nicotine that would keep smokers satisfied—but he immediately backed away from any kind of partnership. "I basically said, 'You're so controversial that I'm afraid that's going to hurt the work of our center,'" Schroeder remembers.

Pax's executives should have known about these dynamics and designed a launch campaign that had no possible link to Big Tobacco, especially after all the time Adam and James had spent studying documents from the Tobacco Master Settlement Agreement in graduate school. But the promise of future growth seemed to trump historical caution. "They had the Silicon Valley mind-set of 'We're a tech company; we're not a tobacco company,'" says Greg Conley, president of the American Vaping Association. "And so, they hired very, very few people with experience in tobacco" early on. If they had, Conley says, they might have had on staff people able to see where things were going and who would never have let a campaign with even a chance of drawing comparisons to Big Tobacco end up on a larger-than-life billboard in Times Square.

The comparisons to cigarette ads and the allegations of targeting teenagers clouded Juul's reputation right from the very beginning. If Juul had a target on its back in the years to come, it was only because it had put one there.

7

DEMOTED (JULY–DECEMBER 2015)

Outwardly, Adam and James had what they'd always wanted: a sleek, sexy product that had people talking online, rave reviews from journalists and bloggers, and fifty million dollars in fresh venture capital funding. But behind the scenes, the picture wasn't quite so pretty.

The good press and the buzz on social media weren't translating into the kind of sales the company had hoped for, in part because it was hard for people to go out and buy a Juul in a store after they'd seen it on Instagram. Since before Juul launched, according to documents included in the multi-district litigation against Juul, Pax's executives had their eyes on mass retailers like Circle K, 7–Eleven, and Speedway. True e-cigarette fans were devoted to vape shops, but hard-core vapers made up a tiny percentage of the U.S. population. Just about everybody stopped in convenience stores at one point or another, so executives knew that if Juul were stocked in these national chains, the possibilities would be enormous. But getting Juul on the shelves was easier said than done. Haunted by memories of slow-selling products like Ploom, many retailers were hesitant to bet big on another e-cigarette they'd never heard of.

The entire industry had grown substantially since Ploom launched, but the e-cigarette category, which was valued at around $3.5 billion in 2015, was still tiny compared to the $97 billion traditional tobacco industry. According to CDC data released in 2015, fewer than 4 percent of U.S. adults regularly used e-cigarettes. If convenience stores sold e-cigarettes, they often minimized the risk mostly by stocking those made by the tobacco brands they already knew—and who they knew were able to pay the bills.

If they wanted to convince shop owners that Juul was worth the risk, Pax's sales team had to be aggressive. They promised to buy back unsold merchandise and flaunted the device's low taxes and high profit margins, saying whatever it took to win over stores, former East Coast sales director Vincent Latronica said in an interview with Reuters. One sales rep remembers repeatedly calling stores himself, posing as customers looking for Juul devices so retailers would think Juul was more popular than it actually was. ("You do that for about three days. A week later, I walk in and I'd go, 'I'm the Juul rep,' and they're like, 'We've been hearing about you!'" the rep remembers with a laugh.) The team also had a trump card not available during the Ploom era: nicotine salt. When they showed buyers the punch each 5 percent nicotine Juul pod delivered, and how closely the Juul mimicked a cigarette, some retailers were suddenly interested.

"We would never use the word *addictive*," one sales rep remembers. "We would say it was strong. We would say it was satisfying" in a way that previous e-cigarettes had not been. The subtext, of course, was that the Juul would keep customers coming back: nicotine dependence is a very good business model.

Even when the sales team did find a willing buyer, the company wasn't making much money on whatever it sold. The Juul vaporizer and pods cost way more to manufacture than anyone had expected, one company source remembers. The company's cost estimates were based on the assumption that Pax would be working with manufacturers that could fully automate the production process, churning out thousands of pods a day. Instead, the company had signed a deal with a small manufacturing company on the East Coast that didn't have the capacity to fully automate production. As a result, Juul products cost about twice as much to make as the engineers had expected, according to one company source. The Juul Starter Kit (a vaporizer and a four-pack of pods) ended up retailing for fifty dollars, while a four-pack of pods alone cost sixteen dollars. Those prices were higher than equivalent products on the market at the time, and enough to make Juul, like Pax before it, seem like a luxury good.

There were also still bugs in the manufacturing process. The engineering team hadn't been able to get the pods to stop leaking before they were released for sale, and customers were calling in pretty regularly to complain about the dreaded juice-in-mouth mishap. As many as 20 percent of the pods from any given production run ended up being leaky or otherwise unusable—which meant that a fifth of the money spent making them was effectively being tossed straight in the trash. Paul Moraes, head of the supply chain department, was scrambling to figure out how to fix this. He remembers coming in one day and personally testing hundreds of pods to see how many leaked. Around 15 percent of them did, a number far too high for his liking—but there didn't seem to be any quick fix, at least not without drastically changing the way the pod was designed. The company didn't have that kind of time or resources.

There were other issues, too. Philip Morris USA, the subsidiary of Altria that makes Marlboro cigarettes for the U.S. market, had sent Pax a cease-and-desist letter shortly after Juul launched, arguing that Pax was infringing on its trade dress. The original Juul device had a transparent, diamond-shaped window between the metallic body and the mouthpiece, so users could see how much e-liquid they had left in their pod. Philip Morris was arguing that this window looked too similar to the red diamonds on its iconic Marlboro packaging, forcing Pax's designers to tweak it to a hexagonal shape to avoid a very costly legal battle with a very rich company.

Around this time, in the fall of 2015, James called a meeting. The company had racked up its fair share of problems during its first few months on the market: sales weren't great, the pods were leaky, social media posts seemed to be attracting the wrong audience, and Philip Morris and public health advocates had found a rare patch of common ground in their belief that Juul was imitating Big Tobacco's branding. So, James had gathered his staff to share some wise words.

That fall, Volkswagen was all over the news because it had installed software in cars that obscured their nitrogen oxide emissions, allowing them to illegally skirt Environmental Protection Agency regulations. When the company got caught, it found itself starring in both an international news story and a hugely expensive lawsuit. With his staff gathered around in the Pax offices, James read aloud from a news story about the lawsuit. When he finished, he looked around the room full of twenty-something employees fresh out of college. "Don't do anything that could get us sued," he concluded. He seemed to want the meeting to be about trust and transparency, but that punch line was a funny way of showing it. "The adults in the room, we all looked at each other," remembers Paul Moraes. "Our jaws were on the floor." If that was the best advice Pax's CEO had to offer, the company was in trouble.

This kind of behavior wasn't unusual for James. As one former employee put it, his leadership style made him "a polarizing figure" around the office. It was harder to be offended by Adam, who was quiet and low-key and generally pretty easy to get along with. With Adam, it could be difficult to tell what he was thinking, but he was generally pleasant around the office. James, however, was more complicated. He was brilliant, but he was also stubborn and exacting, and he liked things the way he liked them. He was funny and charismatic, and he had that trademark loud laugh, but he also had a short fuse. Some employees got along with him well, but others walked on eggshells around him.

By some former employees' accounts, Pax often felt like a workplace divided. What should have been one big team working toward a single goal often splintered into smaller groups of people gathering behind their particular leader. Richard Mumby had his favorites on the marketing staff. Adam had a circle of people with whom he worked closely in the lab. And "James had his favorites, and he had his people he had no tolerance for," says one former employee.

One former employee remembers being caught in a constant tug-of-war between James and Adam, who seemed to be in a power struggle even years after James displaced Adam as CEO. "Adam would say, 'Hey, we need to do this.' Then James would say, 'I don't want you working on this,' [and] Adam would say, 'Let's do it anyway. Don't worry about James. I'll take care of James,'" the former employee remembers. "Then James would have a melt-down." Some company sources don't remember much tension related to James' leadership, but others paint a vastly different picture. By the fall of 2015, it got so bad, a former employee remembers, that multiple senior managers avoided talking to James, their own CEO.

But James wouldn't be CEO for long. In meetings that fall, he and the board had agreed that it was time to try something new. James was a brilliant product designer, but he didn't seem suited to the role of CEO. The manufacturing operation still wasn't where it needed to be, and the Vaporized campaign was turning out to be quite a public relations headache. Under James, both problems just kept lingering on at a slow burn. He was an erratic leader, as likely to be disliked as he was trusted. That was no way to run a business.

In October 2015, Pax's board of directors called for the entire staff to gather in the middle of the company's open-office floor plan for an all-hands meeting. It was an unusual request. The board's role was typically a behind-the-scenes one. It weighed in on major business and financial decisions and offered advice to James, Adam, and the rest of the executive team during monthly meetings. But its members weren't in the office on a regular basis, and only the highest-level Pax staffers interacted with them—so if they were calling an all-staff meeting, it was clear that they had something big to say.

Once everybody had gathered around the tables in the middle of the room and quieted down, a member of the management team stepped forward. He cleared his throat. "We're looking for a new CEO," he announced briskly. "Effective immediately, James is out as CEO."

A hush fell over the room as all eyes turned to James, who sat perched on the edge of a table, feet swinging and eyes downcast. He had known what was coming—after discussions with the board, he had technically resigned from his role—but it couldn't have been easy to hear it announced in front of the entire staff. James would stay with the company, but in the role of chief product officer—a title level with Adam's role as chief technology officer. The announcement left many employees feeling shaken. James had built the company from the ground up. Without his and Adam's vision, it wouldn't even have existed. If even he could be demoted so publicly, what did this mean for the rest of the company? Was anybody safe?

With Pax Labs out of a CEO, board members Hoyoung Huh (a doctor and Silicon Valley health care entrepreneur), Nick Pritzker, and Riaz Valani formed an "executive committee" that, along with a group of senior Pax employees, effectively ran the company while the board searched for James's permanent replacement. If Adam and James had been a "two-headed monster" when they were co-CEOs at Ploom, this scenario was even more chaotic.

To employees from that era, the executive committee seemed to care only about growth after Juul's slow start. Shortly after the committee came together, some of Pax's senior-most employees—including supply chain head Paul Moraes—were let go. Huh took charge of board meetings, which James had previously run. And after years of mostly sticking to the boardroom, Pritzker and Huh made plans to be in the office for most of each week, "to help us manage our people," as the minutes from one executive meeting later included in a consolidated complaint related to multi-district litigation read. Adam and James's names were on the patents, but it wasn't their company anymore.

Within a few weeks of his public demotion, James's schedule became more erratic, employees remember; sometimes, he didn't come into the office at all. As for Adam, his role, at least for the short term, didn't change too much, but there was an unspoken wrinkle. Now that the nicotine salt mixture was finalized and the product was out on the market, there wasn't as much for him to do. Like James, he wasn't a born executive, which was increasingly what the company's success seemed to require.

"Adam was viewed as a critical component to the company, but I think his role, just due to the company's expansion and maybe his lack of leadership skills in certain areas, he was having less and less influence," says one former senior employee. The uncomfortable truth was that Pax seemed to be outgrowing the men who had laid its foundations. James and Adam were both brilliant product designers and practical scientists, but they weren't businessmen. Juul "was born out of a very small company mentality, a couple [of] entrepreneurs sitting down and saying, 'Hey, let's try to do this,'" says former supply chain director Paul Moraes. "It didn't really have any kind of vision for where the e-cigarette industry was going."

That was a problem, because in the decade since Adam and James had put together their Stanford thesis, the U.S. vaping industry had gone from virtually nonexistent to attracting significant interest from the traditional tobacco industry. Mom-and-pop vaping brands were no longer charting the industry's course. Big Tobacco companies were doubling down on the non-combustible market. Tobacco cigarette sales were falling, while the e-cigarette market continued to grow larger and larger—which suggested that at least some smokers were switching to products they hoped were safer. They might not have liked it, but tobacco executives knew that if they were going to survive in the long term, they would have to be part of that trend. And when Big Tobacco companies are your competitors, it's not enough to have a great idea. You have to have a great, and ruthless, business.

Pax's board, newly in control of the company's trajectory, was trying to work tobacco industry trends to its advantage, according to later legal complaints. If cigarette sales were down, cigarette manufacturers weren't the only ones who would lose out. Distributors that sold cigarettes to retailers would also lose money. Pax's executive committee therefore began courting the cigarette industry's major distributors, selling them on the idea that Juul products could help replace some of the revenue they were losing due to plummeting cigarette sales. Even better, they told them, the Juul device's relatively high price tag and lower tax rate meant better profit margins for distributors compared to those for cigarettes. Getting in with these companies was crucial, as they already had relationships with most of the country's largest retail chains. Stores that had been hesitant to take a chance on a brand-new start-up might think twice if that start-up were working with a well-known distributor.

There was another possible way to bring the company some extra legitimacy: finding a partner who already knew, and carried influence in, the tobacco world. Internal documents later included in multi-district litigation suggest

Pax's executives and board members began thinking about the value of an investment from a Big Tobacco company shortly after Juul's release. Such a partnership might raise some eyebrows, but a well-financed, well-known tobacco company could bring sales, marketing, and distribution capabilities Pax could currently only dream about. Japan Tobacco's investment hadn't been quite the boon it had at first seemed to be. But with Juul out in the world, another tobacco company might be next in line.

8

IGNITION (AUGUST 2016–MAY 2017)

Kurt Sonderegger, Ploom's former marketing boss, had started to notice a change afoot. Once upon a time, when he saw someone vaping in public, they tended to be using either cigalikes or the clunky, open-system devices that let them blow out fat, eye-catching clouds of vapor. But increasingly, he was spying Juul's little USB-stick vapes all over town. "Overnight, I saw the big tattooed guys with the giant mods suddenly walking around with a little Juul in their hands," Sonderegger says.

Of course, it hadn't really happened overnight. Business had been slow for most of Juul's first year on the market, even as the product started to make the rounds on Instagram and impress former smokers. Pax Labs's total revenue for 2015 was $49 million, but Juul products made up only a small portion of that total. Finally, though, the sales numbers seemed to be picking up. The company had worked out some of its manufacturing kinks, scaled up production, and convinced more stores to start stocking its products. By the middle of 2016, about a year after Juul was first introduced, sales data showed it was the second-best-selling independent e-cigarette brand in the United States, though still far behind Big Tobacco–backed brands.

With business looking up, the executive committee decided in the summer of 2016, almost a year after James's public demotion, that it was time to bring on a new CEO.

With the board's executive committee in charge, things were going much more smoothly than they had the year before. By early 2016, for example, the company had scrubbed away all traces of its flawed Vaporized campaign, replacing it with the more subdued campaign Mumby and his team had produced. "We heard some feedback that [Vaporized] was too lifestyle-oriented," Adam recalled in a 2019 interview. "We took the criticism to heart."

It would have been hard not to, as scrutiny of e-cigarette advertising had just kept growing. In early 2016, the CDC released a report finding that 70 percent of middle and high school students regularly saw e-cigarette ads. "The same advertising tactics the tobacco industry used years ago to get kids addicted to nicotine are now being used to entice a new generation of young people to use e-cigarettes," the CDC director warned in a statement accompanying the report. Around the same time, the California Department of Public Health released an education campaign for parents, sounding the alarm about kid-friendly e-cigarette ads and flavors. It clearly did not behoove e-cigarette companies to do anything that could draw any more unnecessary attention. Only a year and a half earlier, NJOY and Blu had been forced to defend their ads before a Senate panel. It would not be a good look to be next.

With e-cigarette advertising in the hot seat, even the people who created Vaporized had to admit that this style of marketing could create more problems than profits for Pax. The product seemed to be landing among adult smokers, but the controversial marketing threatened to overshadow this fact. In March 2016, according to court filings related to the multi-district litigation against Juul, Richard Mumby wrote in a postmortem summary of the campaign sent to board member Hoyoung Huh and a number of marketing staffers that "the models that we used for the #Vaporized campaign appeared to be too youthful for many consumers (and the media). . . . We need to be sensitive to the subjectivity of youthfulness by positioning the brand to be mature and reliable."

Already, however, there were signs that Juul was taking off among people much younger than the company's target demographic of twenty-and thirty-somethings. Many of the same things that were supposed to make Juul appealing to adult smokers—small size, discreet look and aroma—were apparently making it very easy for teenagers to sneak them into school and use them around teachers who were none the wiser. Kids could hit the device when their teacher turned to write something on the board, exhale into their backpack or shirtsleeve, and still look like model students. "Freshmen that juul as they are leaving school," one Twitter user wrote in March of 2016, adding a heart-eye emoji and a desperate emoji. "[Shaking my head] when the juul pod runs out @ school," another user wrote in May. Someone else on Twitter joked about writing a horror movie that takes place in "the underground juul clubs that control most of the school bathrooms"—or, as they'd soon come to be known in memes and among teenagers, "the Juul rooms." As one New York City teenager later put it in an interview with *The Cut*, "None of us smoked before we Juuled [in 2016]. At some point we all started it 'cause we thought it was cool and then we kept using it 'cause we got addicted."

Despite concerning posts like these, Pax Labs's business seemed to be righting itself, with Juul sales picking up and the marketing team focusing on less controversial avenues going forward. It was finally time to bring on a full-time CEO.

The board chose Tyler Goldman, a middle-aged serial entrepreneur who'd worked for the music streaming company Deezer. He'd gotten a law degree from Northwestern University before pivoting to the entertainment business, where he'd founded companies that included Buzz Media, a prolific social media publisher that churned out reams of celebrity and entertainment content. Goldman had a unique blend of skills that would have appealed to Pax's board. He understood the social media world, but he also had the legal training necessary to keep Pax out of hot water. This was an especially important task now that the e-cigarette industry finally had to play ball with federal regulators.

In May 2016, a few months before Goldman was hired as Pax's CEO—and seven years after the FDA gained the ability to regulate tobacco products—the Food and Drug Administration published its long-awaited deeming rule for e-cigarettes, the document that would finally allow the agency to oversee vaping products. After years of badgering from people like Illinois senator Dick Durbin and Matthew Myers at the Campaign for Tobacco-Free Kids, the FDA had finally put something on the books to rein in the exploding e-cigarette industry. The rule officially established a federal law that made it illegal to sell e-cigarettes to minors or to offer free samples of vaping products. And effective August 8, 2016, e-cigarette companies could not start selling any new products or modify any existing ones without first getting approval from the FDA, which would evaluate the products based on their potential to give adult smokers a safer alternative to cigarettes versus their risk of causing new health problems or addiction among nonsmokers.

Manufacturers of products already on the market, like Juul, had two years to retroactively draw up a document known as a "pre-market tobacco product application," or PMTA, for their devices. Even with two years to work, the PMTA requirements were no joke. Makers would have to design, orchestrate, and submit the data from dozens of studies on their product's toxicity, its ability to help smokers stop using cigarettes, and its abuse potential among nonsmokers, including underage users. If a maker sold multiple flavors or devices, they'd have to repeat this process for every single one. They'd also have to disclose all the ingredients in each of their e-liquid formulas and provide analyses of how these ingredients could affect human health when inhaled into the lungs. E-cigarette products could stay on the market during the two years that manufacturers had been given to draft these applications, and during the FDA's review process once the applications had been turned in, but manufacturers could not make any significant changes to their products during that time. And if the FDA eventually concluded that a particular product would not have a net-positive effect on the nation's public health, it could be pulled from the market entirely.

The stakes were high for all e-cigarette companies, but particularly for the independent companies that had laid the groundwork for the U.S.

vaping culture. Many of these operations were so small, and produced so many flavors, that they had almost no chance of pulling together the money and scientific expertise necessary to conduct the dozens upon dozens of advanced studies necessary. "The PMTA will force ninety-nine percent of companies out of the industry," says Kurt Sonderegger, who opened a small e-liquid company called Cafe Racer Vape after leaving Ploom's marketing division. "The cost involved is [hundreds of thousands of dollars] or more per product. Only a small handful of companies are going to do that."

In some sense, this was a good thing. If companies couldn't afford to rigorously safety-test their products, there was a strong argument to be made that those products shouldn't be sold. But the wrinkle to the whole situation was that virtually all the companies that had PMTA money at their disposal were those owned by or financially tied to Big Tobacco brands: R.J. Reynolds's Vuse and Altria's MarkTen, for example. Clearing the market of small, independent vaping brands and leaving behind only those brands intimately tied to the interests of cigarette companies didn't sit right with some people. "Big Smoking is selling [e-cigarettes] with a conflict of interest, because they still sell cigarettes," says David Abrams, the smoking-cessation expert and e-cigarette evangelist from NYU. Would cigarette companies really want vaping to take off when it could steal sales away from one of the most successful and profitable consumer products of all time?

For many people in public health, there was a bigger concern. The deeming rule seemed to go very light on flavored products, which many experts blamed for attracting teenagers to e-cigarettes. By 2016, there were more e-liquid flavors on the market than anyone could count, and many of them seemed explicitly targeted to young people. Cigarettes in all flavors except menthol were banned in 2009, when President Obama signed the Family Smoking Prevention and Tobacco Control Act, in large part because they appealed to children. A large study later showed that this decision had led to a 43 percent drop in underage smoking and a 27 percent reduction among young adults. Many tobacco control experts wanted something similar for the vaping industry. "There already was [a belief] that the e-cigarette industry was using flavors to attract kids," says Matt Myers from CTFK. "It already was clear-cut that there was a youth problem, and it was already clear-cut that flavors played a huge role in that."

A draft version of the FDA's deeming rule that circulated in 2015 showed that the agency planned to pull all flavored vaping products off the market within ninety days of the rule's implementation, according to *Los Angeles Times* reporting. When the vaping industry caught wind of this, the pushback was swift and strong. From the end of 2015 into early 2016, according to the *Times*, a steady stream of vape shop owners, e-cigarette makers, and tobacco industry lobbyists came calling on the FDA, arguing that its proposed rules on flavors were unreasonably strict and could drive smokers back into the arms of cigarette companies by limiting their choices.

By the time the final deeming rule was published in May 2016, the seventeen-page passage outlining the science behind the FDA's decision to pull flavors from the market had been scrubbed from the document and replaced with a watered-down promise to weigh "concerns regarding flavored tobacco products' appeal to youth [against] emerging evidence that some adults may potentially use certain flavored tobacco products to transition away from combusted tobacco use." All things considered, it was a huge victory for the vaping industry—even though companies still faced the unenviable task of pulling together PMTAs, an undertaking that would rule their lives for the next two years.

There was a significant amount of pressure on Tyler Goldman to keep things moving forward as Pax did so. The company's sales had improved considerably since Juul's launch, but as of mid-2016, Juul products were still available in only 7 percent of stores in the United States. To push that number up, Goldman would need a much bigger team. Pax employed a fairly small group to oversee manufacturing, marketing, and selling multiple product lines, not to mention dealing with regulators, journalists, customers, and parents angry about their teens vaping. There weren't enough people to get the job done, and Pax was still working with fairly small manufacturers that couldn't turn out thousands upon thousands of pods per day—but executives were pushing for more clients, more customers, more stores anyway. Everybody at Pax seemed to be working at warp speed, 24/7.

Under Goldman's leadership, Pax went on a hiring spree to keep growing, building out a team that could help sell and market Juul to the masses. Erica Halverson, who joined Pax's marketing team as a mid-level manager in late 2016, was one of the many new hires. She remembers that period as a whirlwind.

Pax had a large, open office space in San Francisco's trendy Mission District. As soon as you got past reception, you could look out over the expanse of the company's space. With the exception of a few conference rooms and the laboratories where Adam and his team worked, the whole area was open. Instead of closed-door offices, the staff worked at large communal tables, their seats arranged by department. When Halverson first started at the company, she remembers there being plenty of space. But "about four to five months after [I started], we were clearly running out of room and jam-packing people in and making up office spaces that were not office spaces," she says. "Every single conference room was always in use." The office buzzed with activity, plumes of vapor rising from nearly every seat at every table as staffers vaped at their desks. New employees, sometimes more than a dozen of them at a time, were introduced at virtually every Monday morning meeting.

Sometimes, when it came to hiring, quantity outranked quality. "There were people that were in management and leadership positions that should not have been there, but there was nobody else to fill that spot," Halverson says. "They were thrown into that position . . . to get a body in the role." The result, she says, was a company culture in crisis. Communication between managers and their reports broke down, and a rift started to form between the tight-knit old guard and the dozens of new people flooding the company's San Francisco headquarters.

"A lot of the top echelon of the company was working in silos," Halverson says, and it was difficult for employees at lower levels of the company to get any clear information. When her own boss was fired, Halverson was never told about it directly. She thought he was out sick, and learned the truth only when he'd been gone for several days and she asked someone when he'd back. The answer, she learned, was never.

Pax was growing at warp speed, but its growth felt haphazard and chaotic. Roles were turning over as fast as the company was filling them, and Halverson says efforts were being duplicated across the company. "We were hiring people that were duplicating jobs because we were all in our own silos doing our own things, and we weren't talking to each other," she says. Nobody seemed to want to slow down and build things right. Pax felt like "a start-up who wants to act and feel like a corporation," Halverson says. The board clearly wanted Pax to accelerate out of the start-up phase and skip straight to massive-company status, but Goldman and his team hadn't quite laid the groundwork to do so.

"When I was there," Halverson says, "they were getting a little ahead of themselves." A lot of people left because they couldn't handle the turbulence and the lack of communication. The list of casualties included Richard Mumby, who left the company just before hiring hit a fever pitch.

Halverson technically worked under Richard Mumby in the marketing department, but she says they rarely interacted. By that point, Mumby wasn't intimately involved in many day-to-day operations. He appeared to delegate most of his tasks to other people, from running meetings to actually carrying out marketing plans, and lower-level employees couldn't quite tell what he did on a day-to-day basis, Halverson remembers. This wasn't terribly unusual at Pax, where communication often left something to be desired, but, nonetheless, it no longer felt like he was the one steering the ship. In early 2017, Mumby left his job as Pax's chief marketing officer.

Meanwhile, the people who were left were being worked to the bone. A former member of the customer service team around this time remembers working fourteen- or fifteen-hour days, six days a week. "It was like, no matter what, we've got to keep the momentum moving forward," the employee recalls. "There was no time to stop and reflect on what was happening and see what we could change. People were more concerned with making profits than doing what the original mission statement was."

Employees might have been exhausted and stretched thin, but they were giving the board and executive team exactly what they wanted. Pax sold 2.2 million Juul e-cigarettes in 2016. In fact, the device was becoming successful enough that other companies seemed to be taking notice. By 2017, brands like Pulse and Bo had come out with sleek, rectangular vapes that could easily be mistaken for Juuls. A flood of e-liquid companies also started packaging their flavors in pods explicitly sold as "Juul compatible," meaning they worked with Juul devices. Many of these Juul-compatible products came in funky flavors like Pink Lemonade and "Lush Ice." They weren't made by or authorized by Pax Labs, but there they were, sometimes stamped with a Photoshopped approximation of Juul's logo. This trend opened up a world of legal headaches for Pax, one filled with intellectual property lawsuits and cease-and-desist letters, but it suggested the little Juul device wasn't only selling well; it was shaping consumer preferences and product design across the entire industry.

As Pax grew, no one was keeping a closer eye on it than Altria, the parent company of Philip Morris. As of 2017, Philip Morris's Marlboros accounted for 40 percent of the U.S. cigarette market, with the next-best-selling product, R.J. Reynolds's Newport, in a distant second. Altria's net revenue was on track to exceed $25 billion in 2017.

But the tobacco market was changing. E-cigarettes clearly weren't going away, and sales were down across the cigarette sector as these devices gained popularity. Some customers actually seemed to be switching from cigarettes to vaporizers. This might have been fine for Altria if they had been switching to its products—but many weren't. MarkTen, Altria's e-cigarette brand, was one of the country's largest, but its devices were rapidly beginning to look outdated next to products like the Juul. MarkTen's products weren't sexy. Its slim, white devices looked like the cigalikes that became popular when the vaping industry was just getting started, but consumer preferences were drifting away from gimmicky products that looked just like traditional cigarettes. Reviewers found them pretty blah, nothing special in the increasingly saturated vaping market.

Altria's top executives had been watching Juul practically since it launched. Throughout 2015 and 2016, the brand's sales were far lower than those generated by Big Tobacco–backed e-cigarettes like Vuse and Altria's own MarkTen products, but by the first quarter of 2017, the market was changing. Vuse, by a comfortable margin, was still the country's biggest vaping brand, followed by Blu. But then there was Juul, encroaching on MarkTen's own sales figures. And while MarkTen's sales were fairly stagnant, Juul's were growing steadily each and every quarter.

Altria executives knew that Juul was a better product than MarkTen ever had been. "Although Altria set up [MarkTen] to compete, it did not have scientists or technical experts who were experienced in developing e-vapor products," the company later wrote in court documents filed in response to a complaint from the Federal Trade Commission. "Altria's effort was a failure." Juul had a much sleeker design and better nicotine delivery. Indeed, the MarkTen, in comparison, looked like its frumpy older cousin. If Juul was going to keep siphoning off Altria's sales, why shouldn't Altria take some for itself? It was the oldest trick in the book: if you can't beat 'em, join 'em.

In early 2017, the executive team at Altria decided to test the waters. They informed Pax's team that Altria was very intrigued by Juul's product and its growth and wanted to stay in touch. By the spring of 2017, the two companies' executives were in serious talks about a partnership of some kind.

Adam and James, who still had seats on the board even though Tyler Goldman had taken over as CEO, were "skeptical" of the whole proposition, Adam recalled in a 2019 interview. "There was a lot of deliberation and discussions that went into 'Should we form this partnership with Altria?'" he said. "I really didn't think that we would end up doing the deal." It wasn't that the men were opposed to working with Big Tobacco, exactly. Ploom had taken an investment from Japan Tobacco after all, and attracting potential investors had been part of the strategy ever since Juul launched. Adam and James were practical enough to see that cigarette companies had resources and ties to consumers that could benefit their business, even if, as Adam said, they could understand why people might be confused or cynical about the partnership.

The question was what Altria could do for Pax. Juul was finally selling well, the company was growing, and there were rumors of offers from other Big Tobacco companies—including Altria's rival British American Tobacco, reportedly. If the board was going to invite all the bad press and scrutiny that would surely come with an investment from Big Tobacco, it needed to be absolutely sure it was for the right deal. Who knew what the company's executives could get if they waited things out, played hard to get? "Big tobacco is used to paying high multiples for brands and market share," Adam wrote in an email to his team a few months before Altria came calling, according to the consolidated complaint from the multi-district litigation against Juul. If Pax's executives played their cards right, they might be able to get more than a partner. They could get a massive payout.

9

THE DIVORCE (MAY–NOVEMBER 2017)

Coughs racked Chance Ammirata's body. Bewildered and unimpressed, the high school junior handed the little flash drive–like device back to his friend, who'd given it to him to try during a quiet moment in culinary class. She'd said the Juul produced only flavored water vapor, but it sure didn't feel that way to Chance. His lungs were burning. Nonetheless, at his friend's coaxing, he decided to give it another shot. "I took like three more hits, and the coughing subsided, and I felt this buzz that went through my entire body," Chance remembers. He'd never felt anything like it.

Within two weeks, he'd purchased his own Juul and a pack of Mint e-juice pods from a smoke shop near his school in Miami Beach—which was easy enough to do: the teenager was never asked to show ID. After that, he hardly went anywhere without his Juul. He burned through about half a pod a day, about as much nicotine as one would get from a dozen cigarettes. "I was working almost a full-time job, and I had all of my classes," he remembers. "It was difficult to [vape] everywhere, even though I really wanted to." It helped, though, that just about all his friends had Juuls on them 24/7, so he could steal hits here and there. The devices were so small, and the vapor dissipated so quickly, that it was easy enough to take a quick hit in the hallways or when the teacher's back was turned.

In 2017, when Chance picked up his first Juul, the National Youth Tobacco Survey estimated that about 12 percent of high school students vaped—on paper, actually a decrease from the pre- and early Juul era of 2015, when 16 percent of high schoolers reported using e-cigarettes. But Chance says the reality in his school did not match the story told by national data. So many kids were using Juuls that the device's name had become a verb: *to juul.* "I went to a public school with about four thousand kids in it," Chance says. Within about a month of his first hit, he remembers, "It went from twenty friends I knew were juuling to—it was harder to find someone who wasn't hooked on it than someone who was."

His experience wasn't unique. In May 2017, a student reporter from Loy Norrix High School in Michigan picked up on the juuling trend sweeping schools across the country. She interviewed an anonymous fifteen-year-old freshman who'd become addicted to juuling after hitting one for the first time in the school cafeteria. "I literally cannot go, like, an hour without hitting my Juul," the student confessed. "If I don't have pods, it's a crisis." The student spoke of spending upward of thirty dollars a week on pods, sometimes borrowing or stealing money from a parent to support the habit. The student wasn't eating much, was irritable, and was so addicted to nicotine as to be unable to imagine life without a Juul. "I don't even want to think about stopping," the student said, "so it's probably not going to happen."

Widespread as it was, underage juuling was not a universal phenomenon. It was especially popular in schools where students could afford to drop thirty-five dollars on a device that needed to be constantly refilled with pods that cost about fifteen dollars for a four-pack. National data showed that vaping was particularly common among white teenagers: from 2014 to 2017, almost 34 percent of white high school students reported trying an e-cigarette at least once, compared to almost 20 percent of Black students. White students were also more likely than Black students to report having tried only e-cigarettes but no other tobacco products, a trend that some experts thought could lead to a concerning gateway effect. "Everybody was touting [less] teen cigarette use as such a success in the U.S.," says Dr. Kelly Henning, an epidemiologist who leads the Bloomberg Philanthropies Public Health program. "The idea that you could reverse that was really so alarming."

It may not have been everywhere, but in schools where juuling was ubiquitous, it was becoming more than an activity; it was taking on its own culture. Juul periodically came out with limited-edition devices in colors like royal blue or gold, and third-party companies also sold wallpaper-like "skins" people could use to customize their Juuls with luxury fashion logos, branding from TV shows, or colorful patterns. Kids who got their hands on "good" Juul flavors—basically, anything but Crème Brûlée—could make a killing reselling them to friends. Teenagers were starting to dabble in Juul tricks—blowing vape rings or juuling through their nose or sucking down a whole pod at once—that they could show off at parties or on Snapchat stories. Social media remained at the heart of Juul's cultural takeover.

In May 2017, twenty-year-old Donny Karle bought his first Juul. He'd vaped before, but he mostly used clunky tank-style vapes that were annoying to lug around and often leaked. Karle bought a Juul because it seemed stealthier and more convenient. He decided to make an "unboxing video" of him checking out his new device and learning how it worked. He posted the six-minute clip on YouTube and racked up more than fifty thousand views. After that, he kept making videos about Juul and other e-cigarettes and posting them on YouTube under the username "DonnySmokes." Sometimes they were just reviews or unboxing videos, but he also dabbled in advice. "How to HIDE & HIT Your JUUL at SCHOOL WITHOUT Getting CAUGHT," he titled one video. "How to hide your JUUL from your parents," he labeled another.

While DonnySmokes was building an audience on YouTube, plenty of accounts were doing something similar on Instagram. These accounts posted memes, photos, and videos about all things Juul—including how to use one stealthily at school by hiding it in school supplies or exhaling the vapor into one's sleeve. Next came Reddit, where the page "UnderageJuul" made its debut in July 2017. There, teenagers chatted about their favorite Juul flavors and how they could get the devices themselves. The best way, they agreed, was to get somebody who already had a Juul device to copy down its serial number. Pax had such a lax warranty policy that all you had to do was email the customer service team "your" serial number and claim your device was broken. Typically, they'd have a new one in the mail within days. In one instance, according to the lawsuit filed by the California attorney general, a Pax employee noted that a single customer had made more than three hundred warranty claims in about a month.

The youth-use issue was a topic of discussion within Pax Labs, the complaint alleged. "Fuckin 40 people in checkout right now," one customer service employee wrote on Slack, the company's internal messaging platform, in 2017. A coworker joked back: "40 teenagers trying to buy 200 juuls." Board members and executives couldn't deny the problem, either, because many of them had seen it firsthand. Some of Pax's top employees and board members had kids in the kind of wealthy schools where vaping was everywhere. They'd pick up their children and see kids juuling in the parking lot, remembers a consultant who worked with the company in 2017. "It wasn't hard to figure out who was buying the product," the consultant says. Anecdotal evidence wasn't hard to come by.

To Pax's executive team, it was crystal clear that youth juuling wasn't going away and that dealing with it was going to require an increasingly large portion of the company's time and energy. Experts kept warning them to tamp down this youth problem before it got even further out of hand. "If this spreads among high school kids, you'll be dead," UCSF nicotine researcher Neal Benowitz remembers warning science director Gal Cohen in meetings about Juul. "We know what happened with cigarettes." Already, the spread seemed to be spiraling out of control. "I'm seeing kids starting to get this. I'm seeing the marketing has [reached] the kids, and I'm seeing parents have no idea about these things," a Massachusetts doctor warned a local news station in July 2017.

Juul and Pax devices were two different beasts. Pax had never really caught on with underage users, in large part because of its $250 price tag, but juuling was fast becoming a way of life in certain schools across America. There were plenty of other differences, too.

Pax vaporizers had over time become almost exclusively associated with vaping marijuana rather than tobacco, and they were beloved for that purpose. By 2017, Pax had a whole range of products. There was the Pax 3, a higher-tech version of the original Pax device. It was rectangular with smooth edges and no buttons or switches in sight, and it worked with either loose-leaf marijuana or waxy marijuana concentrates. There was also the Pax Era, a smaller device that looked like a Juul and vaporized cannabis oil. Both Pax and Juul products were popular, but there were fundamental differences between the two markets. Before too long, the Juul team would have to file a PMTA, the lengthy and expensive FDA application requiring dozens of studies and thousands of pages of charts and graphs. Meanwhile, Pax had to deal with the patchwork of marijuana laws across the country, carefully tailoring its sales and marketing depending on whether a state allowed the use of marijuana medicinally versus recreationally versus not at all.

Given the inherent differences between the nicotine and cannabis markets, it seemed natural for different teams to manage Juul versus Pax. In June 2017, Pax and Juul divorced, becoming two separate companies: Pax Labs and Juul Labs.

The split revealed many of the issues marketing staffer Erica Halverson described—namely, that the company's hiring practices had been all over the place. "They had to get rid of a good swath of us because they figured out, 'Oh my god, we have two to three people doing the exact same thing,'" she says. Among those who remained, about 160 employees were assigned to work for Juul, while only 32 were left for Pax. The board likely wasn't happy with the rampant waste exposed by the split. The last thing a start-up needed was unnecessary overhead costs, and plenty of them had been introduced during the Goldman-era hiring boom. Nonetheless, he remained the CEO of both brands, while Adam and James became, respectively, the chief technology officer and chief product officer at Juul Labs.

While Pax and Juul were separating, a leadership shake-up was underway over at the FDA, too. Shortly after President Donald Trump took office in early 2017, he nominated a new FDA commissioner: Dr. Scott Gottlieb, a libertarian-leaning internist in his midforties who had previously served in a couple of high-level positions within the agency. Gottlieb was an interesting character. He spoke rapid-fire, apparently unafraid to offend or step on toes, but he also raised his own chickens at home in Connecticut, tweeted prolifically, joked around with journalists, and was a loving father to three children under ten. As both a trained physician and a cancer survivor who'd beaten lymphoma almost a decade earlier, he had a unique understanding of the American medical system. Despite his medical and bureaucratic experience, Democrats were deeply concerned about Gottlieb's "unprecedented financial entanglements," as Washington senator Patty Murray put it during Gottlieb's confirmation hearing. The man Trump wanted to oversee the country's drug industry had himself made buckets of money investing in pharmaceutical companies, which caused many lawmakers to fear he would be far too friendly to drug companies at a time when prescription drug costs were spiking. The Senate approved him by only a 57–42 margin.

Antivaping advocates were nervous for their own reasons. Gottlieb had previously invested in a company called Kure, which franchised vape shops and lounges. Kure wasn't exactly shy about the reality that e-cigarettes were recreational products. The company's website called vaping "far more than a way for ex-smokers to buck a nasty habit. It has become a way to relax, enjoy and socialize—it's a cultural movement that is being led by Millennials, and in many ways it has nothing to do with smoking." In only two sentences, the company confirmed that people were vaping for fun; young adults were the most likely to do so; and the habit had "nothing to do with" smoking cessation. The fact that the incoming FDA commissioner, the man who would be in charge of finally implementing an e-cigarette deeming rule nearly a decade in the making, had chosen to invest in a company with this mind-set did not bode well for those who wanted to see tighter regulations on e-cigarettes.

The Campaign for Tobacco-Free Kids put out a statement urging Gottlieb to recuse himself from any FDA business involving e-cigarettes. Gottlieb didn't quite do that, though he did resign from Kure's board, and he quickly established tobacco regulation as one of his top priorities at the FDA. The first meeting Gottlieb took as commissioner, on his first day of work, was with Mitch Zeller, who ran the agency's Center for Tobacco Products. On his third day at the agency, he addressed the whole staff to talk about his goals for reducing tobacco-related deaths. And in July, only two months into his tenure, Gottlieb unveiled an ambitious plan that, if it moved forward, would shake up the entire tobacco industry.

He proposed new regulations that would cap the amount of nicotine in cigarettes to make them less addictive, a policy that he hoped would both help current smokers quit and prevent more people from becoming dependent on cigarettes in the first place. Gottlieb knew that if he did something that drastic, he'd need to give current smokers some kind of alternative. "We sought to open up new opportunities for adult smokers who were currently addicted to nicotine and still wanted to enjoy nicotine—to help them find ways to do it through vehicles that didn't have all the death and disease associated with smoking," Gottlieb explains. Medicinal nicotine products like the patch and gum were one option. E-cigarettes were another.

At the same time that Gottlieb announced his ambitious plan for cigarette regulation, he gave e-cigarette manufacturers a four-year extension on their PMTAs. Companies still weren't able to introduce any new products during that period without the FDA's go-ahead, but those that already sold e-cigarettes now had until August 8, 2022, to file any paperwork with the agency. "We didn't want to sweep them off the market at the very time we were seeking to regulate nicotine in combustible products," Gottlieb says, as doing so would have been a brutal move for people who were currently dependent on nicotine. "We thought it was a balanced public health approach." Both Gottlieb and Mitch Zeller believed that e-cigarettes could be a useful tool for adults who wanted a less dangerous way to consume nicotine.

In August 2017, the two published a joint perspective paper in the *New England Journal of Medicine* that seemed to bode quite favorably for the e-cigarette industry. "Led by the best available evidence, the FDA will pursue a regulatory framework that focuses on nicotine and supports innovation to promote harm reduction," they wrote. "This framework will recognize that the core problem of nicotine lies not in the drug itself but in the risk associated with the delivery mechanism." In other words, it was possible that e-cigarettes—along with non-inhaled medicinal nicotine products like the patch and gum—could make it much less dangerous, if not totally safe, to consume nicotine.

"To the consternation of some in the public health and tobacco control communities, we chose to explicitly acknowledge that there is a continuum of risk when it comes to the delivery of nicotine," Zeller says. "There are more harmful and less harmful ways to deliver nicotine. The most harmful, no dispute, is the combustible cigarette. The least harmful, and also no dispute, is medicinal nicotine products [like patches and gum]. Everything else is somewhere along the spectrum."

The debate, of course, is figuring out where e-cigarettes fall on that spectrum. Scientists were still in fierce disagreement about that question when Zeller and Gottlieb's paper came out. There was more research on e-cigarettes than there had been when they first launched, but scientists were still far from consensus on the topic.

One group of scientists, led by Stanton Glantz from UCSF, argued that e-cigarettes belonged right next to cigarettes on the continuum of risk, pointing to papers (many authored by Glantz himself) that suggested that the devices actually made smokers *less* likely to quit, encouraged young people to start smoking, and potentially led to worrying side effects like heart damage. Other papers found that many popular e-cigarettes contained chemicals known to be dangerous to the lungs when inhaled or produced by-products like formaldehyde (thought to be a carcinogen in humans) when heated up. And of course, there was the issue of youth use, which many antivaping scientists viewed as the biggest risk associated with e-cigarettes.

The opposite side, led by people like NYU's David Abrams, fervently believed e-cigarettes were far less dangerous than combustible cigarettes. They believed that vaping could get adults to stop smoking; that many teenagers who vaped were either former smokers or kids doing fairly harmless experimentation, as many do with alcohol and marijuana; and that switching could lead to huge reductions in smoking-related conditions like cancer and heart disease. Zeller and Gottlieb's stance seemed like a big win for the pro-vaping side. Here were the country's top two tobacco regulators acknowledging in one of the nation's most prestigious medical journals that e-cigarettes had a place in the tobacco control world—and backing up those words by giving vaping companies more time on the market, virtually unregulated.

That extra time was a gift for Juul. Newly independent, the company was struggling to figure out how to deal with its success. Sales had increased so quickly over the past year—more than a million vaporizers were sold each month in 2017—that Juul sometimes couldn't fulfill orders. Sometimes it would purposely stock stores only with pods, not vaporizers, as a way to maintain existing users without attracting new ones, and to triage supply issues. Purposely avoiding new customers was hardly a perfect business strategy, but desperate times called for desperate measures. Goldman clearly knew the situation was less than ideal. "If we're not getting enough devices out into the marketplace, it means we're not giving people the option to switch to Juul," he told CNBC in a fall 2017 interview.

PR also remained a struggle. Lawmakers and journalists were starting to catch on to the underage juuling phenomenon in larger numbers than ever before. "'Juuling': The Most Widespread Phenomenon You've Never Heard Of," read one fall 2017 *Boston Globe* headline. "Teenagers Embrace JUUL, Saying It's Discreet Enough to Vape in Class," added NPR. And perhaps worst of all, *USA Today* warned that "Juuling Is Popular with Teens, but Doctor Sees a 'Good Chance' That It Leads to Smoking."

In October 2017, New York senator Chuck Schumer added weight to the trend pieces by urging the FDA to evaluate e-cigarette products faster, specifically citing teen juuling in his argument. "To know that New York kids are much more likely to be using these new-age e-cig devices, like Juul, is not only concerning, but it could be dangerous," Schumer argued at a press conference.

The last thing Juul needed was more bad press. On that front, the company had taken some steps in the right direction. Buyers now needed to be at least twenty-one to purchase a Juul through the company's e-commerce portal, and the marketing department was trying to clean up some of the practices that had gotten it in trouble during the Vaporized era. If ads or social media posts had people in them, the models couldn't look even questionably underage, and they couldn't have lots of followers who were, either. It was somewhat rare that models even showed up in its social media campaigns anymore. Juul's official accounts now veered more toward artfully arranged still-life shots than the kind of sexy lifestyle marketing that had gotten the company in trouble before.

These principles were drilled into marketing staffers' heads, and they were nonnegotiable. "Everything we did—every period on the end of a sentence, every color that we used, every person that was in an ad that we chose—had a purpose behind it," says Erica Halverson, who worked on the company's marketing team until the summer of 2017, when she was laid off. "The purpose was: this cannot, in any way, be geared toward teenagers."

And yet, Juul Labs still seemed tempted to slide back into its old ways. The company could either swear off controversial marketing at all costs or it could push for growth at all costs. It couldn't do both, at least not effectively, but the company's executives often tried anyway.

In September 2017, Juul Labs settled a lawsuit filed by the California-based Center for Environmental Health (CEH). In 2015, CEH sued a number of e-cigarette manufacturers, including Pax, for failing to disclose to California consumers that their devices produced small amounts of formaldehyde as a by-product of heating and aerosolizing e-liquids. At that time, CEH demanded that each manufacturer add a warning label to its packaging and pay a $2,500 fine for each day it failed to warn consumers they could be inhaling formaldehyde. By the time Juul was actually ready to settle the lawsuit, in September 2017, youth vaping was a much bigger issue than it had been in 2015. CEH decided to take advantage of the opportunity and added a few optional provisions about youth marketing to the settlement agreement. In addition to the fines related to formaldehyde, the company could either sign a legally binding agreement not to market to minors or pay a $2,500 fine. Juul opted to pay the fine.

Perhaps it was purely a business decision. A $2,500 fine was tiny, especially now that Juul was one of the top-selling e-cigarettes in the country. It may have just made sense to pay it and move on. But Juul executives also likely balked at one of CEH's stipulations: as part of its clause on marketing to minors, CEH asked Juul not to advertise on Instagram. Even after all the blowback over Vaporized, this was a sacrifice Juul Labs wasn't willing to make.

Christina Zayas, who lives in New York City and runs a popular lifestyle and fashion Instagram account, was in her midthirties in the fall of 2017, when she got an email from Lumanu, an influencer marketing company working with Juul. A Lumanu representative offered Zayas a thousand dollars to create one blog post and one Instagram post about Juul, a tool she pitched as "a genuinely satisfying vapor alternative for adult smokers." It seemed like a great match to Zayas, who had recently taken up smoking as a crutch after she got sober. She'd been interested in trying e-cigarettes anyway, so she said yes without much thought. "I was very honest" about my story, Zayas says of the blog post she turned in. "I wanted to make it about recovery."

Juul's marketing team had other ideas. After Zayas turned in her post, the representative from Lumanu sent her feedback from a member of Juul's marketing team, who had asked for the post to be rewritten to de-emphasize anything about addiction, likely to avoid their getting in trouble with the FDA by making statements that could be perceived as health claims. "We don't need her to be an expert in e-cigs/nicotine, but an expert in lifestyle/fashion and explaining how she incorporates our product into her daily life," the Juul staffer wrote. "It'd also be great if she could talk about the design aesthetics, seeing as she is a fashion figurehead to her audience."

Zayas was upset. She'd been excited for the chance to write openly about addiction and recovery, but Juul didn't seem to care about any of that; they just wanted her to be another Instagram lifestyle influencer selling a cool new product. "What annoyed me most was the back-and-forth and not having the freedom to share what I wanted to share," she says. She collected her check, posted the revised version of her blog post and a photo of herself vaping while reclined on a stoop, and decided never to work with Juul Labs again.

Zayas was one of only four influencers Juul paid to explicitly promote its products. The bulk of its strategy was more sophisticated and subtler. The company dabbled in a little product placement—Juul shows up in a 2017 episode of HBO's Millennial-focused show *Girls*, for example—and it also dove into the world of unpaid influencers. Juul's influencer team hired a consulting firm to sift through the nearly 350,000 addresses on Juul's email list in the fall of 2017 to match them with social media accounts that had influencer potential. The consulting firm sorted the names into various categories. There were "top-tier" influencers, who were either celebrities (like actors Adam Scott and Anna Paquin) or people with social followings of at least one hundred thousand, all the way down to "low-tier" influencers who had social followings of fewer than ten thousand but who were considered "super fans" who could be useful for word-of-mouth marketing. The consulting firm took care to note which "top-tier" influencers were thirty or younger, given that the company was trying to stay away from working with anyone who looked controversially young. Still, the consulting firm wrote that it "recommended keeping [these younger celebrities] on our roster," just in case.

There were benefits attached to finding people who already liked and used Juul and might be willing to post about it. It was free, for one thing. The post also wouldn't need to be marked as an ad, which both made it feel more authentic and meant Juul would have little responsibility over what the influencer ultimately wrote or who saw the post.

Juul had stopped offering influencers free samples in 2016, as soon as the FDA's deeming rule forbade it from doing so. To get around this policy, the company instead gave high-priority influencers a discount code that allowed them to purchase Juul devices and pods online for one dollar. Each person also got access to a VIP portal where they could get Juul-branded swag and early access to new devices and flavors. The rapper and actress

Awkwafina became one of the company's first VIP invitees after she talked about switching from cigarettes to Juul on a podcast in the summer of 2017. "WOW—thank you so much for the codes," she gushed in an email to Juul's influencer manager. "That is so awesome and greatly appreciated. I will forever and always rant about how much I love Juul and how it saved my life." This was exactly the result Juul's influencer team was looking for: a lifetime of free advertising.

Meanwhile, the company was also working on an entirely different way to fix Juul's youth problem. Company executives thought an educational campaign could be one way to dissuade teenagers from using Juul, so in November 2017 Juul Labs hired a veteran educator named Bruce Harter as a consultant. During his nearly fifty-year education career, Harter had been the principal of schools in Arkansas, Iowa, and Colorado and a superintendent in Oregon, Florida, and Delaware. Most recently, he'd been the superintendent of California's West Contra Costa Unified School District. Given these credentials, the company entrusted Harter and his former associate superintendent Wendell Greer with writing a curriculum that could teach kids all about why they shouldn't be vaping—from the ways nicotine could affect a developing brain to the lifelong burden of addiction.

It's hard to say why Juul's executives thought America's coolest and fastest-growing e-cigarette company was in a position to provide antivaping education to children, but there certainly was a need for *someone* to teach these kinds of lessons. In late 2017, shortly after Harter was hired, National Institute on Drug Abuse data showed that almost 30 percent of high school seniors, 25 percent of high school sophomores, and 15 percent of eighth graders said they'd vaped either nicotine or marijuana at some point that year. The data also showed that more than half of them thought their vapor contained only flavoring, not nicotine or THC. This prompted an outcry from advocacy groups like the Campaign for Tobacco-Free Kids, which put out a statement demanding that the FDA ban flavors in all tobacco products.

But to people at Juul, the data may have seemed like an opportunity. If most teens thought they were just inhaling water vapor, and far fewer of them knew they were actually inhaling nicotine or THC, maybe Juul could go straight to the source. Maybe, if it taught teenagers exactly what they were inhaling and why they shouldn't be inhaling it, they could convince some of them to stop. Maybe then everyone would stop insisting that Juul had marketed its product directly to teenagers.

Or maybe not.

10

In the fall of 2017, Juul Labs's board embarked on a new project. Juul had been growing at a steady burn for the last two years, its sales progressively ratcheting up with each quarter, and it was now really starting to take off. The company's revenue approached $100 million in the last quarter of 2017, and its sales were overtaking other e-cigarettes on the market, including big names like Vuse, Blu, and MarkTen. With Juul Labs now an independent company, separate from Pax Labs, it was time to find a CEO who could take things to the next level.

Tyler Goldman had done well by the company in his year and a half as CEO, but if Juul was going to keep growing at the pace it was, the board knew it needed someone who had the expertise to help it scale. Under Goldman, even as sales soared, growth had been sloppy and chaotic. Turnover was a problem, hiring was slapdash, and many of the company's managers didn't have much leadership experience. The company's back-end processes also hadn't caught up to consumer demand—the company still sometimes had trouble filling orders, and it was still plagued by issues like leaky pods. In being unable to meet demand, the company was leaving customers' money on the table. The board knew that if it was going to become the kind of giant corporation they dreamed about, it would need someone who could work out those kinks. And they thought they had just the man for the job: Kevin Burns.

Burns was a gregarious, straight-talking guy in his fifties, the sort of person you could easily picture holding a beer and flipping burgers at a backyard barbecue. He was a good-humored family man, married with two teenage children, but he also didn't take any bullshit. He didn't sugarcoat anything. His language was colorful, peppered with choice words like *idiots* and *mo-fos*. He was also a workaholic with a reputation for building brands into winners.

Burns had most recently worked at the Greek yogurt company Chobani, by way of his private equity firm, TPG. In a financially desperate moment in 2014, the yogurt maker had turned to TPG for a $750 million loan. It also got Burns, who was known as a turnaround guru for struggling companies. Chobani's founder had reportedly called Burns to ask for his help while Burns was at an Easter Mass service with his family in April 2014. Burns not only picked up the call during the service, but he also said yes. He spent a couple years at Chobani, helping improve its back-end processes and distribution capabilities. When he stepped down at the end of 2016, he left behind a booming business.

Juul Labs wasn't in the dire straits Chobani had been—if anything, it was growing faster than it could handle—but the board knew it needed someone who could streamline its operations and implement a solid growth plan. "As the company grew, the role of the CEO also needed to change," says a company source. "Kevin clearly had manufacturing, supply chain, and management experience." Neither Adam nor James had worked out in the CEO role, and Goldman didn't seem to have the chops to help Juul keep scaling. They needed someone like Burns.

But Kevin Burns had no interest in running an e-cigarette company—at least not at first. The nicotine business was very different from the Greek yogurt business, and Burns wasn't a smoker. He'd never even heard of Juul until the fall of 2017, when he started getting calls from the company's board members. Plus, he had purposely taken time off after stepping down from his role at Chobani, and he was enjoying being home with his family in California after years of constant travel.

When Juul's board started calling, "I said, 'Nah,'" Burns remembered in a 2019 interview. "But the board was quite effective at reaching out to people that knew me. I got two or three other calls, so I said, 'Okay, I'll take a meeting.'"

Once Burns finally took a meeting with the board, it wasn't a terribly hard sell. He was intrigued by the size of the opportunity—the number of smokers the company could feasibly switch from cigarettes to Juul—as well as the size of the challenge. When he began interviewing in late 2017, Juul's growth was skyrocketing. The company would sell 16.2 million vaporizers by the end of that year, enough that one in every three e-cigarettes sold in the United States was a Juul—a remarkable feat for a start-up competing against Big Tobacco companies. Juul Labs was in the midst of a $150 million fundraising campaign. But, despite its growth, Juul was still a fairly small operation, with only 225 employees.

Juul was incredibly successful for a small company, which meant it could absolutely be dominant if someone managed its growth the right way—and, maybe someday, guided it toward an initial public offering that would open up its stocks to outside investors and provide quite a cash-out for its executives. This likely held real appeal for Burns. For years, there'd been whispers about Chobani going public, but it hadn't happened during Burns's tenure. Even if it had, he'd been the president, not the CEO—not the one in the top spot. "He's a smart and very competitive guy who had a significant amount of success both as an investor, buying up what was in distress at Chobani and turning it into a machine," says a source who worked with Burns. "The one thing he has not done is take a company public." With Juul, it looked like Burns might have a real shot at doing that.

"I kept coming back to, this could be a massive opportunity, a massive impact," Burns recalled in 2019. Eventually, he said yes to the board and took the job. Still, the decision "was not a slam dunk." His teenage daughter, who was far more familiar with Juul then her father was, thought it would be a bad look for her father to work for a company that made products her classmates liked to hit in the bathroom between classes at school. "My daughter said, 'Dad, I see too many kids using this. I'm really worried about the company,'" Burns remembered. Some of the adults in his life had a similar reaction. "I have a lot of friends that I've known for a long time who kind of look at you and say, 'Really?'" he admitted.

Despite the doubters, Burns decided the opportunity was worth the risk. In December 2017, Juul Labs announced that Kevin Burns would take over as CEO, while Tyler Goldman would leave the company to pursue "new entrepreneurial opportunities."

Almost as soon as Burns walked through the door at Juul's Mission District headquarters, he began to make changes. The company had gone on a hiring spree under Goldman, but it hadn't done the right kind of hiring. Growth didn't necessarily feel strategic or efficient. That was exactly what Burns wanted to change. He couldn't believe the company didn't have a government affairs team, or a robust communications team, or a cadre of scientists working on clinical studies. Virtually all the company's resources were going toward keeping the lights on and keeping the product coming out, and Burns could see that with an FDA application to worry about and lawmakers and journalists investigating underage juuling, this wouldn't always be enough. In addition to streamlining business practices and increasing production, he knew that if Juul Labs were to keep growing and survive the crucible of public opinion, it would have to become politically, scientifically, and publicly savvy.

"The category and the company got out ahead of itself a little bit in terms of the infrastructure around it, the data around it, and being ready for some of the challenges it was facing," Burns said in the summer of 2019. If it was ever going to go from a successful start-up to a blockbuster company, Juul would need more lawyers, more publicists, more lobbyists, more researchers, more people versed in supply chain and quality assurance—and Burns set out to find them.

He also set his sights on a bigger goal: international expansion. Juul's business up to that point had been focused on the United States, but the majority of the world's billion-plus smokers live in other countries, like

China and India. Burns wanted them to buy Juuls, too, and he was convinced he could grow the company enough to make this possible in the near future. "In company meetings, he would say, 'Such-and-such a percentage of our revenue comes from the U.S. and such-and-such percentage comes from international. Our goal in the next five years is to flip that, or at least make it fifty-fifty,'" one company source remembers.

Within months of his hiring, Burns began filling gaps in the company—and simultaneously altering its culture. "This was the point in time when Juul decided, 'We're a real company now,'" says one former Juul executive. "It was still very start-uppy, with the goal to move to an environment that was a top-notch public company." In earlier days, most Juul staffers had been Millennials who liked the freewheeling start-up vibe as much as they did the idea of stamping out cigarettes. They were smart people and good employees, but they'd come up mostly through the Silicon Valley tech start-up system, which meant that Juul functioned a lot like a Silicon Valley tech company. Burns and the board wanted "people who worked at Big Fortune Five Hundred companies, who had the traditional blue-chip experience," the former employee says, as well as people with experience in the health care and pharmaceutical worlds—people who could help Juul grow from a start-up to a global corporation.

In a 2019 interview, Burns said his immediate focus, upon taking the job, was building out a team that could establish Juul as a responsible company and help guide it past obstacles like the PMTA process. That, he said, necessitated expanding Juul's quality control, supply chain, and legal departments, as well as making "sure that we're doing all the right things in terms of interfacing with the regulators." But to some people within the company, growth seemed to be a higher priority for Burns than following FDA regulations.

In early 2018, after more than two years on the market, some of Juul's pods still leaked. Since the product's launch, Juul had received more than one hundred thousand customer complaints about leaky pods, and some of them were gruesome. People reported burning in their mouths and lungs, canker sores, blistering, numbness, and vomiting after the juice got in their mouths. This was a problem on several levels. It was concerning from a health standpoint, of course, but it was also a ticking time bomb for sales and public relations. After years of tinkering, Juul's engineers thought they'd finally figured out a way to stop the leakage without compromising the pod's look or size. If they passed instructions about the fix along to the manufacturing facility that made Juul's pods, they could start getting the improved design out into circulation. Burns and the rest of the executive team allowed the change to go forward.

This was a logical decision, except that when the FDA's deeming rule had gone into effect in 2016, it said that companies—with very few exceptions—could not make modifications to products already on the market without clearing them with the FDA. In essence, modifying an existing product made it a new product in the eyes of the FDA.

If redesigning Juul's pods didn't fall into that category, it certainly came dangerously close. But Juul had made other, subtle changes to its product, and nothing bad had happened yet. Employees had tinkered with the device's circuitry and software in 2017, too.

Juul's leaky pods weren't only a problem for users. When fluid escaped the pods, it sometimes caused the device's sensor (which registered when a user inhaled and told the battery to kick on) to short out, shutting down the whole device. In 2017, according to *Bloomberg* reporting, Juul's engineers swapped the original sensor for a sturdier one. But swapping the sensor forced the engineers to tweak the device's circuitry and firmware to accommodate the new piece. What had started as one simple tweak was turning into quite the ripple effect.

These fixes predated Burns, but by the time he joined the company in late 2017, the Juul device had essentially been gut-renovated. The outside looked the same, and the average user wouldn't have known that anything was different, but the engineering team had made so many tweaks that, from a technological standpoint, the revamped device was essentially brand-new. It reportedly even had a new nickname within the company, "Jagwar," after the muscled, humanoid jaguar character in *Teenage Mutant Ninja Turtles*. A cautious company probably would have reported those alterations to the FDA, for fear of violating the deeming rule's provisions on product modifications. But the changes to the device and its pods went undisclosed. (In a statement about product changes, a Juul spokesperson maintained that Juul "comp[lies] with the requirements applicable to our products.")

The decision not to report may have been less about purposefully flouting the FDA, and more a sign that Juul's top executives didn't yet understand how carefully the FDA's policies needed to be followed. Regulatory affairs were certainly discussed within the company, but it sometimes seemed that their magnitude didn't sink in, that executives did not realize the company could live or die by the FDA's word. "Kevin, coming from yogurt, had no aptitude for this stuff," says a company source. He "didn't understand the gravity of" FDA regulations. (When asked in a 2019 interview about the challenges of building a brand in a highly regulated and scrutinized industry, Burns quipped, "Shit happens. We've got to respond.") Oversight of the luxury yogurt business was very different from that of the nicotine business, and Burns seemingly couldn't or didn't want to grasp that the same growth strategies that had worked at Chobani weren't necessarily going to work at Juul, in the opinions of some of his employees.

One company source says Burns seemed to think the FDA should be pleased with Juul's decision to alter its pods and vaporizer, because improving Juul's product meant improving the experience for customers, which in turn meant more smokers might want to stop using cigarettes. Of course, it also meant that Juul could quietly release a superior product that would rake in more money without going through the laborious and expensive FDA approval process.

Much of Juul's board didn't seem opposed to this approach, either. Members of "the board wanted to scale as quickly as possible," says a former Juul Labs employee. "There was never any impetus to fix the youth problem. There was no one saying, 'We need to make the regulators happy.' There was always an emphasis on better growth, faster growth."

Then again, even if anyone had pushed back and tried to slow things down, they probably wouldn't have succeeded. Burns wasn't one to spare feelings, and he wasn't afraid to put people in their places. Nobody was above his reproach, even the founders of the company he now worked for.

If Adam and James had been in the back seat at Juul after their respective demotions from CEO, they were now clinging to the car's rear bumper. They were still in executive meetings, but "James and Adam weren't telling

[Burns] what to do," says a former Juul executive. If anything, it was the opposite. Burns's relationship with Adam didn't seem to be terribly adversarial, in large part because Adam didn't really have adversarial relationships with anyone; he kept to himself and rarely ruffled feathers. With stubborn, outspoken James, though, it was another story. "Kevin openly dismissed James in large meetings many times," a company insider remembers. It was his company now, and he seemed to want James to know it. "I heard stories that he was the first to bark at someone, or [that he] had a temper," says a former staffer. It was best, in short, to stay on his good side—and nobody wanted that more than Howard Willard at Altria.

A few months into Burns's tenure at Juul, Altria once again came calling. The cigarette giant was no longer interested in simply investing in Juul. It reportedly wanted to buy the company outright, to the tune of eight billion dollars. Altria was apparently so fixated on Juul's growth that it acquired from a Chinese company a pod-based e-cigarette that looked like a chunkier version of the Juul. In February 2018, it rebranded the product as the "MarkTen Elite." (By this time, the market was full of Juul look-alikes, so Altria was just joining the club.) Even with the MarkTen Elite on the market, Willard likely knew the company had almost zero chance of catching up to Juul in the long run. From 2016 to 2017, Juul's sales jumped by more than 600 percent. "The previously flat e-vapor category had begun to grow rapidly" from late 2017 into 2018, and "JUUL was responsible for much of that category growth," Altria CEO Howard Willard explained in documents later provided to Illinois senator Dick Durbin. Altria wanted in on that growth, and Willard was prepared to pay billions for it.

Juul's executives turned down the acquisition offer, uninterested in handing total control of the company over to Altria. But this didn't mean they were opposed to the idea of working with the Big Tobacco company; they just didn't want to sell outright.

Though some company sources deny it, a few employees of that era thought Juul Labs executives were playing a very expensive game of cat-and-mouse. "Kevin, the rest of the management team, and the board said, 'Look, what we could do is get an equity investment out of this that would get us richer,'" says a source with knowledge of the negotiations. An eight-billion-dollar offer would make the executive team rich, to be sure. But if Juul kept growing, maybe it could force Altria's price tag up higher and higher, ideally without selling the company outright. With plans for international expansion and domestic sales soaring, this didn't seem at all impossible. Burns turned down Altria's offer and focused on shifting Juul into hypergrowth mode. Says a source familiar with the company's inner workings, "Everything Kevin was doing in 2018"— the strategic hiring, the fluid relationship with FDA regulations, the push for international expansion—"was scaling up to get a bigger check from Altria."

Another former staffer says he got the distinct sense that Juul was adding employees in departments with fancy names—Scientific Affairs, Government Affairs, Medical Affairs, Public Affairs—to make the company seem more legitimate to potential buyers. This source worked in one such department, and he says he was rarely given the data or resources he needed to deliver on his job description. He was constantly learning things about the toxicology and efficacy of Juul's product from outside researchers at conferences when he really should have had access to that data, and more, in-house. It made him think he had been hired mostly for show. "Is this just a farce, to hire a scientific team, in order to sell this thing to a tobacco company?" he remembers wondering. "It didn't seem like . . . they really, truly cared about the science"—or, at least, not as much as they cared about making money.

A third company source disagrees, noting that Juul "was growing quickly, but it wasn't pushing for growth vis-à-vis a larger number from Altria."

Even if Juul's growth wasn't meant to seduce Altria, entertaining an eventual investment from Big Tobacco was an extraordinary move. Perhaps it shouldn't have been so surprising, given Adam and James's prior relationship with Japan Tobacco International and the history of Big Tobacco acquisitions within the e-cigarette industry. But to accept an investment as a young, financially struggling start-up was different from doing so as a thriving business at the top of its industry. Juul's executives knew that Altria promised resources and expertise that could really help the business explode. Its regulatory scientists could guide the FDA application process, and its relationships with retailers and existing smokers could help Juul's sales truly dominate the market. And, of course, Altria had the kind of money Juul, for all its success, could still only dream about. This fact was never far from executives' minds as they negotiated a deal, company sources say. Indeed, it was apparently important enough to consider forging a very strong link with the industry Juul was, theoretically, meant to replace. If Ploom had been created to give smokers a better version of the cigarette, it now appeared that Juul's purpose was to become a better version of Big Tobacco.

The disruptor had become the co-conspirator.

11

In January 2018, as Kevin Burns was settling into his new digs at Juul, Wesley Cedros, the senior director of student services at California's Tamalpais Union High School District, received an unusual proposal from educational consultant Bruce Harter.

Harter told Cedros that he was working with a company called Juul. It was prepared to offer the district twenty thousand dollars if San Andreas High School, a public school in Cedros's district, taught Juul's anti-teen-vaping curriculum during either "Saturday School" sessions for students facing disciplinary consequences or during regular class time. The proposal stipulated that a Juul consultant would be on hand to "observe program sessions without participating in them," and that the school would provide the consultant with progress assessment tests taken by the students at the end of the session.

Cedros was skeptical but intrigued. "Twenty thousand dollars, to a public school, is a lot," he says. "But as we looked over the proposal and looked into who was funding the proposal and looked at the sample curriculum, it was a pretty easy ethical decision to turn the money down." First and foremost, Cedros knew he couldn't accept the offer because his district receives funding from California's Tobacco-Use Prevention Education

Program, which explicitly forbids schools from taking money from tobacco companies. But Cedros also didn't feel that the curriculum was particularly rigorous compared to what the school was already using to teach students about substance abuse. Juul's curriculum covered the basics of addiction and discussed how nicotine dependence can affect the still-developing teenage brain, and it came with a discussion guide meant to get kids talking about topics such as peer pressure, parental influence, and substance abuse. Still, Cedros was confident his health teachers could come up with something better.

Something else also struck Cedros as odd: Juul's curriculum seemed awfully similar to an antivaping tool kit created and widely circulated by researchers at the Stanford University School of Medicine. "It seemed like a pretty blatant rip-off of the work done at Stanford," Cedros says. "Right there was a red flag." The whole thing felt a little odd, so Cedros turned down Harter's offer and called the California Department of Education to let them know what he had received. It turned out the department already knew what Juul was up to. About a week later, the department sent out a letter to schools across the state, urging them to reject any outreach from Juul Labs.

By this point, Bonnie Halpern-Felsher, the Stanford developmental psychologist who'd created the university's antivaping tool kit, had heard rumors that Juul was circulating its own antivaping curriculum. "I said, 'Huh, that's a little bit scary. No tobacco company should be creating its own prevention curriculum,'" she says. The rumor motivated Halpern-Felsher to update her tool kit so it would directly address Juul, by far the most popular e-cigarette among teenagers, rather than focusing on e-cigarettes as a uniform category.

That work was well under way when Halpern-Felsher got an email from a colleague who had attended an academic lecture about vaping in early 2018. The presenter had mentioned Juul and had specifically said the company was working with Stanford on a prevention curriculum. This got Halpern-Felsher's attention. Under no circumstances did she want people thinking she had worked with an e-cigarette company. She started trying to find a copy of Juul's curriculum to review it herself, and not long after, Stanford issued Juul a cease-and-desist letter, directing it to stop mentioning Stanford in its curriculum. Juul denied doing so and said it would not in the future, Halpern-Felsher says.

Her concerns about being linked to Juul's curriculum were well-founded. The idea of tobacco companies leading anti-tobacco education had a sordid history. In the late 1990s, the tobacco company Philip Morris set out to offer similar antismoking programs through youth-focused groups like the 4-H Club, the Boys and Girls Clubs, and the YMCA. In 1998, Philip Morris executives even offered 4-H a $4.3 million grant in exchange for the privilege of developing an antismoking curriculum for the organization. A couple of years later, the company started distributing special book covers in elementary, middle, and high schools around the United States, each one emblazoned with the slogan "Think. Don't Smoke," accompanied by the Philip Morris logo.

The campaign was pitched as a way to dissuade kids from smoking, but critics argued that Philip Morris was effectively advertising directly to schoolchildren in their classrooms. A study later concluded that kids who had seen materials from the "Think. Don't Smoke" campaign, including television commercials, actually looked more favorably upon the tobacco industry than those who hadn't. Cheryl Healton, who is now the dean of New York University's School of Global Public Health and was the president and CEO of the antismoking American Legacy Foundation (renamed Truth Initiative in 2015), didn't mince words in a 2002 study on the program's effectiveness. The discovery that the ads made kids friendlier toward tobacco, she and her coauthors wrote, "lends support to the assertion of tobacco control activists that the purpose of the Philip Morris campaign is to buy respectability and not to prevent youth smoking." Philip Morris scrapped its controversial program in 2002, the same year Healton's study came out.

Juul Labs executives may not have known about this program when they hired Bruce Harter at the end of 2017, but its chief administrative officer, Ashley Gould, certainly knew about it by the spring of 2018.

By that time, Juul had hired a dedicated youth prevention coordinator, a woman named Julie Henderson, and Gould was seeking advice from public health experts including Cheryl Healton, a respected researcher who saw potential in e-cigarettes.

Healton agreed to take Gould's call, but as soon as she mentioned Juul representatives visiting schools, Healton was horrified. "I remember saying, 'What are you, Philip Morris?'" Healton says. "I said, 'You're kind of following the playbook of a major tobacco company that just got into a lot of trouble for this.'"

But Healton's shock wasn't enough to stop Juul from exploring the idea of a school outreach program. "Every corporation that wants to be a good guy wants to run their own good-guy program," Healton says. The businesses always think they're showing off "corporate responsibility" when often they're doing the opposite. "To take the mantle of harm reduction into schools with their own staff," Healton says, "was suicidal." Regardless of whether Juul was purposely targeting students, it was absolutely going to come off that way. That much was obvious to Healton.

Some educators weren't as concerned. Dennis Runyan, the superintendent at Arizona's Agua Fria Union High School District, knew Bruce Harter from work they'd done together years earlier in Florida. In the spring of 2018, Harter pitched Runyan on Juul's grant program, and Runyan invited his old colleague out to meet with district leadership. Vaping "was just emerging as an issue in our schools," Runyan says, and he and his colleagues were looking for funding to teach students about abuse of opioids and other substances. Juul was prepared to offer "open-ended, no-strings-attached" grants of ten thousand dollars for each school in the district, which seemed like the perfect solution. Runyan used the first ten-thousand-dollar grant to pay a local health teacher to develop, with guidance from Harter, a summer program for roughly three hundred rising freshmen. Runyan says the curriculum turned out well. He had no hesitation about offering it to students and says he'd probably do it again.

Around the same time, Juul's youth prevention team got a call from a mental health services provider that worked with the Dwight School, an exclusive private school on Manhattan's Upper West Side. Vaping was becoming an increasingly big problem for Dwight, in a way cigarette smoking hadn't been for a long time. Dwight was exactly the kind of school where vaping was everywhere. Most of its students had plenty of disposable income, and the school was located in a big city, where it was pretty easy for underage students to buy substances. The administration was looking for a speaker who could educate Dwight students about nicotine addiction and the health risks of vaping. Someone from the mental health services provider happened to know someone who worked at Juul, and they arranged for a representative to speak at Dwight as part of the school's mental health and addiction seminar series.

Caleb Mintz was a Dwight ninth grader at the time. On the day of the presentation, he settled into his desk, ready to be bored for the next hour. He already knew about and had tried juuling, as had just about everyone else he went to school with; many of them already owned Juuls or borrowed them off friends. His friend and classmate Phillip Fuhrman, sitting just a few desks away, was addicted to Juul. It seemed highly unlikely that Caleb and his friends were going to learn anything from this presentation that they hadn't already learned by watching their classmates vape in the school bathroom.

As Caleb listened, the man sent by Juul Labs launched into a spiel about the risks of youth nicotine addiction and why teenagers shouldn't vape. It was pretty standard stuff—except, Caleb says, that the representative kept sprinkling in references to how safe Juul was and how it was going to get FDA approval any day now. Something felt off to Caleb. He and Phillip approached the speaker afterward, and Caleb asked him what to do for a friend who was addicted to nicotine. The speaker, not realizing that Caleb wasn't referring to cigarettes but, rather, to Phillip's juuling addiction, whipped out his Juul and showed the boys how it worked—again emphasizing just how safe it was. Again, the whole thing didn't sit right with Caleb. "I really felt like there was an ulterior motive [to the presentation] besides just curbing teen vaping," Caleb says. "I knew that if I told my mom, she'd create a whole scene out of it."

Caleb knew his mother well. Meredith Berkman, a mainstay of the New York City philanthropy scene, was the daughter-in-law of a *Washington Post* reporter who'd covered Big Tobacco for years. She couldn't believe what she was hearing from her son, and she called the school, demanding to know what was going on. The first person she spoke with brushed her off, saying Caleb must have misunderstood what the speaker meant. Undeterred, Berkman called the headmaster and told him everything. "He was apoplectic," she says. He'd had no idea the presentation had even happened.

Equally apoplectic, Berkman called Caleb's friend Phillip's mother, Dorian Fuhrman, and filled her in on everything. Fuhrman was horrified. She already knew about Juul—she'd done her research after she found one of the devices in Phillip's pants pocket—but she couldn't believe her son's school was actually working with the company. "We said, 'We can't let [Juul] get away with this,'" Fuhrman remembers. They filled in one other friend, and together the three women began researching Juul and other e-cigarette companies, vowing to do whatever they could to get Juul out of schools and prevent more kids from becoming addicted. They started laying the groundwork for an advocacy group they would eventually call "Parents Against Vaping E-cigarettes," or PAVE. They began hosting educational forums for other parents in New York City and registered their group as a lobbying organization. None of them had experience in politics per se, but they knew people would listen when they spoke, and they wanted every parent in the country to know Juul's name. "If we weren't talking about it," Fuhrman says, "no one else was."

While the mothers of PAVE were doing their research, Julie Henderson and Ashley Gould were starting to have second thoughts about the whole school outreach experiment. They had stayed in touch with Cheryl Healton from NYU, who remained steadfastly opposed to Juul Labs's having any kind of contact with kids in school. It finally seemed to be sinking in for Henderson and Gould that this program, malicious or not, had some very bad optics.

That spring, Juul's education team had flown out to Illinois to meet with Bill Walsh, the principal at Hinsdale Central High School. Walsh had heard about Juul's grant program from colleagues in the education world, and he wanted to see its curriculum for himself. When he read it, he wasn't impressed. The curriculum seemed fairly basic, better suited to an elementary or middle school audience than his high school students. Instead of using it, Walsh negotiated a deal: Juul would fund Hinsdale through its grant program, but the school would use that money to pay its own health teachers to write a stronger antivaping curriculum. If Juul wanted to distribute its own materials, its representatives could come to the school's health fair later that spring. "I fully support the way we went about it," Walsh says.

Henderson wasn't so sure. In mid-April 2018, about a week before the health fair at Hinsdale Central High School, she drafted a tense email to education consultants Bruce Harter and Wendell Greer. "Just spoke w/ Ashley & she shares my concern about the optics of us attending a student health fair given our new understanding of how much our efforts seem to duplicate those of big tobacco," she wrote, adding that Philip Morris had done the same thing "under the guise of 'youth prevention.'" She suggested that, instead of sending Juul reps to the school, they send some flyers and ask school administrators to hand them out. Harter wrote back the next morning: "While I don't disagree about the comparison of big tobacco, I'd be very concerned about withdrawing a week before the fair," he wrote. "Hinsdale Central invited us. . . . I also think we lose credibility by revoking a commitment."

Harter's reply seemed to clear Henderson's conscience. "Thanks, Bruce, for this candid and affirming response," she wrote back. "Thanks, too, for verifying that Hinsdale Central invited us. I'll be sure to stress that point as I confirm participation w/ Ashley & Kevin."

As the spring went on, Juul kept doling out grants. One went to Larry Lewis, the director of California's Richmond Police Activities League. RPAL ran a program that dismissed minors' criminal charges if they completed a ten-week training course on making better life choices. Lewis wanted to include information on vaping prevention in the program, but he couldn't get anybody to fund it—until he found Juul's grant program. The company gave RPAL $89,000 to develop and teach its "life skills" curriculum, which included a unit on the risks of abusing substances, including nicotine. That kind of money, absolutely vital for Lewis, was a drop in the bucket to Juul, which had just launched a $1.2 billion fundraising campaign and had money to spare. Lewis says he has no regrets about the partnership. "When you're trying to save low-income kids, especially Black and brown kids, not a lot of people want to fund those programs," Lewis says. "If they're willing to save lives, we are willing to work with them."

As the education program moved forward, Henderson and Gould seemed to seesaw between enthusiasm and worry. They kept going back to Healton at NYU, who kept offering additional proof that the whole thing was a bad idea. A couple of weeks after Juul offered its grant to RPAL, Healton sent Gould what she calls "iron-clad proof that they should not be doing this": a copy of a paper she'd coauthored on Philip Morris's school program, detailing all the ways it perniciously encouraged teen tobacco use. "Here is the paper that ended the Think. Don't Smoke campaign undertaken by Philip Morris," Healton wrote in an email, which Gould then forwarded to several other members of the Juul team.

Not long after, Henderson drafted an email to Greer and Harter detailing the numerous similarities between Juul's program and Philip Morris's. She attached several articles, including Healton's study, that she said "help explain current executive concerns & discussion re: discontinuing our work w/ schools." Executives finally seemed to be serious about ending the program—but not before Harter circulated one last contract. In June, he proposed to offer Baltimore's Freedom and Democracy schools $134,000 to create a summer school program for children as young as eight.

The next month, Juul's leadership finally decided to listen to Healton and end its education program. Runyan, the superintendent from Arizona, stopped hearing from Juul that summer, even though the company had agreed to give ten-thousand-dollar grants to several other schools in his district. "The communication just dwindled and stopped," he says. "We did one or two inquiries about the grant, and there was just no more communication after that."

By the summer, Stanford's Bonnie Halpern-Felsher had finally gotten the full copy of Juul's curriculum. She hired a summer intern to go through the presentation slide by slide, looking for places where Juul had stolen her work. "We found an entire set of slides that were literally lifted and taken verbatim from our tool kit into their curriculum," Halpern-Felsher says. "Not only did they do that, [but] we [had] by accident left a couple [of comments] to each other in the curriculum we put online. They left those in there." It couldn't have been clearer to Halpern-Felsher that Juul had stolen her presentation. In a BuzzFeed.News story about the curriculum, a Juul representative declined to comment on that allegation, but said the company halted its education initiative "in response to feedback from those who thought our efforts to dissuade youth from using nicotine were being misunderstood."

Halpern-Felsher was also beginning to see why many schools didn't find the curriculum terribly rigorous. According to a commentary she published in the *Journal of Adolescent Health* in 2018, Juul's presentation never mentioned the role that tobacco industry marketing had played in getting young people hooked; nor did it teach any media literacy skills that could help students realize when they were being targeted by social media posts or advertisements. And while the curriculum mentioned the risks of nicotine addiction and its impact on the developing brain, "they never then link nicotine and the brain to Juul. They never mention the word 'Juul' in the curriculum, period," Halpern-Felsher says. "They don't put the pieces together. If your entire curriculum is on 'e-cigarettes,' [kids are] not going to think it [applies to] 'Juul.'" Multiple studies have shown that even kids who admit to vaping don't always know the specifics of their chosen brand or its nicotine content. By purposely leaving its own name out of the presentation, Halpern-Felsher thought, Juul seemed to be attempting to imply that other forms of e-cigarettes were risky to use but that the Juul was not. (A company source says Juul did not include its name in the curriculum for fear of coming off as promotional.) "One would hope [the curriculum] was [made] for good," Halpern-Felsher says. "But I'll be honest: That's really hard to believe."

With school outreach out of the picture, Juul shifted its youth prevention efforts to other areas. The marketing team decided to stop using models in its own social media posts and instead began featuring bland testimonials from adult smokers who had used Juul to switch from smoking to vaping. The company was also working on lower-strength, 3 percent–nicotine versions of its tobacco and menthol products and on new Juul product packaging that would feature a huge (FDA-required) warning about the addictive nicotine inside. Biggest of all, Juul had committed thirty million dollars to a youth prevention plan that involved developing better age-verification systems online and in retail stores, stepping up secret shopper programs meant to catch stores that sold to minors, and patrolling social media and resale sites that posted youth-friendly content. These all seemed like safer plans than sending Juul reps into schools, which invited inevitable comparisons to Big Tobacco.

Around the same time as all the back-and-forth over school visits, Gould, during a business trip to New York City, asked Healton and several of her colleagues to have dinner. She arranged a reservation, telling Healton she hoped to talk in more depth about how Juul Labs could improve its youth prevention and public health programming. But when Healton and her colleagues arrived at the restaurant, they found no trace of their guest from Juul. Minute after minute ticked by, and still Gould didn't show. Finally, she hurried into the restaurant almost an hour late, apologizing before she'd even sat down at the table. "I'm so sorry," she blurted out. "I got tied up in a meeting at the Plaza."

Healton felt her stomach drop. Philip Morris was famous for conducting its business at the Plaza. The hotel wasn't far from the tobacco company's New York City offices on ritzy Park Avenue. In the 1950s, Philip Morris executives famously used a suite at the Plaza to meet with other tobacco magnates to cook up a plan to downplay the health risks of smoking. More than sixty years later, Healton feared that Altria, Philip Morris's parent company, was using the Plaza as a place to bait Juul into a partnership.

"The minute I heard that," Healton remembers, "I thought, 'They're being bought out by Philip Morris.'"

12

"My 20 year old son is incredibly addicted to Juul and wants to quit," Katherine Snedaker wrote on May 3, 2018. "He is using three pods a day. Do you have any research or advice [on] how to quit?"

She hit send, hoping the email would finally bring her family some relief. Her son had started juuling during his freshman year of college, and it was now abundantly clear that he had a problem. He was so addicted that he once punched a hole in the wall of the Snedakers' Connecticut home when he couldn't find his Juul. He was coughing all the time. And neither he nor his doctor had any idea how to help him stop. Out of options, Snedaker decided to go to the source: Juul.

"Okay, here's your product," she remembers thinking. "What's the exit plan?"

When she finally got a response from a company lawyer three days later, it sank in that Juul didn't have the answers, either. The lawyer sent over a few generic resources about e-cigarettes and nicotine addiction and punted Snedaker's question back to her son's doctor, noting that the company couldn't make health recommendations and had no knowledge of her son's unique situation. To Snedaker, it suggested, no one, not even the people who made Juul, knew how to get someone off the device.

Snedaker had tried so hard to raise kids who would never smoke cigarettes. She thought she knew the warning signs to look for. But here she was, stuck. "As consumers, we were pretty stupid, considering we had grown up with Joe the Camel," Snedaker says. "Yet, in the end, I'm sitting there on an airplane watching my son smoke Juul."

FDA commissioner Scott Gottlieb may not have known Katherine Snedaker personally, but he was deeply concerned with stories like hers. "By 2018, people had brought to our attention the appeal of Juul to kids," remembers a former agency official. "It was always 'juuling'; it wasn't e-cigarettes," the official said of the verb that had by now entered the lexicon. "It became like 'Kleenex.'" Juul was a brand, and a problem, all its own.

The commissioner hadn't seen this coming the previous summer, when he announced his bold plan to revamp tobacco regulation. He and Mitch Zeller had honestly seen potential in e-cigarettes. They seemed like a valuable option for adult smokers. But this one company, and its takeoff among youth, was complicating Gottlieb's efforts around harm reduction.

Gottlieb could see, based on the 2017 National Youth Tobacco Survey, that more than two million U.S. middle and high school students were using e-cigarettes. There was plenty of anecdotal evidence to suggest that many of these teen vapers were juuling. Every day seemed to bring a troubling new headline, like one the *Washington Post* ran in the spring of 2018: "The Juul's So Cool, Kids Smoke It in School." There were scores of news articles describing this phenomenon, recounting kids disguising their habit through stunts like blowing vapor "into their backpacks . . . or into their sweater when the teacher isn't looking," as one California high school sophomore told NBC News in March 2018. (Juul Labs repeatedly denied allegations that it purposely hooked kids, offering variations on the same statement: "We have never marketed to youth, period. . . . We have no higher priority than to prevent youth usage of our products.")

Kids were definitely using other e-cigarettes, but none had risen to the level of a cultural phenomenon quite like Juul had. As the vaping industry's biggest name, and the apparent favorite among underage users, Juul was about to pay the price for its skyrocketing growth.

In April 2018, a few weeks before Snedaker begged Juul for help, Gottlieb's agency began a "blitz" targeted directly at Juul. Agency investigators went undercover into stores and resale websites to root out which ones were selling Juul products to underage kids. Gottlieb's Center for Tobacco Products also wrote to Juul's vice president of regulatory and clinical affairs and demanded that he turn over a slew of internal documents related to Juul's marketing practices, product design, health research, and consumer complaints. In those papers, Gottlieb hoped to find some explanation for the youth juuling explosion.

Juul complied and handed over tens of thousands of documents, but it omitted some information. The team did not disclose that company engineers had been quietly tweaking the Juul device over the years, taking it from the original "Splinter" model—with its leaky pods and sensitive sensor—to the newer, better "Jagwar" device. These changes could have been interpreted as a violation of the FDA's deeming rule, which specified that companies had to file PMTAs anytime they introduced a new or modified product. But Juul executives "didn't give a shit about regulatory engagement," says a company source. That characterization may have been a bit strong—Juul representatives maintain that the company follows and respects FDA requirements, including those related to the PMTA process— but former employees say deference to federal regulators did not always seem like the guiding principle within the company. Top executives often seemed more interested in growth and profit than playing it safe and adhering to the FDA's byzantine regulations, and a better-functioning product was crucial to facilitating that growth.

Still, the FDA's document request was a vivid reminder that Juul had more critics than friends. Journalists were constantly writing about kids juuling in school and pointing to the Vaporized ad campaign as evidence that Juul had hooked them on purpose. Anti-tobacco advocacy groups such as the Campaign for Tobacco-Free Kids were raising hell about vaping, calling for dramatic measures like bans on all flavored products. A group of Democratic senators had written to Juul in April 2018 demanding that Kevin Burns explain why so many kids seemed to be hooked on its product. "Your company's product purports to help people quit smoking cigarettes, yet we are concerned that JUUL—with its kid-appealing design and flavorings—will only lead to further nicotine addiction and adverse health consequences," they wrote. Angry emails like Katherine Snedaker's showed that parents weren't happy, as did the fact that a group of Juul users, some of them underage, had recently sued the company for allegedly downplaying the product's nicotine content and getting them addicted—claims that Juul denied and said it planned to defend itself against in court.

Building some political influence looked like one way Juul could protect itself. And while that strategy certainly wasn't new—Capitol Hill is crawling with lobbyists and special interest groups associated with just about every industry under the sun—Juul's lobbying campaign was about to turn some heads. By the end of 2018, Juul would spend $1.6 million on lobbying, compared to just $120,000 the year prior.

By April 2018, when the FDA demanded Juul's documents, Burns had already hired Tevi Troy and Jim Esquea, both of whom had previously been high-ranking officials in the Department of Health and Human Services. Their jobs were to direct public policy and federal affairs from Juul's brand-new Washington, DC, offices, while a network of people beneath them handled lobbying in different regions of the country. Those people then hired contract lobbyists on the ground in their particular regions—people who knew the ins and outs of the local political scene and which lawmakers might be receptive to working with an e-cigarette company like Juul as it tried to build influence on Capitol Hill.

Broadly speaking, this list tended to include Republicans, who are historically friendlier toward the tobacco industry than Democrats. Tobacco had long been a pillar of the economy in some ruby-red states like Kentucky and North Carolina, which makes some representatives from those areas more inclined to protect it. Juul wasn't a tobacco company in the strictest sense of the word, but it at least got a warmer welcome from lawmakers used to working with Big Tobacco. Plus, in conversations with conservatives, its lobbyists could fall back on arguments about free choice and government overregulation of vice products.

With Democrats, who were on the whole anti-tobacco and pro-regulation, the conversation tended to be a harder sell. Democrats, like anti-tobacco crusader Dick Durbin, were also more likely to work closely with advocacy groups like the Campaign for Tobacco-Free Kids, the American Lung Association, and the American Cancer Society, who were worthy opponents for Juul on Capitol Hill. In 2018, CTFK spent $680,000 on lobbying, mostly to push for stricter regulations on tobacco and nicotine products. The American Lung Association spent $500,000 to lobby for a number of issues, including bans on kid-friendly e-cigarette flavors. The American Cancer Society spent a whopping $4.3 million, though only a small portion of this went toward pushing for stricter regulations on e-cigarettes and flavored e-liquids.

One former Juul lobbyist remembers telling Burns that Juul Labs would be smart to push for certain regulations, too. E-cigarettes had been available for purchase in the United States for more than a decade, and the FDA had made only cursory steps toward regulating them. Without oversight or government review, "the industry was viewed as illegitimate," the lobbyist says. If Juul proactively embraced regulation, the lobbyist thought it could help change that perception. He wanted rules that would require e-cigarette makers to disclose their e-liquid ingredients, clear sales and marketing guidelines for vaping companies, a better licensing structure for tobacco retailers, and penalties for retailers that sold to minors. But Burns didn't seem all that interested in these suggestions. He was fixated on one policy above all others: "Tobacco 21" laws, which would raise the minimum legal age for tobacco purchasing from eighteen to twenty-one.

Tobacco 21 laws work not only by barring teenagers from buying tobacco themselves, but also by preventing eighteen-year-old high schoolers from passing cigarettes down to younger friends or siblings. Back in 2005, Needham, Massachusetts, had become the first U.S. town to implement a Tobacco 21 policy, and its underage smoking rate subsequently plummeted by nearly 50 percent. In the years following, a number of cities and states, including California, had adopted similar legislation. Burns thought it was a no-brainer for Juul Labs to support these policies and push for their expansion. The company would lose money by shutting out the eighteen-to-twenty-one age group, but it seemed a small price to pay in the long run.

All anybody could seem to talk about was Juul's youth use problem, and the data clearly showed that Tobacco 21 laws could help keep young people away from tobacco products. If fewer teenagers could buy and use Juul pods, that was a plus on its own. And as an added bonus, if public conversation and media coverage shifted away from the youth vaping epidemic, Juul Labs could finally step out of the hot seat and focus on selling more vaporizers, making more money, and maybe even moving toward an initial public offering (IPO).

One of Juul's former lobbyists says Burns became obsessed with the idea that Tobacco 21 laws were going to put an end to the youth vaping epidemic and save Juul's reputation. He "latched onto this idea of raising the purchase age to twenty-one and said we should just be going all in," the lobbyist remembers. To the lobbyist, Tobacco 21 seemed like one piece of a larger regulatory framework that Juul should have been supporting—but try explaining that to Kevin Burns. "He has a lot of opinions about what we should and should not be doing, and can be quite forceful about that," the lobbyist says. If Burns thought Tobacco 21 should be Juul's priority, then so it was.

On the surface, Juul should have had allies in health groups like the American Cancer Society and the American Lung Association, which had long supported Tobacco 21 policies. But these groups, vocal critics of the tobacco industry, were less than eager to join forces with an e-cigarette company. Many public-health groups—not to mention the wealthy benefactors who funded them, like Michael Bloomberg—were coming out increasingly strongly against e-cigarettes, fueled by concern about the youth vaping problem. "The priority of Bloomberg Philanthropies is to protect kids," says Dr. Kelly Henning, who leads the organization's public health program. "Whether or not there's a role for these products for older adults who are highly addicted . . . that's not the focus of our campaigns."

Many groups felt that way, which meant Juul, even if it could potentially benefit adult smokers and push for policies like Tobacco 21, was not high on their list of preferred allies. "The Juul experience was the first time I have ever experienced a situation where an opposing lobbyist would not have anything to do with me. Even when Juul adopted their Tobacco 21 initiative, they would not have any conversation about it," says a former Juul lobbyist. "I have been called a number of things," the lobbyist says, "including 'the devil.'" The message was clear: Juul could support Tobacco 21 all it wanted, but it wasn't going to get a hand from lobbyists representing public health groups.

Juul did have at least one powerful ally: Iowa attorney general Tom Miller, a Democrat and the country's longest-serving current attorney general. Miller had been one of the attorneys general who orchestrated the Tobacco Master Settlement Agreement back in the 1990s. He saw great promise in e-cigarettes and their ability to save lives that would otherwise be lost to smoking, but he also feared that youth use was a big enough liability to sink e-cigarette companies forever. "I didn't want kids to use e-cigarettes, and I didn't want kids' use to bring about restrictions on e-cigarettes that would diminish their use among adults who are smokers," Miller says. In the spring of 2018, he decided to give Juul a call to offer his decades of institutional knowledge about tobacco and smoking cessation. After his first call with Ashley Gould in April 2018, Miller quickly became a trusted adviser for the company—to an unusual extent for a sitting attorney general. Emails released through public records requests showed Miller's office regularly corresponding with Gould and her staff at Juul. "There have been 870 articles [about Juul] since we started tracking in mid-January," Gould wrote to Miller's office in one April 2018 email, while coordinating a meeting with the AG. "Most of them the same negative story."

Miller says he was never compensated by Juul and never provided any substantial advice on press or regulatory matters. His primary role, he says, was to set up an advisory council that could help Juul Labs with its youth use problem.

Miller recruited several former attorneys general to join the group, including Georgia's Thurbert Baker, Tennessee's Mike Cody, Illinois's Neil Hartigan, and Arizona's Grant Woods. He also reached out to a few people from the public health world, including Clive Bates, the former director of the United Kingdom's Action on Smoking and Health, and Dr. Margaret Stager, an adolescent medicine specialist from Ohio. NYU's David Abrams acted as an informal adviser, sometimes weighing in by email. It was an impressive collection of experts, but one of the group's meetings did not go exactly as Miller or Juul Labs probably planned.

During a conference call in the summer of 2018, Burns told the assembled group about Juul's mission to give adult smokers an alternative to cigarettes and its deep commitment to dissuading teenagers from vaping. When he was finished, Miller turned the mic over to the advisory group, asking if anybody had questions or suggestions.

Grant Woods, the former attorney general of Arizona who had worked with Miller on the Tobacco Master Settlement Agreement in the 1990s, had some thoughts. "Unless you get rid of all of the flavored e-cigarettes," Woods told Burns, "I think attorneys general around the country are going to come after you for marketing to children." Burns pushed back, Woods remembers, pointing to research that says adults like to use flavored products when they switch from cigarettes to vaping.

Woods remained unconvinced. "Here's the thing," he responded. "You're lucky I'm not attorney general right now, because I would sue you. After this phone call, I would sue you, because you're marketing to children. If you want to avoid people like me, I'm telling you what you need to do: you need to stop it."

This was not advice Burns was likely to follow. Aside from the fact that many adults like to use flavored vaping products, flavored pods were the company's moneymaker, accounting for about 80 percent of all Juul pods sold. Mango pods, which were first introduced in 2017, brought in millions of dollars each year, as roughly a third of all pods sold were Mango.

Woods could tell that Burns wasn't going to take his advice and probably wouldn't want to take any other advice that could hurt his sales, so after that call, Woods dropped out of Miller's advisory group. The rest of the group kept meeting throughout the summer, recommending that Juul adopt youth prevention practices such as stricter online age-verification policies and penalties for retailers who were caught selling to minors. They also floated the idea of endowing an independent philanthropic foundation that could educate kids and their parents on vaping. At least some members wanted Juul to stop selling its fruity flavors, thinking they appealed to kids, but the group couldn't reach consensus.

The advisory group didn't bring about any major changes to Juul's business, but one of its suggestions dovetailed nicely with something Juul's scientists were already considering. Members of the advisory committee suggested that Juul Labs commission independent research on youth use of its products, and this seemed like a great idea. In April 2018, the same month the FDA asked for documents, Juul paid outside research firms to poll teenagers about their favorite Juul flavors in an effort to better understand underage use (the results turned out to be Mint and Mango), according to documents related to the multidistrict litigation against Juul, but it hadn't at that point done anything close to a nationally representative study on youth vaping. Having that data could help Juul understand exactly how many teenagers were using its products and others, and, perhaps, how to stop them from doing so. Plus, Burns and his team had a hunch that the data wouldn't match the agency's narrative about a ubiquitous teen vaping problem. Nobody was denying that teenagers were juuling, but to Burns's team, the FDA's rhetoric about a youth vaping crisis seemed to be getting increasingly dramatic—and increasingly aggressive toward Juul, specifically.

Some kids, like Katherine Snedaker's son, absolutely were addicted to vaping, and this was cause for concern. But Juul's internal researchers thought the numbers pushed out by the FDA and the Centers for Disease Control and Prevention might be overblown. Just because kids vaped once, or even once a month, it didn't mean they were addicts; nor did it mean they hadn't been smoking cigarettes previously—and if most kids who juuled were former or current cigarette smokers, there was an argument to be made that e-cigarettes had actually *improved* their health. They also took issue with the idea that Juul, the de facto face of the industry, was the only brand teenagers were using.

"It wasn't just a Juul problem, and we had a feeling that a number of other bad actors out there, making compatible pods, were a big part of this issue," says a company source. Just as the advisory committee suggested, Juul's researchers decided to commission a youth study to find out for sure.

The advisory committee also seemed to give Burns another idea. As 2018 pressed on, Juul's government affairs team requested meetings with other attorneys general across the country, perhaps trying to engender the same support the company had won from Tom Miller in Iowa. Juul Labs also donated fifty thousand dollars to both the Republican and Democratic fundraising campaigns for attorneys general. "They were really working the crowd," says Woods, the former Arizona attorney general. "They tried to persuade everyone that they were a good player and they were doing the right thing. They wanted the attorneys general to support them."

Some attorneys general refused to meet with the company at all, but plenty did. Among those who took meetings, the outcomes were hit or miss, says a lobbyist who sat in. Burns would give his spiel about Juul's ability to give smokers a better option and try to develop a rapport, sometimes successfully and sometimes not, with the attorney general and whoever on his or her staff handled tobacco issues. The outcome usually broke down along party lines. Democrats tended to be more combative than Republicans, and more likely to think Juul was intentionally hooking kids. Burns fielded their comments and did his best to assure them that Juul was interested only in selling to adults.

"There was no real ask of the AG," says the lobbyist. It was more: "If there's any talk of regulation, let's have a conversation about it. We would rather have a seat at the table than be on the table." But Burns was a bright guy. He probably knew—and had in fact recently been warned by Grant Woods from Arizona—that lawsuits against Juul were likely coming down the pike just as they had for cigarette companies, and that state attorneys general would likely be the ones doing the suing. Building relationships with attorneys general of both parties early, before any documents were subpoenaed or depositions taken, seemed like a smart play.

While Juul was learning to play the game in Washington, Scott Gottlieb was holed up in the FDA's headquarters in Silver Spring, Maryland, continuing to study Juul. In May 2018, while Juul was going on its political influence tour around the country, he'd gotten an interesting tip from a few of his investigators. They'd inspected a facility operated by one of the contractors Juul paid to fill its pods with e-liquid. There, they'd noticed some changes to the Juul pods. It seemed awfully convenient that Juul's executives hadn't thought to mention this change in the fifty thousand pages of documents they'd handed over to the FDA earlier that spring. If they thought they'd heard the last of Scott Gottlieb, they were in for a rude awakening.

13

GROWING PAINS (JULY–AUGUST 2018)

Less than a year into Kevin Burns's tenure as CEO, Juul made history: on the heels of a $650 million influx of venture capital funding, analysts valued the company at $15 billion. This made it the youngest company ever to surpass "decacorn" valuation—the nickname for companies whose valuation had reached $10 billion (as compared with the $1 billion–valued "unicorns"). Juul reached that benchmark faster than Facebook, Snapchat, or Twitter had.

The company was a juggernaut. Despite, or perhaps because of, all the talk of youth vaping, by the summer of 2018, Juul Labs was widely reported to control almost 70 percent of the U.S. e-cigarette market and, perhaps more impressively, to account for nearly all the e-cigarette category's growth. Its "competitors" were really just fighting for second place, and even the traditional cigarette industry had reason to worry. A June 2018 Morgan Stanley report called Juul's growth a "headwind" to the traditional tobacco industry, noting that cigarette sale volumes in the United States had decreased by 5.5 percent in the first quarter of 2018, coinciding with Juul's growth. "We believe JUUL is different [from other e-cigarettes] because of its enhanced technology[,] which is based on a nicotine salt that more closely mimics the nicotine delivery of smoking a cigarette," the Morgan Stanley report read. "Moreover, no other e-cig has been able to capture such a meaningful share of the overall cigarette category."

Though Juul's success seemed only to breed more scrutiny from regulators and the media, at least financially, it was a good time to be Juul Labs. The company was on track to earn $1.3 billion in revenue in 2018, with more money pouring in each financial quarter. Fifty new employees were starting each week, enough that the company had outgrown its Mission District headquarters and moved to a new, larger space on the waterfront in San Francisco's industrial but up-and-coming Dogpatch neighborhood.

Juul Labs now occupied a historic redbrick building on city-owned Pier 70, in a complex that had previously served as the headquarters for Union Iron Works and Bethlehem Steel. Many people on Juul's staff couldn't quite remember what the building had been—a school? maybe a factory?—but it was undeniably beautiful, with soaring, wood-beamed ceilings and big windows with green trim. (Lovely as it looked, the afternoon sun turned the building's un-air-conditioned upper levels into a sauna on warm days.) On the building's top floor, Burns had commissioned a full replica of a convenience store, with fake display racks showing off not only Juul's products, but also the cigarettes Juul was trying to displace and the counterfeit and Juul-compatible products other brands made to try to steal Juul's market share. The company used this space as a teaching and meeting area, where employees could see everything they were up against and brainstorm new ways to sell Juul products.

The headquarters had some other unique features. The building's original safe was still intact, though it now held nothing more glamorous than cleaning products and toilet paper. There was a deck where employees could step out for fresh air or a vape break. (Many simply vaped at their desks, the scent of Mango vapor drifting through the air.) And employees could brainstorm in the 2018 version of a 1970s-style conversation pit: a hodgepodge of pillows and mats stacked in a pyramid beneath a neon sign reading, "Goodbye Smoke Breaks. Hello Juul." In the cafeteria, where a free lunch spread was set out every afternoon for the company's roughly five hundred employees, staffers could look into a glass curiosity case displaying the Ploom and Pax prototypes Adam and James had built by hand. Framed posters in the hallway spelled out the company's guiding principles: "Mission First. Think Big. Deliver Quality. Debate & Commit. Go. Own It. Give Back."

That summer, in addition to the new San Francisco headquarters, Juul opened its first international office in London, only months after rolling out its product in Israel, its first overseas market. The company's executive team had high hopes for the United Kingdom—they expected to make up to $180 million there during Juul's first year in that market. It was logical to think Juul would succeed in the United Kingdom, given that the country was culturally similar to the United States but far friendlier toward e-cigarettes. While many experts and public health groups in the United States vocally opposed vaping, Public Health England explicitly recommended it as a 95 percent safer alternative to smoking. British addiction scientist Michael Russell's old truism that people smoke for the nicotine but die from the tar is "deeply hardwired into the U.K. expert community," says Clive Bates, the man who previously ran the country's Action on Smoking and Health. "Once they started to follow that insight truthfully, that, I think, led them to the place they are now"—a place where tobacco harm reduction is seen not just as an option, but as one of the best ways to get smokers to quit.

There was one obvious problem for Juul, though. In the United Kingdom, as in many European countries, e-liquids can contain, by law, no more than 20 milligrams per millileter of nicotine, which means a formula can be up to about 1.7 percent nicotine by weight. This nicotine cap proved a stumbling block for Juul, a brand built upon the success of potent, 5 percent nicotine solutions. In part because of this nicotine regulation, executives knew sales were unlikely to be as high in the United Kingdom as they were in the United States. Nonetheless, Juul introduced a 1.7 percent nicotine version of its e-liquid in the United Kingdom in the summer of 2018.

While Juul's products, even at 1.7 percent nicotine, carved out a decent chunk of the United Kingdom's e-cigarette market share, staffers back at Juul's San Francisco headquarters were working on an innovation they thought could supercharge the company's sales overseas. Before spreading out even further, into the rest of Europe and Asia, Juul needed to prove that its products could thrive in the United Kingdom. Kevin Burns was betting big on international expansion, and it wasn't going to look good if sales in Juul's first European market fell flat. Plus, the United Kingdom wasn't the only country that capped nicotine content at much lower levels than Juul's U.S. products. If the company were to succeed on a global scale, it would need to think strategically.

Company executives devised a plan: if they could manipulate the design of pods sold abroad to make their nicotine delivery more efficient, perhaps they could achieve the *feeling* of a 3 percent nicotine solution without actually increasing the liquid's nicotine content. Doing so wouldn't violate the FDA's policy on product changes, as the United Kingdom and other international markets were out of its jurisdiction, and such changes wouldn't technically violate nicotine cap laws. Informally, the extra-strength pod was nicknamed "Turbo." Officially, it was known as J2.

The crux of Turbo was an invisible design change: tweaking the pod's wick. The wick is the part of the pod that gets saturated with e-liquid, helping it travel from the fluid reservoir to the heating element where it is vaporized. In the United States, Juul wicks are made from braided silica.

But in 2018, Juul's engineers began experimenting with cotton wicks. A cotton wick can hold more liquid and saturates faster than silica, in theory producing more vapor per puff and giving users a bigger hit. A cotton wick seemed like the perfect way to get around the 1.7 percent nicotine cap. Even though the liquid itself was weaker than that in a normal Juul pod, each hit would deliver a vapor twice as dense as what users could get from a traditional U.S. Juul pod—essentially rivaling the experience of a 3 percent nicotine solution with a lower-strength liquid.

To test Turbo, a company source remembers, R&D engineer Ari Atkins and his team did what they'd done for years, ever since Adam first mixed together nicotine salt solutions for the first Juul device. They tested the new product on themselves, and offered test hits to any curious employees who wanted to give it a try. Says a former Juul Labs employee with knowledge of the testing, "They were all of the opinion, 'Well, look, it's going to be [fine]. We've tested it downstairs'" in the lab.

The company did begin some more formal testing in 2018, including toxicology testing required by U.K. regulators and some exploratory studies of how a cotton wick would deliver nicotine. But they left one crucial box unticked, sources say: testing whether the product actually improved upon the experience of using the original Juul pod. Some employees who tested it had their doubts. "I remember telling them, 'You guys, this isn't very strong,'" says one tester. Even still, the people in charge of J2's launch didn't at that point design and orchestrate a study that compared users' experiences with the new pod versus the old one, and so the project moved ahead without one.

Meanwhile, the company's executives had other priorities. On August 1, 2018, Kevin Burns, Nick Pritzker, and Riaz Valani met with Altria's CEO and CFO, Howard Willard and Billy Gifford, at the Park Hyatt, one of the Pritzker family's hotels in Washington, DC, to continue hashing out the terms of a possible deal. Within Juul's upper echelons, sources say, it felt like the Altria investment was a question of when, not if. The founders' original "skepticism" about the Altria proposition appeared to have faded, though the warnings from experts hadn't.

Within the insular tobacco control world, rumors had been swirling all summer about Juul potentially accepting money from a tobacco company. Stanford's Thomas Glynn asked about it that summer during a coffee meeting with a big group of Juul executives that included James and Adam. "They were honest and said that was something they'd always consider if it made sense to them," Glynn remembers. He thought taking the money would make their lives harder, that partnering with Altria would make it almost impossible for Juul to effectively argue that they were out only to improve public health. Nobody at the company seemed overly concerned, though. "They were businesspeople first. They weren't public health; they were businesspeople," Glynn says. "The fact that e-cigarettes could help people stop [smoking] was a side benefit." The primary benefit seemed to be making boatloads of money.

While executives waited for the Altria deal to close, James was deep in another project. Adam had become somewhat withdrawn from daily life at Juul, sources say. James, however, still harbored certain passion projects. During the summer of 2018, he was full of ideas for an app that would use Bluetooth to sync with a next-generation Juul device (nick-named "Bebop") that the engineering team was working to develop for international markets.

The smart-device concept was meant to be a tool for youth prevention. The idea was that adult Juul customers could verify their ages in the app, then link their app to their Juul device. Once the two were synced, the device would "lock" unless the corresponding smartphone were nearby, verifying that the right person was about to take a puff and, it was hoped, preventing underage users from getting access to Juuls.

The app also opened up a world of data. It could display exactly how much nicotine someone used each day—which could, in theory, help people taper their consumption over time (and help them decide when it was time to buy a new pod of e-liquid). "If a consumer wants to quit our product, they can," James said at *TechCrunch*'s 2018 Disrupt conference. "We will give them the tool set to do that in the smoothest possible way."

Except, according to a source with knowledge of the app's development, it didn't really include such a tool set. It could indeed show people how much nicotine they were consuming, but it didn't offer any advice on how to stop using a Juul or any feature that could help users limit their intake. All it provided was raw data, and the company's executives couldn't agree on exactly what to do with the data the app collected. Any data about use of an addictive product, particularly when gathered by the company *selling* that addictive product, must be handled carefully, and some executives were nervous about opening that door.

James was one of the people pushing to do more with the data, company sources say. In his mind, one of Juul Labs's biggest problems was its "churn" rate—or the number of people who bought a Juul, didn't like it, and never tried it again. To James, each of these people represented a lost opportunity—a smoker who might have switched to Juul but who didn't stick with it long enough to do so fully. Ever since it ran focus groups in the lead-up to Juul's launch, the company had known one possible reason for this: the first puff on a Juul can feel extremely strong. Vapor feels different than cigarette smoke when it hits the lungs, so a deep pull sometimes sent even seasoned smokers into coughing fits and scared them off. The company's website urged users to "start with light puffs to get a feel for Juul's vapor without inhaling." James wanted to do something similar with the app, using real-time data to coach people into finding their perfect puff, so they wouldn't get scared off early.

A company source says employees in the science division immediately had concerns. "Don't coach people about how to use an addictive chemical," the source says. "Frankly, it looks like it's engineering addiction." At least one Juul scientist allegedly urged James to consult with behavioral researchers before he attempted to do anything that would change the way people used nicotine—especially when regulators were deeply concerned about Juul's appeal to young people who had never used the drug before—but it could be difficult to dissuade him when he was excited about an idea.

When he wasn't working on the app, James was trying to meet with tobacco control experts around the Bay Area, apparently still in search of people who could lend their credibility to Juul and its research team.

Unbeknownst to Stanford's Robert Jackler, he was on James's list. Ever since it launched with its Vaporized ad campaign in 2015, Jackler had been keeping an eye on Juul. Jackler, a head and neck surgeon by training, ran the Stanford Research into the Impact of Tobacco Advertising (SRITA) center with his wife, Laurie. He was deeply concerned by Juul's popularity among young people, and by the striking similarities between some of its early advertising and the old tobacco ads he and Laurie kept preserved in their archive. Now, three years after the company's launch, he had some new concerns.

During the summer of 2018, Jackler brought on a group of interns to help with his research. He gave a couple of them, both rising college sophomores, a special project. Jackler wanted to see if the interns could clear Juul's online age-verification system even though they were younger than twenty-one, the minimum age of purchase on Juul's website. The system successfully blocked them from buying Juuls, but something else interesting happened.

"After they were rejected, they started getting a stream of marketing emails, including discount coupons for purchase of Juul, praises of [the] Mango-flavored pods, and all this kind of stuff," Jackler says. In theory, Juul wasn't supposed to let anyone younger than twenty-one subscribe to its marketing emails, given that it sold an age-restricted product. But if his interns had gamed the system without even trying, he was pretty sure thousands of teenagers who'd tried and failed to buy Juul products online were now being directly targeted by the company's marketing outreach. (When Juul employees ran an audit of their email lists, according to documents cited in the California attorney general's lawsuit, they found that more than 529,000 subscribers had never been age-verified.)

Jackler couldn't believe Juul could be so sloppy. It seemed pretty easy for the company's software engineers to write some code that barred any user who'd failed age verification from being added to the company's marketing email list. At best, the slipup showed gross negligence on Juul's part. At worst, it showed malice.

On July 31, 2018, Jackler called Julie Henderson, Juul's youth prevention director. When she didn't answer, he followed up by email. "I was calling to suggest that your IT team look into the fact that rejected under age purchasers are subscribed to JUULs [sic] marketing emails," Jackler wrote. "Also, under age individuals can sign up for your newsletter (despite the >21 requirement[,] as there is no age gate). I am hoping that these are just glitches in the code which runs the systems as opposed to an intentional policy."

Jackler's email hit a nerve within the company. Juul's employees had known for years that Veratad's age-verification software had flaws. Over the years, they'd heard from plenty of angry parents whose kids had somehow bypassed it and purchased Juuls online, so the problem had been fairly hard to ignore.

Earlier in 2018, compliance manager Annie Kennedy had run an experiment, according to the California attorney general's legal complaint. She purposely used an incorrect date of birth for a test purchase and found that without ever having to upload an ID, she still passed

Veratad's system because she'd entered her name, address, and *year* of birth correctly. When she raised this issue with the company's director of product, he said her order technically met the standards jointly set by Veratad and Juul. Still, he admitted that he "was not a fan" of that policy, because it "makes it really easy for a kid to pass with their parents' info." He asked Kennedy if she knew why that loophole even existed. She explained that Juul's executive team had implemented the policy years earlier.

"It was initially a compromise," Kennedy wrote back on the company's messaging platform, Slack, according to the complaint. "We wanted to hard check the complete [date of birth but] got a lot of push back (prior to [age verification] and youth prevention being some of our main company goals), so we settled with a hard check on [year of birth] at that time." Kennedy's note suggested customers could pass Veratad's system if the information they entered corresponded to a real person who had been born in the year they specified, even if the entire date of birth wasn't correct. This meant that a twenty-year-old could easily buy Juul products in the months leading up to his or her twenty-first birthday, or a teenager could fool the program fairly easily by entering a parent's name, address, and year of birth. Theoretically, they'd need an adult to sign for the delivery when it arrived, but it was still a significant loophole.

Jackler's point about the marketing emails provided another example of an age-verification problem—and, worse, one that people outside the company could clearly recognize. Days after Jackler pointed out the company's mistake, Juul implemented a new system that barred anyone younger than twenty-one from signing up for its email list. But Matt David, the company's director of communications, was explicit in his instructions for how this development should be described publicly, according to the California legal complaint. He strictly forbade his employees from sending out a blast that would notify people under twenty-one that they'd no longer receive emails. "Telling [non-age-verified] users that they need to pass an [age-verification] test is a massive red flag to press. [It would then have been] crystal clear [that] we didn't do it in the past," he wrote in an email.

"Better to frame it as a broader policy; we can mention other things we're doing." As a compromise, the complaint alleges, the company emailed its entire list of non-age-verified followers to say it was strengthening its age-verification process and asked them to provide the last four digits of their Social Security number or a photo of government-issued ID. Fewer than three thousand people responded to the prompt, and fewer than two thousand passed.

Even before Jackler's interns started getting emails from Juul, he'd been trying to set up a meeting with Julie Henderson. After years of skeptical observation, he wanted to meet with Henderson, Ashley Gould, and their staff to talk about how Juul could improve its youth prevention program. Juul had made a few steps in the right direction. It had its thirty-million-dollar youth prevention campaign, and it had stopped using models in its social media marketing. Under Gould's supervision, an entire team of Juul employees now trolled social media all day long, asking for youth-oriented posts to be taken down, but the effort clearly wasn't working perfectly. About half of Juul's Twitter followers in 2018 were younger than eighteen, one study estimated. On Instagram, Jackler and his team counted tens of thousands of posts tagged with hashtags from teen-friendly fan accounts, like #JuulNation and #DoItForJuul. On YouTube, when Jackler's team searched "Juul at School," more than fifteen thousand videos came up. Almost two thousand came up when they searched "Hiding Juul from parents." One popular YouTube video posted in April 2018 showed two apparently teenaged boys sitting in a car hitting a Juul as many times as they could without exhaling. Clearly, Juul's team couldn't keep up with the amount of illicit Juul content online. Henderson agreed to meet with Jackler and his research team that summer.

On the morning of August 13, 2018, Jackler's group arrived at Juul's sprawling new headquarters in San Francisco's Dogpatch neighborhood. They were asked to sign a nondisclosure agreement as soon as they got to reception. As an academic who planned to write about Juul, Jackler refused to do this. After some deliberation, one of Juul's in-house lawyers decided that without signed NDAs, it would be best to hold the meeting in an outpost building down the street, which served as spillover office space and had less proprietary information lying around. Jackler's team, Henderson, and the lawyer walked down the street together, making polite small talk until they got to the annex building. When they opened the door to the conference room, there sat Gould and James Monsees, "which I didn't expect," Jackler says. "I thought we were meeting with their education people." And yet there was Juul's cofounder, wearing a hooded sweatshirt, puffing on a Crème Brûlée Juul pod, and casually waiting for the start of a meeting he hadn't even been asked to attend.

James turned to Jackler immediately: "You know, Dr. Jackler, we've met before," he said with a grin.

"Oh?" Jackler replied, confused. He'd spent plenty of time and energy studying Juul, but he couldn't remember ever meeting James in person.

"Oh, yes," James said. "We came to you as we were considering how to market our product. You know, your repository of tobacco advertising online was extremely helpful to us as we planned how to market our product."

Immediately, Jackler's mind flashed to his tobacco advertising archive. He and his wife, Laurie, had started their collection back in 2007. Back then, it consisted of only about three hundred historical tobacco ads, which they'd showcased at a museum exhibition on Stanford's campus. That would have been right around the time James and Adam were getting Ploom off the ground. Was that how they'd met? Had James been at the archive's opening? Jackler couldn't remember. But what he did know, without a doubt, was how extensive his archive had gotten over the years. If they had spent some time going through it, Adam and James could have seen thousands of the ads that had made cigarettes an American institution—ads that had convinced Americans that cigarettes kept them slim and that their doctor smoked Camels, so they should, too. There were ads that targeted a customer's ego ("You're so smart to smoke Parliaments!") and those that sold sex (bikinis, bikinis, and more bikinis). There were those that convinced smokers that a company's cigarettes were "fresh" and "pure," "relaxing," and "good for the nerves." And, of course, there were those ads Jackler considered explicitly youth-oriented, with their fresh-faced cheerleaders and perfectly marketed teenage rebellion. To Jackler, Juul's fun, colorful Vaporized campaign had seemed eerily similar to those earlier ads from Big Tobacco. Even as the company evolved and cleaned up its marketing, Jackler had heard echoes of Big Tobacco in Juul's slogans about its device being "smoking evolved" and "built to satisfy."

James Monsees hadn't personally developed the Vaporized campaign, nor any of Juul's advertising. Richard Mumby and Steven Baillie, the minds behind Vaporized, seemed to have been thinking more about social media marketing than old print ads. But in Jackler's eyes, Juul's cofounder was now all but admitting to copying advertising from cigarette companies—an opinion James would later deny. "It's as clear as the nose on my face that they were inspired by the most successful genre of contemporary tobacco advertising"—that is, ads depicting attractive twenty-somethings having fun, socializing, and partying, Jackler says. "They decided, very simply, 'Why reinvent the wheel? Let's emulate the single most popular and successful tobacco brand: Marlboro.'"

As these thoughts raced through his mind, Jackler tried not to show his surprise. Now that he had James Monsees in a room, he was going to try to get some answers about his choices over the years—why Juul had launched with Vaporized, why it used social media so much, why it relied so heavily on marketing its flavored products, why it insisted on selling such strong nicotine pods. Even though the meeting was supposed to be all about youth prevention, Henderson was "quiet as a church mouse," Jackler remembers. Occasionally, the company's lawyer would lean over and whisper something into James's or Gould's ear. But for the most part, it was just Jackler and James, locked in a verbal two-step.

For most of the two-hour meeting, Jackler says, he lobbed question after question at James, who would answer with what basically amounted to a well-rehearsed sales pitch about Juul's mission to save a billion smokers from smoking-related deaths. James seemed set on finding a credible scientist will-ing to support Juul. Apparently, though incorrectly, he thought he had a shot with Robert Jackler.

Jackler says he left the meeting convinced that James Monsees cared more about making money than he did about public health. His pitch about Juul's mission was so polished, Jackler says it felt like a "stump speech" rather than a heartfelt belief. In Jackler's opinion—which company sources later denied—"What he was worried about was the perception of his investors. It was one of those take-homes that he was so transparent about."

With a deal between Altria and Juul seeming more imminent by the day, it wouldn't have been shocking if James had investors on the brain. But, of course, Jackler didn't know about that yet.

As the summer of 2018 came to a close, Juul hosted another visitor who was upset about youth vaping—this one unexpected. One afternoon, a knock rang out through Juul's lobby, echoing off the imposing solid wood doors. Confused, the receptionist got up to see who could be outside knocking. When she opened the door, she discovered that the pounding had come from a slender, well-put-together blond woman. She introduced herself as Christine Chessen, said she lived nearby, and demanded to speak with Kevin Burns.

The day before, Chessen had found a Juul in her teenage son's backpack as he packed up to return to boarding school for the fall. She'd been hearing about the teen juuling problem with increasing frequency lately and held out hope that her three children wouldn't get mixed up with it. "I was so bummed" to find out otherwise, Chessen says. She confiscated the Juul and channeled her frustrations into a letter she planned to send to Burns. In the letter, she begged Burns, who had teenage children himself, to consider what it would feel like to find out his kids were using an addictive product without his knowledge. She even asked him to speak to her son and dissuade him from vaping.

"It was an emotional letter from a mom," Chessen says. When she looked into where to send the letter, she saw that Juul's headquarters were in San Francisco, not far from where she and her family lived. "I'm driving down there," Chessen decided. It was an impulsive decision, totally out of character. But radiating with anger, Chessen couldn't help herself.

No one at Juul knew quite what to make of Chessen. Hordes of Juul's young employees were passing through the lobby on their way back from lunch, throwing curious glances toward the fuming middle-aged woman standing by the reception desk. Plenty of parents had called and emailed before, but a furious mother standing in the lobby and demanding to speak with their CEO had to be a first. A security guard tried to calm her down, but Chessen demanded to speak with an executive from the company. Finally, an executive assistant came down, took Chessen's letter, and promised to give it to the right people.

Two hours later, she got a call from communications director Matt David. "He was so apologetic," Chessen remembers. At the time, he had a young child himself, and he spoke like a concerned fellow parent, she says. At her request, he even called Chessen's son and told him to stop juuling, and he invited Chessen to come back to Juul's offices—invited, this time—to continue the conversation about how Juul could do better. They were saying all the right things on the surface, but Chessen wasn't convinced. "You could just tell it was a line of BS, in my opinion," she says.

Chessen couldn't stop thinking about Juul. She felt as if the company followed her wherever she went, as if it were taking over the city of San Francisco. "We'd go out to dinner, and we'd see someone with a Juul backpack on. We'd see the advertisements," she says. "It just irritated me." She knew there was more to do. She just didn't know what yet.

14

On September 24, 2018, three FDA investigators arrived on Juul's doorstep. They informed Kevin Burns that they were there to perform a high-priority inspection requested by the FDA's Center for Tobacco Products and that they'd need to come inside—now.

The staff was ready for this moment. The FDA routinely dropped by to inspect companies that fell under its jurisdiction, looking for anything that felt amiss or suggested that a company wasn't following FDA regulations. This time, though the team at Juul didn't know it yet, the agency's inspectors were looking for clarity on the things Commissioner Gottlieb felt Juul had been less than forthcoming about over the years: product modifications, health complaints, youth marketing, underage vaping, and more.

The moment Burns let the inspectors inside the building, his employees slipped into a well-rehearsed dance. The receptionist knew to call Juul's director of compliance, who escorted the investigators to a conference room, where they'd essentially live over the next several days. A team of Juul employees set up in a nearby back room, ready to pull any document the investigators asked for—which totaled thousands over the course of the inspection. The FDA's inspectors were also free to pull Juul staffers into their conference room to answer questions.

The investigators called in Julie Henderson, Juul's youth prevention director. She told them about Juul Labs's youth prevention plans, claiming that the company had distributed educational materials, but never to youth—only to teachers, parents, and principals. If the company ever developed a new curriculum, she promised, it would be through a third-party group. The investigators took notes, requested a few documents on Juul's curriculum, and let her go.

Chelsea Kania, who'd been with Juul's marketing team since the company was called Pax, answered questions about Juul Labs's marketing and advertising. Investigators asked her about Juul's influencer program and why a company making a product for adult smokers had advertised so heavily on Instagram. Kania calmly told the investigators that Juul had paid only four social media influencers in its entire history, which was true—she just glossed over the unpaid influencers who had posted about Juul after getting vaporizers at a dollar a pop, a company source recalls. She admitted that the company had given out free products right after Juul launched, but she stressed that free sampling had stopped as soon as the FDA's deeming rule went into effect in 2016. Now, she said, Juul focused on a different kind of marketing: testimonials from adult smokers who felt their lives had been saved by Juul's products.

As the investigation moved along, Josh Vose, the company's vice president of medical and clinical affairs, walked the FDA team through the numerous studies that would make up Juul's PMTA. The FDA's team also grilled Vose and a few other staffers, including the company's senior vice president of engineering, hardware, and firmware, Bryan White, about the pod changes FDA inspectors had discovered at a Juul contractor's facility that spring—but that Juul had failed to report on its own.

White admitted that Juul had, indeed, changed its pod design earlier that year to stop e-juice from leaking out. He and Vose cast the update as a safety fix. More than 150,000 people had complained to the company about leaky pods since 2015, many describing burning or blistering on their mouths, tongues, and lips. Nicotine can be poisonous when swallowed, and Juul wanted to do everything in its power to stop this from happening, so it had made the design change and asked its pod-producing contractor to start implementing it.

That was all true; it just conveniently glossed over the additional changes to the device's firmware and circuitry that Juul's employees had sat on for years. (A company source swears White mentioned changes made to the device's circuitry, sensors, and firmware, too, but there's no mention of those comments in the FDA's postinspection report.) The investigators nodded and took down some notes before responding. One of them reminded Juul that the FDA policy that forbade product modifications without agency approval extended to contractors, too. But because the pods had been updated for safety reasons, it didn't seem like a huge deal. "We don't really see this as a problem," one investigator said, according to a company source. "We'll have to address it in the PMTA."

All in all, the investigation had been pretty civil. No bombshells, no smoking guns. It was hardly the explosive raid that would be splashed across front pages the following week. When the reports did come out, describing an FDA "raid" of Juul's headquarters, "We were all sitting around thinking, 'Oh my god, look at these headlines,'" remembers a former high-level employee, scoffing at the sensational tone in the reporting. "The result of the 'raid' was, they found nothing."

The FDA did eventually post the results of its "raid" online: "NAI," which stands for "no action indicated." "We thanked the firm for their cooperation and efficiency," one investigator wrote in the final report—though the FDA's tone would change later on, after *Bloomberg* in 2020 published a story about Juul's other, undisclosed product changes. "The FDA is aware that other allegations have been made about additional modifications to Juul's products, which were not disclosed to the FDA during the 2018 investigation," an FDA spokesperson says. "The FDA is looking into these allegations. The FDA closely monitors retailer, manufacturer, importer and distributor compliance with federal tobacco laws and regulations and investigates to determine whether violations of the law have occurred."

Even without these disclosures, the FDA's investigators didn't exactly find nothing during their site inspection. The agency passed several tidbits along to other federal agencies, including the Federal Bureau of Investigation and the Federal Trade Commission, just in case they wanted to open investigations of their own. And now the FDA had thousands of Juul's internal documents at its fingertips.

The FDA's facility inspection was the third act in a play Commissioner Gottlieb had been directing for weeks. It all started in early September 2018, when Mitch Zeller, who ran the FDA's Center for Tobacco Products, received data from the National Youth Tobacco Survey. The data weren't good at all. The survey showed that between 2017 and 2018, youth vaping had shot up in popularity by a staggering 78 percent. By the fall of 2018, according to the survey, almost 21 percent of high school students—about three million teenagers, 1.3 million more than the previous year—said they had vaped in the past thirty days.

Gottlieb was horrified by these numbers. He truly believed in e-cigarettes' potential for adult smokers who wanted to quit, but he was also a physician, a father of three, and a public health advocate. He couldn't stand by and do nothing, especially when news reports suggested that schools were taking more and more dramatic actions to stop youth vaping—and when public opinion was swinging against the e-cigarette industry, and Juul in particular. A school in Philadelphia had recently banned flash drives because teachers couldn't tell the difference between them and Juuls. The whole thing was getting out of control.

Within minutes of getting the results from Mitch Zeller, Gottlieb made a phone call to the White House "to let them know about it, and also to let them know that I was going to have to take pretty aggressive action in the coming days," Gottlieb says. "I had all the license I needed to do that."

Just days later, on September 11, Gottlieb delivered a speech at the FDA's headquarters in Maryland—act two in his Juul offensive. He began by reiterating his belief that e-cigarettes could serve as an important "off-ramp" for smokers who no longer wanted to use cigarettes. The problem, he continued, was that they had become a wider "on-ramp" to nicotine addiction for kids than he had predicted. "Unfortunately, I now have good reason to believe that it's reached nothing short of an epidemic proportion of growth," Gottlieb said. "I use the word *epidemic* with great care. E-cigs have become an almost ubiquitous—and dangerous—trend among teens. The disturbing and accelerating trajectory of use we're seeing in youth, and the resulting path to addiction, must end. It's simply not tolerable. I'll be clear. The FDA won't tolerate a whole generation of young people becoming addicted to nicotine as a tradeoff for enabling adults to have unfettered access to these same products."

On that very day, he continued, the FDA had issued a dozen warning letters to companies that were selling explicitly kid-friendly products, like vapes that looked like juice boxes or candy, informing them that the FDA was ready to issue fines, seize products, or do whatever else it took to get their products off the market if they didn't stop selling them voluntarily. Since the spring, the FDA had also been conducting an undercover secret shopper program, looking for retailers who were selling Juuls to underage kids. That effort had produced fifty-six warning letters. Now, Gottlieb announced, the FDA was going much further. It had issued an additional 1,100 warning letters to stores that continued selling e-cigarettes, including Juuls, to kids. Already, 131 of those stores had been forced to pay fines for their bad actions.

And, Gottlieb continued, the FDA was looking seriously at how it could better regulate the e-cigarette industry as a whole. Just a year earlier, Gottlieb had given vaping companies extra time to put together their FDA applications. Now he was considering taking that time back—and even more catastrophically for e-cigarette companies like Juul, which cashed in on flavored pods, he said he was seriously considering a policy that would ban flavored products completely.

Finally, Gottlieb addressed the five e-cigarette brands he thought were driving the youth vaping epidemic: Vuse, Blu, Logic, MarkTen, and Juul. "I've been warning the e-cigarette industry for more than a year that they needed to do much more to stem the youth trends," Gottlieb said. "In my view, they treated these issues like a public relations challenge rather than seriously considering their legal obligations, the public health mandate, and the existential threat to these products. And the risks mounted." Now he demanded that executives from each of the five companies behind these brands produce within sixty days detailed plans for curbing youth use, and he recommended that they brace themselves for investigations and further actions from the FDA. "Let me be clear," Gottlieb said. "Everything is on the table," including, as it would soon turn out for Juul, a facility inspection— act three.

A few weeks after the September site inspection at Juul's headquarters, Kevin Burns and Scott Gottlieb came together for a "constructive" meeting to discuss Juul's plans for youth prevention, as Gottlieb had demanded. Burns described an ambitious plan that would involve shutting down Juul's long-controversial social media pages in the United States and, more dramatically, removing Juul's Mango, Fruit Medley, Cucumber, and Crème Brûlée pods from retail stores at a time when Mango accounted for about a third of the company's pod sales. (The company decided that Mint, Menthol, and Tobacco didn't count as flavors and kept them on store shelves.) Anyone who wanted their Fruit, Mango, Crème Brûlée, or Cucumber fix would need to buy pods on Juul's website, which accepted only customers who were twenty-one or older. Considering how important flavored pods were to Juul's bottom line, this seemed like a big action. James Monsees would later say he "could not imagine a more responsive, proactive step," but it was not quite as proactive as he wanted it to appear. Gottlieb had just warned the entire industry that he was thinking about aggressively regulating flavored products, and Juul's executives wanted to make it look like the decision had been voluntary rather than forced. The move was clever, sure, but it wasn't exactly proactive; nor did it happen in a vacuum.

Toward the end of 2018, the company's political arm kicked into high gear, with lobbyists blanketing Capitol Hill to push out Juul-approved talking points about flavor bans, FDA regulations, and Tobacco 21 laws. "I want to make sure we're protecting the category," Burns would tell his lobbyists.

He viewed the FDA's crackdown as not just annoying, but also possibly the end of the vape industry as he knew it. Juul's best defense seemed like a good offense. Every lawmaker on the Hill, up to and including those in the White House, should know that Juul wasn't happy about Gottlieb's threats. But Juul's full-court-press lobbying style wasn't having the effect he thought it would, according to one former lobbyist. "None of those moves curried any favor or won them any brownie points with policy makers," says the former lobbyist. "The detractors were still being detractors," and now it looked like Juul was just trying to get around federal regulators.

Burns also neglected to mention something rather large in his meeting with Scott Gottlieb that fall: Juul and Altria were back at the bargaining table and had been for weeks. A deal was looking increasingly imminent, but Burns didn't mention it.

Altria's Howard Willard was in his own meetings with Scott Gottlieb that fall, but he didn't say anything about the proposed deal, either. ("As a publicly traded company, Altria does not discuss potential investments in advance due to materiality and public disclosure requirements," says a company spokesperson.) In a late-October letter to Gottlieb, Willard told the commissioner that Altria planned to remove its pod-based e-cigarettes from the market in light of the troubling new data on youth vaping. "Although we do not believe we have a current issue with youth access to or use of our pod-based products, we do not want to risk contributing to the issue," Willard wrote. "To avoid such a risk, we will remove from the market our MarkTen Elite and Apex by MarkTen pod-based products until we receive a market order from the FDA or the youth issue is otherwise addressed." Altria's non-pod products, like its old-school cigalikes, would remain for sale, but only in the Menthol and Tobacco flavors thought to be less appealing to kids.

Perhaps trying to capitalize on whatever goodwill these meetings with the FDA had inspired, Juul's team sent the results of the company's inaugural youth use study to the FDA on November 5. The research had started the prior summer, after suggestions from Attorney General Tom Miller's youth advisory group, and Juul finally had results worth sharing. After polling about one thousand teenagers, the company believed that only 1.5% of kids ages thirteen through seventeen had used a Juul before and that less than 1 percent had done so in the last thirty days. These still worked out to large numbers—there are about 21 million Americans that age, so even 1 percent of that group would be more than 200,000 teenagers—but it suggested that teen juuling was not, at least, universal.

The research team also found that many kids who were vaping were not using Juul products; many were, instead, using cheap knockoffs implicitly or explicitly branded like Juuls. Says a former employee with direct knowledge of the study, "We listed like forty flavors of competitors and compatibles, and those were all top of the list" in terms of what respondents were using. This was certainly not the experience of teenagers in some areas, who said nearly everyone in their high schools juuled, but a company source says it reflected the fact that Juul's e-cigarettes were far less common in schools in lower-income areas or communities of color. Juul was "aggravating the living daylights out of very rich, white suburban constituencies," as one Washington, DC, insider put it, but that experience wasn't necessarily the same everywhere.

The study also found that most teenagers who were habitually using Juuls, as opposed to those who used them socially or infrequently, were current or former smokers—a partial win for Juul Labs, as it meant that its device was not attracting as many new nicotine addicts as people feared. "The top-line result was there was an epidemic, but it was an epidemic of experimentation," says a source involved with the study. That is, Juul's results suggested that most underage users vaped only sporadically, just as most teen drinkers typically get drunk only at parties. (The difference, of course, being that nicotine is highly addictive, whereas alcohol is not for most people.) The company was not denying that it had a youth vaping problem—it had been fielding calls, emails, and lawsuits from concerned parents long enough to know that teenagers were indeed getting addicted—but its data suggested that things could have been worse. The data at least showed that Juul and Juul alone had not caused the teen vaping trend and that most young vapers were not ripping through multiple pods per day.

Company-funded studies are hardly the gold standard of scientific research—data can be manipulated to suit a certain goal, hence why the cigarette industry for years funded studies meant to deflect real and accurate concerns about their products' safety. And Juul's results were wildly out of step with federal estimates about youth juuling prevalence, as well as the conclusions of some independent researchers. A late 2018 study published in the journal *Tobacco Control* found that as of May 2018, about 9.5 percent of teenagers ages fifteen to seventeen had ever tried a Juul. In an October 2018 survey by the Truth Initiative—itself not unbiased, as a vocal anti-tobacco-use group—more than 15 percent of fifteen-to seventeen-year-olds said they had tried Juul. (By contrast, almost 30 percent of teenagers in 2017 said they'd ever tried a cigarette.)

Still, Juul's study highlighted some points pro-e-cigarette scientists had been trying to make for years: that many kids who tried e-cigarettes did not end up addicted, and that others who picked up the products had previously smoked. An analysis of the 2018 National Youth Tobacco Survey later published by scientists including NYU's David Abrams and Ray Niaura argued that only 4 percent of vapers ages nine to nineteen had never used another tobacco product—though it was impossible to tell whether they picked up cigarettes or e-cigarettes first. The point, Abrams says, is that youth use—while concerning—isn't so different from teen experimentation with alcohol, marijuana, or cigarettes, nor should it be enough to cancel out the benefits e-cigarettes could bring to adult smokers. Concerns about teen vaping are warranted, Abrams says. "But what about a billion smokers?"

If Gottlieb saw Juul's letter about its study, or if he thought it was at all legitimate, he gave no indication. Only days after Juul Labs submitted its data, he released the data from the National Youth Tobacco Survey. In a statement released along with data about the 78 percent increase in youth vaping that year, Gottlieb again threatened to use "the full range of our regulatory authorities" to keep kids from getting access to e-cigarettes and vowed—just as scientists like Abrams feared—not to let the promise of e-cigarettes for adults come before their threat to kids. "We must close the on-ramp of nicotine addiction for kids even if it risks narrowing the off-ramp from smoking for adults," he said. "These are the hard tradeoffs we must take to keep these products out of the hands of kids and confront this troubling epidemic."

That same day, he backed up that promise by introducing a new suggested policy on e-cigarette regulation. Just as Juul had predicted, the policy proposed to prohibit e-cigarettes in flavors except Tobacco, Mint, and Menthol from being sold in convenience stores, gas stations, and other stores where minors can shop. Gottlieb was even entertaining the idea of banning menthol cigarettes while he was at it. He seemed not to care if it pissed off big players like Juul and Altria (not to mention the entire convenience store industry), or if it put smaller vaping companies out of business. Youth vaping was "at a level that's simply not tolerable from a public health standpoint," Gottlieb said, and his first and only priority was changing that.

While Gottlieb was throwing out new proposed regulations, Juul and Altria executives were getting closer and closer to a deal that would reshape the vaping industry in a different way. The paperwork was as good as signed, but after a year of growth at all costs, Burns reportedly wanted to milk the situation for everything it was worth. Burns wanted the shelf space reserved for Altria products in convenience stories, now that MarkTen wouldn't be using much of it. Willard agreed. Burns wanted access to Altria's database of consumers so Juul could contact them directly with promotions. Willard said okay. Burns wanted to be able to advertise Juul's products on Marlboro cigarette packs. Willard said fine. Altria also agreed not to invest in any other e-cigarette companies, or to develop new e-cigarette products of its own.

Things were looking as good as final when news of the eighteen-month-long negotiation process leaked to the *Wall Street Journal*. On November 28, 2018, the newspaper reported that Altria was in talks with Juul about acquiring a "significant minority stake" in the company. As soon as the article made the rounds on Juul's instant messaging platform, chaos erupted at Juul headquarters.

Some employees refused to believe the news. Many felt deeply uneasy about the prospect of Juul working with the country's largest tobacco company. "People were saying, 'I didn't sign up to join Big Tobacco,'" remembers one former employee. Many staffers thought of Juul as a technology company, not a tobacco company. Adam and James's early deal with Japan Tobacco was ancient history by that point, and most Juulers hadn't worked for the company when it happened. Many Juul employees bristled at the mere suggestion that their company belonged in the same league as traditional Big Tobacco brands. "The philosophy at Juul was 'We're different. They're bad, we're good,'" says one former employee who'd previously worked for Altria. The idea of taking money from Altria clouded that whole image.

The *Wall Street Journal* story dominated office conversation so much that Juul's senior leaders decided to hold a companywide meeting to calm everyone down. But instead of telling staffers about the months and months of negotiations with Altria, which were now very close to complete, Burns hedged his bets. For about an hour, remembers a former employee, he talked around the issue without ever confirming or denying the *Wall Street Journal*'s report. He admitted that several major tobacco companies had expressed interest in Juul, but he repeatedly tried to downplay the magnitude of the situation. Burns and other "senior leaders at Juul were saying to staff members, 'That doesn't make any sense. Why would we do that?'" says an employee who was in the meeting. Burns pointed to Juul's dominant market share and $15 billion valuation, using both to suggest that the company did not need support from Altria or any of the other Big Tobacco companies that had come calling.

But after an hour of trying to quash suspicions without actually denying anything, Burns showed his hand. "If we did it," he said, "we know what we'd ask for": namely, access to the company's consumer database and retail shelf space. To some people in the room, that one comment, "if we did it," was a tacit admission that everything the *Wall Street Journal* had reported was true: Juul Labs was seriously considering a partnership with Altria. And, indeed, it was.

In early December 2018, Altria announced that it was discontinuing its entire MarkTen e-cigarette line. (Later, the Federal Trade Commission would allege that Juul made this a condition of the investment agreement, which both Juul and Altria denied.) "We remain committed to being the leader in providing adult smokers innovative alternative products that reduce risk, including e-vapor," Willard said in a statement. "We do not see a path to leadership with these particular products and believe that now is the time to refocus our resources."

The world learned what he meant just a few days later, when Altria announced that it had paid $12.8 billion for a 35 percent stake in Juul Labs. Under the terms of the agreement, Altria would support Juul's product distribution, marketing, sales, and regulatory services operations, perhaps most crucially by helping it draft its PMTA for the FDA. The deal valued Juul at $38 billion, more than double the already massive valuation it had hit earlier that year. It made Juul Labs, a start-up constantly in hot water with the FDA and the media, more valuable than start-ups like Airbnb, Lyft, and SpaceX. And overnight, it made billionaires out of two Stanford grads with a bright idea.

The investment also made FDA commissioner Scott Gottlieb extremely angry. Gottlieb saw the deal as a betrayal. In recent months, executives from both Juul Labs and Altria had made a big show of doing what the FDA wanted with smiles on their faces. Altria had pulled its pod-based products off the market, specifically because this type of product seemed to be driving the youth vaping epidemic. Burns had talked up Juul's new youth vaping prevention plan, which included pulling Juul's profitable flavored products off store shelves. Now Gottlieb could see they'd been hiding their true intentions.

Willard from Altria had sat there waxing poetic about taking proactive actions to prevent youth vaping when he knew his company was only months away from buying a chunk of the country's dominant e-cigarette brand, one that had made its name selling the very pod-based e-cigarettes Gottlieb thought to be at the heart of the youth vaping crisis. Meanwhile, Juul Labs had emphasized the ways it would cut down on underage sales in stores all while negotiating for the very same retail shelf space that America's largest cigarette company used for its products. "There were multiple aspects of the Altria transaction that were inconsistent with, at [the] very least, the spirit, if not the letter, of what they had said to the agency and the commitment they made," Gottlieb says.

According to one company insider with knowledge of the fallout, this was putting it nicely. Gottlieb was furious with the way he'd been yanked around. If he had been tough on Juul before, now he was ready to bring down the hammer. "He decided to wage [war] on Juul, because he felt like he had been taken for a ride," says the company insider. "After that, you had embarrassed Scott Gottlieb," and there was no going back.

PART III

Up in Smoke

15

Walking down the streets of San Francisco, taking in the colorful Victorians and multimillion-dollar town houses, "Jake" had always wondered what those people's stories were. "You see people that can afford houses in San Francisco, and you're like, 'What the hell did they do?'" he says. When he joined Juul Labs at the end of 2018, he got his answer.

Jake started interviewing for a position at Juul in December 2018, right around the time negotiations with Altria were wrapping up. He signed his contract halfway through the month and planned to start after the holidays. Then the Altria deal closed, and it included a staggering $2 billion set aside for employee bonuses. Because Jake was technically a Juul employee when the investment came in, before even setting up his desk he qualified for a $120,000 payout over the next two years on top of his salary. "I had a serious fortune fall in my lap right away," he says. "Literally, a serious fortune." Suddenly, buying real estate in one of the most expensive markets in the country didn't seem quite so ludicrous. Tech money made anything possible. "It was life-changing," he says.

Life-changing though it was for Jake, a $120,000 payout was actually on the low end of what Juul employees received when the Altria investment closed. The $2 billion bonus fund was divvied up depending on each

employee's job title, equity, and tenure at the company. The payouts reportedly averaged out to $1.3 million per person, though that number was driven
way up by senior and longtime employees who became millionaires several
times over with the stroke of Howard Willard's pen. Twenty- and thirty-
something employees who'd been lucky enough to join Juul back when it
was called Ploom suddenly had the money to buy vacation homes and sports
cars, to put in swimming pools and plan luxury vacations. It was the Silicon
Valley dream come to life—for no one more so than James, Adam, and their
executive team.

Though the exact amount hasn't been reported, company sources
say James, Adam, and Kevin Burns made massive amounts of money
when the Altria money came through. Adam and James each owned less
than 5 percent of the company by that point, but they still made enough
off the investment to become billionaires—and at least one of them was
acting like it. Shortly after the Altria deal, James closed on an imposing,
multimillion-dollar mansion fit for a tech scion, with sweeping floor-
to-ceiling windows and balconies with scenic views of the hills of San
Francisco.

Juul's investors were also rewarded handily for pushing through the
early lean years, reportedly receiving a dividend of $150 for each share
they held in the company. Major investors like Tiger Global Management
walked away with more than $1 billion, taken directly from Altria's pay-
ment to Juul. Less than $300 million of Altria's massive investment actually
went into the company. Much of it went toward making a few people very,
very rich.

But even while the executives celebrated and serious fortunes fell into
laps, morale at Juul Labs was strained. Many employees felt betrayed by
management's about-face. Just a month ago, Burns had stood up in front
of the entire company and said that Juul didn't need any help from tobacco
companies. Now the largest cigarette maker in the country owned 35 percent of the brand. Some people viewed Altria's involvement as a betrayal
of Juul's mission, a sign that Juul had sold its moral backbone. If Juul had
been created to make the cigarette obsolete, why take billions of dollars

from a major tobacco company? For many people who worked at the company, the glass had shattered. "I don't know if *defeat* is the word," says a former employee who worked at the company when Altria invested. "But we thought we were going to kill the cigarette industry. And then accepting Altria as an investor—it wasn't the future we imagined for ourselves." Even if employees could see the logic of partnering with Altria, a company with massive resources and regulatory experience, it was a tough pill to swallow.

It felt like the company's whole culture was changing. With a Big Tobacco company as a major investor and business partner, it was no longer possible to pretend Juul was just another innovative San Francisco technology start-up. "It just hurt because you were fighting for something as an underdog for so long," says a former employee from the legal team. "Then you get in bed with one of these well-rooted companies. You're basically saying, 'We are now the establishment.'" Some employees quit after the news broke. "I didn't want to work for a tobacco company," says a lobbyist who left shortly after the Altria investment. "It's not what I set out to do."

Many employees were more than happy to collect their checks and move on, but it was still hard to deny that Altria's money was about to make their lives a lot harder, at least in the public sphere. The constant influx of bad press over youth vaping—"#Juul: How Social Media Hyped Nicotine for a New Generation," read one CNN headline published days before news of the Altria investment broke—already made it hard to report to work every day with heads held high, amped about the company's mission. It felt like nobody cared to talk about the adults who used Juul for its intended purpose, only the youth vaping epidemic. "To see the amount of negative press about us . . . was kind of demoralizing," says a former employee. "It got to the point where people didn't want to show up." The Altria investment only gave journalists, tobacco control advocates, and the public more ammunition to work with.

On the same day that Juul Labs announced its partnership with Altria, it tried to promote the results of company-sponsored research on Juul's effectiveness for adult smokers. Ninety days after 4,200 adult smokers bought Juuls, 56 percent said they had completely switched to vaping for at least a month—an impressive result, albeit one that came from a study Juul itself had commissioned. This finding was completely lost in the sea of criticism about Juul Labs's relationship with Big Tobacco and its contribution to the youth vaping epidemic. Juul "has lost all credibility in claiming that it cares about public health," Campaign for Tobacco-Free Kids president Matt Myers said in a statement the day the deal was announced. "There is no longer any question that Juul has been the driving force behind the skyrocketing youth e-cigarette epidemic that has teens and families across the country struggling to deal with nicotine addiction."

Plus, if public perception of Juul grew even worse, it was hard to imagine Burns ever delivering on the dream of taking the company public, which many employees had wanted for years. "The market totally turned against Juul," a former employee says. "You can't go public in that type of situation." Already, its detractors were calling Juul Labs "Big Tobacco 2.0," and the investment from Altria only galvanized them.

Burns did his best to spin the investment when the news broke, but he was fighting a losing battle. People in tobacco control already saw the Altria deal as "the death knell for Juul," as NYU's Cheryl Healton called it—the final tear in Juul's already tattered reputation. Burns admitted in a statement that Altria was an "unlikely" and "seemingly counterintuitive partner" for Juul, but he stressed that the larger company's resources, connections to smokers, and knowledge about regulatory science, sales, and marketing could help "accelerate our success switching adult smokers" to e-cigarettes. That may have been true, but very few of Juul's adversaries saw it that way. To them, the deal was evidence that Juul's executives had never cared about health at all—or, at least, not as much as they cared about money and power.

FDA commissioner Scott Gottlieb was angrier than just about anyone; he was seething. He did not like to be embarrassed, and he had little tolerance for obfuscation. Two of the companies he was in charge of regulating had just gone around him, and he wasn't about to let that go. In an interview with the *New York Times* in January 2019, he called out the companies publicly. "Juul and Altria made very specific assertions in their letters and statements to the FDA about the drivers of the youth epidemic," Gottlieb told the newspaper. "Their recent actions and statements appear to be inconsistent with those commitments."

In Gottlieb's opinion, Juul and Altria had not only misrepresented their intentions and relationship, but they were also actively trying to undermine the FDA. A month after pulling flavored pods off store shelves to stay in line with proposed agency policy, Juul had accepted money and retail shelf space from a major tobacco company, making it that much easier for the company to sell its remaining products in stores. And Altria, for its part, had acknowledged that pod-based e-cigarettes were driving the youth vaping epidemic right before it invested in the country's dominant maker of pod-based e-cigarettes. Neither decision smacked of respect for the FDA's authority.

Gottlieb's staff had never found Juul Labs's team to be particularly authentic. Juul's executives periodically sent FDA officials letters about the company's youth prevention plans or its internal research or its efforts to clear the market of counterfeit vapes, but then the company would turn around and bad-mouth the FDA all over Washington, DC. Gottlieb would later say Juul and Altria were the "worst offenders," in terms of going around the FDA to lobby lawmakers directly. "I have never seen a lobbying campaign like this before," a senior congressional aide told the *Daily Beast* in 2019. "It's just crazy."

Tevi Troy, who had worked at the Department of Health and Human Services before joining Juul's public affairs staff, was a fixture at the White House, Gottlieb says. "The joke in the White House was that Tevi was still working there because they saw him up there so much," Gottlieb says. But the joke wasn't funny to Gottlieb. To him, Juul's constant lobbying was an effort to belittle the work the FDA was doing to make sure e-cigarettes were safe and appropriately used.

Gottlieb had always been caught in a political crucible. On one side, he had lawmakers tight with well-funded and well-connected advocacy groups like the CTFK, Bloomberg Philanthropies, PAVE, and the American Lung Association. These advocacy groups were very good at getting lawmakers, mostly Democrats, to rally behind ending the youth vaping epidemic—an epidemic that disproportionately affected upper-middle-class white kids. "The funders of the groups that are in the antivaping camp tend to be the same funders that are worried about their kids and grandkids vaping," says Steve Schroeder, the smoking cessation expert from UCSF. As a result, these groups often threw their weight behind advocating for tighter controls on e-cigarettes, such as restrictions on flavored products, stricter guidelines on where e-cigarettes could be sold, or all-out prohibition. Their single-highest priority was getting e-cigarettes out of underage hands, even if it meant that adults who used the products as cigarette alternatives might have a harder time getting them. For the Campaign for Tobacco-Free Kids, this intention was built right into its name. Stopping youth nicotine use was CTFK's entire guiding purpose, and issues involving kids always came first.

It seemed in part because of these voices, and the widespread cultural outrage related to youth vaping, that Gottlieb had come down as hard on e-cigarettes as he had. Matt Myers, the head of CTFK, says he met with Gottlieb frequently over the years and watched him grow more skeptical of e-cigarettes with time. "What changed for him was he realized that [between] the combination of marketing, and how the products deliver nicotine, and the flavors, that in fact there was a huge youth downside," Myers says. Gottlieb, for his part, says the numbers around youth vaping just became too dramatic to ignore.

Across the aisle, Gottlieb had to deal with conservative lawmakers who were deeply opposed to policies they thought restricted adults' choices or that might put small businesses like vape shops at risk. Their priorities were more in line with those of experts who preached harm reduction—both wanted e-cigarettes available to adults—but the lawmakers were often motivated as much by economic and anti-regulatory arguments as by public health. Smokers, who tend to be lower-income or from communities underrepresented in Washington, don't have too many big-money advocates on the Hill, Schroeder says.

In January 2019, Sen. Richard Burr, a Republican from North Carolina who in 2018 accepted eighty-seven thousand dollars from Altria, stood on the Senate floor and asked for Gottlieb's head on a silver platter. Gottlieb had recently floated the idea of banning menthol cigarettes, given that the minty flavoring arguably made them more appealing to young people. Burr was furious at this suggestion, arguing that a menthol ban would deprive Americans of free choice and states of tax money. "If you believe my argument is half accurate and this is ill-advised, for God's sake, pick up the phone and call the White House switchboard and tell the president that came in to reduce regulation that there's an agency that's not listening," Burr bellowed on the Senate floor.

These were the lawmakers who tended to be most receptive to tobacco companies' complaints about the FDA. And if they raised enough of a fuss, it could get back to the White House, where Juul's own lobbyists were often camped out, trying to make friends in the administration. If Juul could convince President Donald Trump that Gottlieb was going too far on vaping, and that it was making the Trump administration look bad, they might be able to get somewhere.

Under the best of circumstances, the FDA has to clear many hurdles to push through meaningful reforms, as the agency's rules undergo review at multiple levels of government. "We have those divergent points of view that we have to deal with when somebody wants to engage in a discussion with us, whether it's a member of Congress who's on one side or the other," says Mitch Zeller from the Center for Tobacco Products. "I'll just say that comes with the territory." Eric Lindblom, who used to work at the Center for Tobacco Products, says the agency's job was even harder with Trump as president. "Under Trump [it was] even more hostile, with an antiregulatory administration," Lindblom says. In that kind of climate, it's not hard to imagine Juul's lobbyists hitting a nerve.

In the midst of this partisan tug-of-war, Gottlieb shocked the public health world by announcing his sudden resignation from the FDA on March 5, 2019. He said he would finish out the month, then go home to spend time with his wife and three young children in Connecticut. The announcement sparked all kinds of speculation. Gottlieb plainly loved his position at the FDA. He called it "the best job I'll ever have," and yet he was leaving less than two years into it. He thrived in the spotlight, tweeting prolifically and rarely turning down a journalist's interview request. He did not seem like a man who would want to retire from government in his forties to go spend more time at home. People wondered if Trump had pushed him out, or if the pressure of regulating e-cigarettes had gotten to be too much, but Gottlieb dismissed all the speculation. He said the weekly commute from Connecticut to DC had become a grind—waking up at 3 a.m. every Monday to be on a flight by 6—and he insisted that he was tired of being away from his family. "It was getting lonely being in Washington all week," Gottlieb says.

Whatever the reason for Gottlieb's decision to leave, he wasn't gone yet. As one of his final acts as FDA commissioner, he demanded that Kevin Burns and Altria CEO Howard Willard come to the FDA's headquarters to explain what, exactly, had gone on behind his back at the end of 2018. Later, Gottlieb would describe the meeting as "very tense." This was putting it lightly.

On March 13, 2019, Burns, Willard, and their teams arrived at the FDA's imposing White Oak campus in Silver Spring, Maryland. Dotted with fifteen enormous brick buildings that, together, look not unlike a federal prison, White Oak was not the warmest or most welcoming of places to take a meeting—especially given that the FDA had announced just that morning that it was again moving the deadline for the PMTA, the document the e-cigarette companies needed to file to get FDA authorization for their products.

Gottlieb was reclaiming the borrowed time he'd lent the e-cigarette industry when he first joined the FDA. The agency had decided to shave off one of the four years Gottlieb had given e-cigarette companies to prepare their applications, moving the deadline for manufacturers of flavored products up from August 2022 to August 2021. For companies juggling dozens of studies and multimillion-dollar research budgets—or for smaller players trying to scrounge up the money required to piece together a solid application—having one less year to prepare was catastrophic. But Gottlieb didn't seem to care. In a press statement, he cited "the epidemic-level rise in youth e-cigarette use" as his motivation. When all was said and done, he warned, "We expect that some flavored e-cigarette products will no longer be sold at all."

With those words on his tongue, Gottlieb sat down to speak with Burns and Willard. Gottlieb had his senior staff with him, including Zeller from the Center for Tobacco Products. Burns brought his chief legal officer, his chief regulatory officer, and his chief public affairs officer. Willard brought his own executive team. Everyone settled around a conference table in the brick building that housed the commissioner's office, the tension in the air unmistakable. After they exchanged pleasantries, Gottlieb got down to business. He was deeply upset, and he wanted Burns and Willard to know exactly why. He launched into a monologue, his words flying out lightning fast as he grew more and more impassioned. He had nothing to lose, and he wasn't holding back.

"No other company that I've worked with at FDA behaves the way you do," Gottlieb began, his dark eyes fixed on Burns. "No other industry that we regulate behaves the way that you did, where you come in and make representations that you want to work with us on a critical public health problem and then you constantly go around us. You don't even try to work with us. The first thing you do is go to the White House to start to complain about what we're doing before you've really even given us a chance and engaged with us. No other company operates this way," he spat.

Gottlieb's words hung in the air. There wasn't much Burns could say in response, nor anything, at this point, that would change Gottlieb's mind. In that moment, all Burns could do was take the commissioner's verbal tirade on the chin, do his best to calm him down, and wait for the meeting to end. After all, Gottlieb would soon be ancient history.

16

Months after news of the Altria investment broke, Juul's public opinion ratings were at rock bottom—fewer than 10 percent of respondents said they viewed the company favorably in a Morning Consult poll conducted in March 2019.

Researchers who used to consult for Juul stopped returning employees' calls. Others said they'd talk, but only if there was no record of their conversations, anywhere. Employees kept turning in resignations—though there were hundreds of people waiting in the wings to take their spots, perhaps enchanted by headlines about $1.3 million payouts.

One former lobbyist says even other e-cigarette companies had come to see Juul as "the enemy that's throwing them under the bus" by souring the FDA, the media, and Congress on the entire vaping industry. The industry "really didn't have too much heat [on it], and then Juul came around," says Rob Crossley, CEO of Cosmic Fog Vapors. "Juul comes in with a high-powered nicotine device, huge numbers of youth using it, and now it's plastered all over the news 24/7." As the first vaping company to become a household name—and not in a good way—Juul was blamed by many in the industry for the increasingly strict regulations coming out of the FDA.

San Francisco residents were also up in arms, with some people who lived in the neighborhoods around Juul's headquarters rallying to kick the company off the city-owned land it currently occupied. "We demand that the Port of San Francisco take whatever measures available to it to remediate this slap to the face of our community," a local advisory group wrote to the San Francisco Port Commission, furious that it was allowing a tobacco company to occupy city property. Christine Chessen, the concerned mother who'd turned up at Juul's headquarters the previous summer, was part of this crowd and more fired up than ever.

In early 2019, Chessen started emailing back and forth with Meredith Berkman, the New York City mom who started Parents Against Vaping E-cigarettes after Juul representatives visited her son's school. Chessen and Berkman came from similar backgrounds. They were both politically connected and both well acquainted with the social scenes in their respective cities. They knew how to play the game and get people to listen to what they had to say, and they were brainstorming ways to take PAVE's message national. PAVE had become the de facto resource for parents struggling to help their kids quit vaping. The women had started to gain influence on the East Coast—Berkman and her friends hosted vaping education sessions for parents in New York City, personally responded to desperate letters from parents, collaborated with advocacy groups like Bloomberg Philanthropies and CTFK, and regularly wrote to lawmakers to ask for stricter regulations on vaping—but they could use motivated people like Chessen out in California, too.

Chessen had also started reaching out to people she knew around town, trying to capitalize on the anti-Juul momentum currently sweeping San Francisco. That list happened to include City Supervisor Shamann Walton and City Attorney Dennis Herrera, whom Chessen and her husband knew from working the San Francisco fundraising circuit. Herrera lived in San Francisco's Dogpatch neighborhood, so Chessen thought she might have some luck convincing him that a tobacco company had no place in his backyard. At the time, California's state lawmakers were considering a pair of bills that would limit or ban the availability of fla-vored vaping products statewide. As Herrera learned more about Juul and its presence in San Francisco, he grew intrigued.

"San Francisco has always had a history of getting involved in issues, especially when there's been federal inaction," he says. "In the face of this void [of federal regulation], I just thought it was incumbent on us and other states and localities to step up and protect our young people." In March 2019, Herrera announced that he was considering a plan more dramatic than any introduced by a U.S. city so far. He wanted to ban the sale of any e-cigarette product, flavored or unflavored, that had not been approved by the FDA—that is, all of them, including the products made by San Francisco's very own Juul Labs. "San Francisco has never been afraid to lead," Herrera said when he announced the plan, "and we're certainly not afraid to do so when the health and lives of our children are at stake."

Kevin Burns and his team at Juul, not to mention their customers, weren't moved by Herrera's rhetoric. In Herrera's ban, they saw a version of the future in which it would be easier to buy traditional cigarettes than e-cigarettes. Yes, youth vaping was a problem, and yes, it would take years to fully understand the long-term health effects of vaping; already, there were some worrying preliminary links to heart disease, respiratory issues, and DNA damage, all of which demanded further study. But everyone already knew, conclu-sively, that smoking was terrible for people's health. It seemed backward to ban vaping products without any commensurate action against combustible cigarettes, even in a progressive city like San Francisco, where relatively few people smoked. "It just absolutely makes no sense to say, 'We're not going to let you sell this safer product—but [cigarettes], which are the number one killer of consumers in the country, is perfectly fine,'" says Dr. Michael Siegel, a professor of community health sciences at the Boston University School of Public Health. "We're squandering the potential value of these products by essentially regulating them out of existence."

"You're talking about leaving a product, the single-most-lethal legalized product in the history of mankind, the cigarette, but not having [e-cigarettes available]," Burns marveled in a 2019 interview. Once again, it felt like smokers were being forgotten—that in lawmakers' increasingly dramatic attempts to get teenagers to stop vaping, the baby was being thrown out with the bathwater.

Shortly after Herrera's announcement, Ashley Gould and a few members of Juul's government affairs and scientific teams met with the city attorney at his office in San Francisco's grand Beaux Arts–style City Hall building, in the hope of stopping the plan before it went any further.

As they settled into the carved wooden chairs in Herrera's sun-dappled office, Gould laid out the company's case. "If you do this," she said evenly, "smokers are going to go back to cigarettes."

For plenty of adult smokers, vaping was the only thing that kept them from giving in to cigarette cravings, she argued. If Herrera banned vaping products while leaving cigarettes on the market, many of those people would be in danger of relapse, and people who wanted to experiment with nicotine might pick up cigarettes instead of vapes. A better strategy, she and her team argued, would be cracking down on retailers who sold e-cigarettes to minors. If it meant avoiding a ban, Burns was willing to pay for every store in San Francisco to install a high-tech new age-verification system the company was trying out. When a clerk scanned a Juul product, the store's sales system would lock up until the customer provided a valid, scannable government ID. The system also wouldn't let anyone buy multiple devices or more than four packs of pods in the same transaction, to cut down on the chances of people buying in bulk with the intent to resell. It would cost at least four million dollars to implement the system citywide, but Burns was willing to do it if it meant Herrera's staying away from an all-out ban.

Herrera listened politely to Gould's pitch, but it was clear she wasn't getting through. "I don't have any choice," he countered when she was finished, according to a source in the meeting. Youth vaping had become such a hot-button issue that he felt he had to react, and dramatically. The ban was going to move forward whether Juul liked it or not.

Juul was used to having harsh critics, but Herrera's ban was something else entirely. For Juul's own hometown, one of the country's largest cities, to ban vapor products outright seemed like not only a slap in the face, but also the start of a bad trend. If other cities followed San Francisco's lead, Juul's future looked very uncertain. Not only that, but the policy seemed like a bad indication of where nicotine regulations were going. If lawmakers were so keen on reining in youth vaping that they'd take e-cigarettes off the market while combustible cigarettes were still in just about every convenience store in America, it seemed like a bad sign not just for e-cigarette companies but also for the adults who were using vapor products legally. "I personally feel that it's ruining things for adults," a forty-nine-year-old Juul user and former clove cigarette smoker said in an interview shortly after the ban was proposed. Juul is "definitely a good avenue for adults to either quit or slow down. Now that the ban is proposed, it's going to make things a lot harder."

Rather than letting the ban go through, "Juul decided to pick up arms and fight it," says a company insider.

Shortly after the meeting with Herrera, the company began funneling money into a group called the Coalition for Reasonable Vaping Regulation, which was pushing for new e-cigarette sales standards in San Francisco rather than than an all-out ban. While the coalition was technically independent, it was propped up by Juul funding. Once it collected enough signatures to get a measure on the ballot, voters in San Francisco's November 2019 elections could opt to replace Herrera's ban with the coalition's alternative plan. The Juul-backed policy sought to keep vaping sales legal in San Francisco, with some added provisions to help eliminate youth use. Any store that sold e-cigarette products would need a permit and would be required to place limits on the number of products any one person could buy. There would be stricter penalties for stores caught selling to underage kids, and e-cigarettes would be available only in stores where you could also buy cigarettes. By the time Herrera's ban became final in June 2019, Juul had poured millions of dollars into the opposition campaign.

The decision to fight back against Herrera seemed like a mistake to some Juul Labs staffers, even if the ban did set a bad precedent. One high-level employee remembers stressing to a colleague that Juul should "disappear from the fight, because the harder we fight, the harder we get overwhelmed." With the youth vaping epidemic getting more airtime than ever, and with the Altria investment tanking Juul's reputation, the public, not to mention lawmakers and regulators, were already predisposed to be suspicious of everything Juul did. Even if its counter-legislation was spotless, anything Juul did to fight a ban on vaping in San Francisco would make it look bad, the employee thought.

All over the country, the Altria investment seemed to have awoken regulators and lawmakers who for years had mostly stood back and watched the e-cigarette industry operate. In May 2019, a federal judge ruled that the FDA needed to move faster on its efforts to regulate e-cigarettes and required the agency to set a new deadline for the filing of PMTAs: May 9, 2020, just a year away. The same month, North Carolina's Josh Stein became the first state attorney general to sue Juul Labs, arguing that the company had violated fair trade practices by purposely trying to attract and addict underage users with its flashy advertising and sleek, concealable device. (Juul later denied many of the complaint's allegations and filed a motion to dismiss the case, which was denied. As of January 2021, it was set for trial sometime later that year.) The anti-Juul outcry in San Francisco had grown fierce enough that Burns was actually planning to buy a twenty-eight-story, multimillion-dollar office tower downtown, just in case the city did evict the company from Pier 70. Things were not looking good. Some employees thought the company's only hope of pulling itself out of the swamp of public opinion was launching an all-out apology offensive, rather than fighting back against these various threats.

Step one was a marketing makeover. In the first half of 2019 alone, Juul paid an ad agency more than $100 million to design and place somber ads that were the polar opposite of the Vaporized campaign. Each ad opened with a title card warning that nicotine is an addictive chemical. Then an adult smoker, indisputably of legal age, would come on-screen to talk about his or her switch from cigarettes to the Juul. "I was a pack-a-day smoker for thirty-three years," a fifty-two-year-old woman says in one ad. Surrounded by colorful throw pillows on her couch in Florida, she described her switch to Juul "like a weight lifted off of you." The ad was noncontroversial, safe, boring. It was the campaign Juul should have launched with. The company had finally gotten the message—three years too late.

Marketing was only one piece of the puzzle, though. As Juul continued its influence campaign in Washington, a few political angles for redemption presented themselves. First and foremost, Kevin Burns continued to believe that Tobacco 21 laws, which raised the minimum age for purchasing tobacco to twenty-one, were the best way to curb the "existential threat" of teen vaping. Backing a policy that made it harder for teenagers to buy Juul products also seemed like a rare public relations victory for Juul. "We're more than willing to take any cut in sales or revenue to do the right thing and prevent underage use," Adam stressed in a 2019 interview.

It seemed like a win-win, especially now that Juul had the option of collaborating with strategists from Altria, whose political operation was a well-oiled, multimillion-dollar machine. Though the two companies didn't share a lobbying budget—Juul spent $4.3 million on lobbying in 2019, while Altria dropped more than $10.4 million—they were widely assumed to push the same priorities. "It's hard to say where Altria ends and Juul begins," a Campaign for Tobacco-Free Kids spokesperson told the New York *Times* in 2019.

In 2019, both companies doubled down on their support for Tobacco 21 laws. By the spring, Juul had spent $2 million on pro–Tobacco 21 advertising, while its national network of lobbyists set to work finding lawmakers who were open to the idea of pushing through Tobacco 21 legislation.

Meanwhile, in what seemed like an effort to get some much-needed Democratic support in Washington, the company began bringing on lobbyists with deep ties to the Black community, says a Republican lobbyist with knowledge of the company's strategy. The pitch was twofold. The first part was positioning vaping bans as a potential criminal justice issue, as such bans could criminalize the use of another vice product. Second was chipping away at the long and complicated history between the tobacco industry and Black America.

In the 1950s, a consumer preferences survey showed that Black Americans were slightly more likely than white Americans to say they preferred cigarettes flavored with menthol, a chemical found in mint plants. Over the next two decades, Brown and Williamson channeled marketing for its Kool menthol cigarettes toward heavily Black neighborhoods and publications, and the tobacco industry donated money to groups like the NAACP and the National Urban League. In part because of those campaigns, Black

Americans to this day smoke menthol cigarettes at much higher rates than people of other racial backgrounds, and according to CDC data, 70 percent of Black kids and teenagers who smoke choose menthols.

If Juul could frame itself as the product that would reverse that damage, offering communities of color a safer option than menthol cigarettes, it had a prayer of a chance at winning support from liberal elected officials from predominantly Black areas. The whole strategy had echoes of what Brown and Williamson had done decades earlier, but Juul tried to spin it as a public health intervention for communities that sorely needed one. "Do I think it's unseemly? Yes," says the Republican lobbyist. "Do I think Juul is the only company doing it? No." (In a statement to the *Daily Beast*, Juul said it works with people from all backgrounds to encourage vaping among adult smokers and discourage it among teenagers.)

Maybe so, but Juul's outreach to the Black community came crumbling down around the same time that its Tobacco 21 push blew up in its face. In June 2019, Juul gave a $7.5 million grant to Tennessee's Meharry Medical College, one of the nation's Historically Black Colleges and Universities. The backlash was swift, with activists accusing Juul of trying to make nicotine addicts out of a new generation of Black Americans. "Juul doesn't have African-Americans' best interests in mind," a spokeswoman for the National African American Tobacco Prevention Network told the *New York Times*. "The truth is that Juul is a tobacco product, not much unlike its demon predecessors."

Around the same time, health groups began pushing back on Juul- and Altria-supported Tobacco 21 bills introduced in states such as Florida, Arizona, and Virginia. The bills, they said, were full of holes. Sometimes they exempted certain populations, like members of the military. Sometimes they included weak enforcement provisions, if any at all, and let retailers that were caught selling to minors largely off the hook. Sometimes they preempted stricter local laws, like those that prohibited certain types of tobacco advertising or the sale of other kinds of flavored tobacco, or made it harder for local authorities to pass more aggressive legislation in the future.

Burns denied that Juul was purposely trying to get loose legislation passed, but he admitted that there were some things he just wouldn't stand for. "We've been supportive of T21, very clean T21," he said in 2019. "There are some things included in T21 state bills we'd be fine with. There are others [to which] we'd say no"— flavor bans, for example, since Juul stood by the rationale that adults use flavored products to switch away from cigarettes. Instead of backing bills with these additions, Juul's government affairs team would work with sympathetic lawmakers on getting alternative legislation passed, sometimes even by drafting new language in-house.

With these insertions and exemptions on the books, even health groups that supported Tobacco 21 took any opportunity they could to bash Juul. "The tobacco companies are masters at proposing or supporting bills that look good on the surface but often include provisions that are harmful to public health," a CTFK spokesperson told the Center for Public Integrity. "This is more a PR strategy than a serious effort to prevent youth use." Even when Juul tried to be on its best behavior, it sparked outrage—much to the chagrin of some people inside the company, who truly believed Juul's product could make a difference. "If what [health groups] wanted was for no one to smoke cigarettes and to save lives, then we'd all be on the same page," says one former employee. At times, the employee says, it felt like health groups just wanted to take their shots at Juul, rather than finding ways to work with the e-cigarette industry.

The company's image rehabilitation campaign extended to its own staff during the summer of 2019. A rumor started going around that Juul's executives had taken money budgeted for the company holiday party and used it to put together mandatory all-staff training in youth vaping prevention. Once upon a time, when it felt as if Juul were on an unstoppable rise to the top, its holiday parties had been big. In 2018, the company toasted the end of the year with a blowout bash at the San Francisco Giants baseball stadium. To go from that to a required youth prevention training course was, unsurprisingly, not a popular decision. "It just felt like we were going through the motions because we felt like we had to more so than we really wanted to," says an employee who worked there at the time. "Morale sucked at that point, so to say, 'Oh yeah, we're not doing a holiday party. Instead, we're going to do youth prevention training,' that's kind of a kick in the nuts."

"No one wanted to go, obviously," remembers another employee.

That feeling only intensified when everyone arrived at the venue. Every Juul employee based in San Francisco had been directed to report to a ballroom at one of the Pritzker family's Hyatt Hotels for the training. Holiday party money seemed to have gone toward Juul "swag" for employees, plus professionally printed booklets on youth prevention—and little else. The conference center quickly ran out of food, and everything got started late because Burns was stuck in another meeting across town. When things finally kicked off, Juul Labs's employees were hungry, bored, and annoyed.

Blissfully unaware, the company's head of HR made her big entrance. While employees gaped, she "galloped" down the ballroom's aisle to Tupac Shakur and Dr. Dre's "California Love"—a classic hip-hop song about partying in California that was released after Tupac spent much of 1995 in prison for a sexual abuse conviction. "For her to come out to that song, white as hell, to Tupac, at a youth prevention convention, it was so effing inappropriate," says an employee who was there. "My mind was blown."

Cheryl Healton, the dean at the NYU School of Global Public Health, watched the public parts of Juul's apology campaign with a mixture of sympathy and scorn. She'd been one of many, many public health experts who'd tried to steer Juul onto the right path as it grew, because she believed in e-cigarettes' potential for smokers. She'd warned Ashley Gould that the school visits were a bad idea, and she'd told Gould and other Juul executives that they needed to take the youth vaping epidemic seriously. They'd taken little of her advice, she says, pressing forward with ill-advised programs and paying the price for it later on. Numerous other tobacco control experts had similar stories.

If Juul was apologizing now, it was only because the company had ignored reason earlier. It had gone with its flashy launch campaign, organized an educational program, failed to understand the regulatory environment, and now it was rich with Big Tobacco's money. It was little surprise that people didn't take its product's merits seriously. "There was a point when they were the darling company, and they blew it," Healton says. "They've been walking it back ever since. All of the things they were trying to do to control youth access on the back end should have been done on the front end."

As Healton knew well, there was no way for Juul to un-ring the bell it had rung. The company's product had contributed to what the nation's top health officials called a youth nicotine addiction epidemic and stirred up an arguably more widespread epidemic of public derision. Neither problem would be easy to solve, but Juul was determined to try anyway.

At one point, Healton remembers getting a call from Gould and several other Juul executives. "They called me up and said, 'We really need to know about how to get kids off [e-cigarettes], because there are so many kids on nicotine,'" Healton remembers. "I said, 'Well I've got some bad news for you: There is no known treatment. That's what you've created, and it can't be fixed.'"

She hung up on the stammering Juul executives on the other end of the line and never advised them again.

17

ON TRIAL (JULY 2019)

Raja Krishnamoorthi never thought vaping would be his issue. The Illinois congressman had campaigned on promises to help the middle class and protect families like the one he had grown up in—families just trying to stay afloat and find a foothold in the United States. Krishnamoorthi's parents immigrated to the United States from India in 1973, when he was three months old, and his childhood had been defined by struggle. While his father studied engineering in Buffalo, New York, the family scraped by, trying desperately to make a new home for themselves in a foreign country that was sinking deeply into an economic recession. They made it through thanks to the "enormous generosity of the American people," which for the Krishnamoorthis came in the form of food stamps and public housing. Despite his difficult childhood, Krishnamoorthi worked hard in school and attended Princeton University, where he studied engineering. After a few years in consulting, he returned to school and got a degree from Harvard Law School. That degree eventually turned into a career in public service, which then turned into a successful U.S. House of Representatives run in 2016. When Krishnamoorthi took office in 2017, he did so with the goal of protecting hardworking Americans and their children. He just didn't know exactly what form that pledge would take.

When the father of three kept hearing from colleagues and reading news stories about a company blamed for getting teenagers addicted to nicotine, he felt compelled to look into it. The more he learned, the more concerned he became. He couldn't believe how many young people were vaping, or how much nicotine they were taking into their bodies when they did. "Given that we have kids at home and given how this thing, vaping, has just completely overtaken us in terms of a cultural phenomenon . . . I decided, 'This is something we have to look into, given that I have the power to do so,'" Krishnamoorthi says.

In June 2019, his team requested thousands upon thousands of pages of internal documents from Juul in the hope of learning more about the people who, depending on whom you asked, had either created the best smoking alternative in the world or had reversed decades of progress on youth anti-smoking efforts. "What really got me going was reviewing the documents," Krishnamoorthi says. As he and his team read through the files, he became increasingly suspicious. Much of what the company did in its early days— the splashy Vaporized ad campaign, the social media marketing, the launch parties, even the design of the product and its flavors—seemed intended to hook the very same young people the company now swore up and down it had never wanted as customers.

Krishnamoorthi wanted answers that old emails and marketing plans couldn't provide. As the chairman of the congressional Subcommittee on Economic and Consumer Policy, he decided to hold a hearing at which he could question the man whom he believed to be behind it all: James Monsees. (Krishnamoorthi was less interested in questioning Juul's cofounder, Adam Bowen.)

James had always been the vocal cofounder, the one who talked to the press and who had seemed to be, for better or worse, the visionary behind Juul and its direction as a company. He'd been CEO when Juul launched and when Ploom started taking money from Big Tobacco, and he'd been the one to spout off in interviews about how Ploom wasn't "an activist company" and that he didn't care if people smoked cigarettes instead. More recently, he'd taken to bragging about Juul's success, calling it in a spring 2019 interview "one of the greatest opportunities for public health in the history of mankind." Adam, for his part, had mostly worked behind the scenes. "We didn't feel [Adam] had a lot to add," Krishnamoorthi says. Republicans on his subcommittee suggested Ashley Gould, the company's chief administrative officer, as an alternative witness. Krishnamoorthi decided Gould could have her time to talk, but he wanted to question James face-to-face and under oath, so he couldn't "point the finger at someone else."

When Krishnamoorthi's office gave Juul official notice about the hearing, the company offered up CEO Kevin Burns to testify. The congressman's team declined. Krishnamoorthi wanted James, the man who had built Juul with his own two hands, to be alone in the hot seat. The hearing was set to go forward on July 24 and 25, 2019.

During the hearing's first day, Krishnamoorthi's subcommittee would hear from a variety of tobacco control experts and advocates, many of whom were staunchly opposed to vaping, motivated largely by the teen juuling epidemic. Ray Niaura, one of NYU's smoking experts, served as the lone harm-reduction advocate on the panel, trying, without much success, to make the case for e-cigarettes' potential for adult smokers. The hearing "was pure scripted TV," Niaura says, suggesting that it was meant to be antivaping propaganda. "Not a single Democrat asked me a question. I don't think they even looked at me."

Indeed, much of the hearing's two hours were taken up by doctors and activists bashing Juul and other vaping companies. Dr. Jonathan Winickoff, a pediatrician from Massachusetts General Hospital and a member of the American Academy of Pediatrics, spoke about the health risks of vaping, from addiction to potential lung disease.

Stanford's Robert Jackler testified about what he called Juul's "patently youth-oriented" early marketing and recalled his meeting with James Monsees the previous summer—the one during which, as Jackler described it, James admitted to modeling Juul's launch campaign after cigarette ads. "He thanked us for a database that we have of fifty thousand traditional tobacco ads online," Jackler told Congress. "He said they were very helpful as they designed Juul's advertising."

Meredith Berkman from Parents Against Vaping E-cigarettes gave a dramatic statement about Juul's effects on children across the country—including her son, Caleb, who also testified to recount the visit Juul's representatives paid to his ninth-grade classroom the year before. Berkman begged Congress to hold Juul accountable for hooking teenagers on nicotine. "It is not a political issue, but a moral one," Berkman said gravely. "If we don't take action now, we face an entire generation of kids addicted to nicotine, who are human guinea pigs for the Juul experiment overall."

Despite all the powerful doctors and activists on the panel, perhaps the most stirring testimony of the day came from a woman whose name few people knew. Rae O'Leary came from a small South Dakota–based organization called the Canli Coalition of the Cheyenne River Sioux Tribe (CRST). O'Leary, herself a member of the Turtle Mountain Band of Chippewa, founded the Canli Coalition in 2009 to help the CRST commit to a tobacco-free lifestyle after decades of rampant tobacco use and high rates of smoking-related disease. American Indians smoke at much higher rates than any other demographic group in the United States, in part because of cultural traditions that involve tobacco and in part because, as sovereign nations, tribes are not subject to most U.S. laws and regulations around tobacco use. O'Leary's work focused on reversing that trend.

Testifying before Congress, O'Leary re-created the day earlier that year when she'd gotten a cryptic text message from a member of the CRST's tribal leadership. "I think you'd better come down here," the message read.

O'Leary hurried over to the room where she knew tribal leaders were meeting. There, she found some unexpected guests: representatives from Juul Labs. They were midway through a pitch about their proposed "switching program" for Native American tribes, which the company later described to the congressional subcommittee as a possible option for "individuals aged 21+ who were current smokers and sought to switch away from using combustible cigarettes." As part of the program, Juul would provide tribal leaders with heavily discounted Juul devices and pods, which they could then distribute for free to adult tribe members who wanted to stop using combustible cigarettes. The Juul representatives said they would build out and foot the bill for an online portal where participants could record information about their health and smoking behaviors, tracking their progress as they switched from smoking to juuling. The company was prepared to spend six hundred thousand dollars just to get the program off the ground, the Juul representatives said, and roughly thirty thousand dollars a month to keep it going. Some tribal leaders were intrigued, O'Leary told lawmakers during the congressional hearing, but she was immediately horrified.

Nothing about the pitch, one similar to Juul's outreach to the Black community, sat right with O'Leary. "The CRST may have looked like an easy target for Juul because of the FDA's inability to enforce tobacco regulations [due to tribal sovereignty] or publish reports of our 51 percent adult smoking prevalence, coupled with our genetic predisposition to addiction," O'Leary told Congress. "Or maybe they were drawn to CRST because of our young population base or recent status as the poorest county in the nation."

To O'Leary, the whole thing had too many echoes of Big Tobacco, which had tried to foist cigarettes on Native American tribes by taking advantage of tribal autonomy and playing up cultural associations with tobacco, a plant considered sacred by many tribes. Cigarette companies had tried every trick in the book to get American Indians smoking—offering discounts, giving away free products, making charitable contributions to tribal causes—and in O'Leary's eyes, Juul was doing the same thing, albeit with a slicker pitch and a techier product.

Whatever benefits Juul's products might have brought to the CRST, she felt, were outweighed by the company's behavior in pitching them. "It's a little bit of a case of smoke and mirrors," O'Leary said in an interview. "It's saddening. The tobacco industry and e-cigarette industry sees us as a vulnerable population, one they can take advantage of." (A few months after O'Leary's testimony, Krishnamoorthi's office published documents from Juul that showed that the company had made similar pitches to at least seven other tribes between late 2018 and early 2019.) If they hadn't before, some of the nation's top lawmakers now seemed fairly convinced that Juul Labs was a sinister company out to hook the nation's most vulnerable people on nicotine. Senator Dick Durbin, who sat in on the hearing, drove that point home in his closing statement. "Make no mistake," Durbin said. "Juul, now partnered with tobacco giant Altria, is driving this epidemic, even as they come before this committee and pose for holy pictures."

The previous day's statements hung heavy in the air as James Monsees and Ashley Gould entered the congressional chamber on July 25 to take their turns in front of Krishnamoorthi's panel. James was up first. He sat at a long table, a notepad and a bottle of water beside him. He wore a dark tailored suit and tie, but hadn't bothered to shave the beard on his chin. He couldn't hide the dark circles under his eyes, and his voice sounded gravelly. He did not give off the essence of a man in charge of his own destiny, nor that of a tech billionaire. He looked like a man about to walk the plank.

Still, he had no choice but to clear his throat and give an opening statement. "Thank you, Mr. Chairman, ranking member, distinguished Members of Congress. My name is James Monsees," he began. "Adam Bowen and I founded Juul Labs, and I now serve as the chief product officer of that company. I am really quite grateful for the opportunity to be here today and address you all. From the moment Adam and I began the journey that would lead to the Juul system, we were clear in our goal—to help improve the lives of adult smokers." James's opening statement sounded like every press statement Juul Labs had given over the last year: part apology, part mission statement, part plea for someone, anyone, to listen when they said they had only tried to do the right thing. "Mr. Chairman, put simply, Juul Labs isn't Big Tobacco," James said. "We are here to eliminate its product, the cigarette."

Chairman Krishnamoorthi, seated at an imposing wooden dais directly across from James, sat stone-faced throughout his opening statement. When James wrapped up, Krishnamoorthi set the tone with his initial five minutes of questioning. Almost immediately, he zeroed in on Robert Jackler's claims from the previous day—specifically, his allegation that James had thanked Jackler for compiling tobacco ads, as they had been so inspirational when he and Adam were designing Juul's marketing. Mere minutes into the hearing, James was forced onto the defensive.

"I think that, unfortunately, Dr. Jackler may have misheard my commentary," he told Krishnamoorthi, choosing his words carefully. "In fact, the resource that he compiled is a useful resource. Back when Adam and I were at Stanford we were very interested in understanding more about the historical bad actions of tobacco companies, and at that point we were very interested in using [Jackler's] research to understand exactly what bad actions those tobacco companies have taken, to familiarize ourselves with how *not* to run a business." Krishnamoorthi looked and sounded unconvinced. His questioning was surely not the reception James had hoped for, but it was good preparation for what was to come.

As each lawmaker took his or her turn questioning James, asking about everything from Juul Labs's flavors to its marketing to the way it branded its packaging, James again and again emphasized that Juul had never meant for kids to use its product, that all he had ever wanted was to give smokers like him a better choice. The words were right, but this was not the swaggering, charismatic braggadocio of even a few years ago. He seemed defeated, subdued into submission.

There were flashes of the old James, at times. "This isn't my favorite thing, to be here today," he quipped after Republican Jim Jordan, one of a few lawmakers on the panel who applauded Juul's work, threw him a lifeboat by voicing support for Juul and its mission. Then, apparently remembering where he was, he quickly added, "But I'm happy to do it." Occasionally he gave answers with his trademark smirk. But, by and large, he did not give off the air of an untouchable Silicon Valley billionaire. Quietly, he was showing cracks in the foundation. "I don't think he acquitted himself as well as he could have," Krishnamoorthi said afterward. "Some of the lawmakers perceived him to be a little casual with the facts."

This was on full display nearly an hour into James's testimony, when California congresswoman Katie Hill took the microphone. She began to read from Juul's 2015 contract with Grit Creative Group, the marketing firm that had pledged to provide at least 280 social media influencers with free products as Juul got off the ground. A letter prepared by Juul executives before the hearing claimed that the company had never used a formal celebrity or influencer marketing program to sell its products and had paid only four social media influencers throughout the company's entire history. This contract seemed to refute that claim directly, as Hill pointed out to James during the hearing.

"Uh, I—I'm sorry," James stammered. "I don't have a copy of that document."

"Is there a reason Juul failed to mention these 280 influencers in your response to the subcommittee?" Hill asked.

"I'm sorry, I'd have to at least take a look at the document," he replied.

"It's information you provided us," she shot back.

"There were a lot of documents we provided," James said, visibly flustered. "I'm sorry."

Hill forged on, pressing James again and again on how the company had used influencers. If it didn't use influencers, why had it needed Grit? Why did internal documents highlight celebrities who could potentially serve as Juul influencers? "You said, a moment ago, that you did not have a traditional celebrity or influencer program. Do you want to maintain that?" Hill asked.

"It sounds like we're getting into territory I'm not completely familiar with," Monsees replied, "so I, um, I'm more than happy to look into it."

The exchange was painful, but it was not unique. Multiple times, James claimed not to recall or know the answers to lawmakers' questions. Other times, he punted by saying he'd need to consult with his staff. "That is mind-boggling that you don't know the answer," Florida congresswoman Debbie Wasserman Schultz marveled after James claimed not to understand a question about the device's temperature-control features. Later, Michigan representative Rashida Tlaib reminded James that "when you say, 'I don't know' and you actually know, it is actually lying, too." The Democrats seemed to be enjoying the opportunity to rake James over the coals—perhaps none more so than California congressman Mark DeSaulnier. "You, sir, are an example to me of the worst of the Bay Area," he spat at James. "You don't ask for permission—you ask for forgiveness. You are nothing but a marketer of a poison, and your target has been young people."

Finally, Texas Republican representative Michael Cloud addressed the elephant in the room: he asked James why Kevin Burns, the company's CEO, wasn't there to testify alongside him. The answer, of course, was that Krishnamoorthi's office had denied Juul's request for Burns to appear. But James, probably truthfully, said he didn't know. "Kevin," James admitted, "could have certainly helped answer some of these questions more defin-itively, or with some more clarity." To the members of Krishnamoorthi's panel, the answer probably came off as flippant—after all, why should the company's founder, one of only two men who had been there since the beginning, stumble over their questions? It must have seemed like yet another dodge. But, in reality, James had just showed his hand: there really was a lot he didn't know about the inner workings of Juul. In fact, it had been years since he'd been the one calling the shots.

Things didn't improve much when Ashley Gould took her turn before the subcommittee. Lawmakers grilled her about Juul's school visits, which she had overseen the previous year. She emphasized that all the vaping education programs were over and had ended as soon as public health experts warned Juul about their implications. "We had hired educational experts to help us come up with a program that we felt would be helpful to stop kids using Juul," Gould explained. "We then received feedback that that was not well perceived, and, in addition, received input from a public health expert telling us what tobacco companies had previously done, which we were not aware of. As a result of all that information, we stopped that program."

But for Krishnamoorthi, Gould had said all he needed to hear within moments of beginning her opening statement: "I do not want my sons to ever touch Juul products," she said. "I have told them that directly, and many times." In this statement, Krishnamoorthi says he heard an admission of guilt—proof that Gould and other Juul Labs executives cared enough to keep their own children away from the company's products, but not enough to do the same for teenagers across the country.

18

Daniel Ament was going to die. Dr. Hassan Nemeh realized this clearly as he looked down at the emaciated sixteen-year-old boy in the bed before him. The once-athletic, healthy teenager lay incapacitated in a room at the Children's Hospital of Michigan, hooked up to an ECMO life support machine that had taken over when his lungs could no longer do their job. It was obvious to Nemeh, a thoracic surgeon at Detroit's Henry Ford Hospital, that Daniel didn't have much time left. A lung transplant could save him, but he would need to be transferred from Children's Hospital to Henry Ford for the surgery—and Nemeh wasn't at all sure the teen's fragile body could survive even a few seconds off ECMO as he was prepped for transfer.

But Nemeh's hands were tied. Even on ECMO, Daniel wasn't getting any better and, indeed, seemed to be slowly spiraling toward death. Transferring him to a portable ECMO machine that might sustain him for as long as it took to travel the few miles to Henry Ford was the only feasible solution, but even that was no guarantee. Nemeh and his team knew, even as they unhooked him, that Daniel might die in the eight to ten seconds it would take to get him reattached to the portable version. His lungs were that spent. "We were against the wall," the surgeon remembers. "We had only one option: we had to transplant him."

The teen's saga began during the summer of 2019, when a friend left a Juul in Daniel's car and he kept it. Because he was an athlete, he'd long resisted vaping, even though his classmates had been using e-cigarettes since the eighth grade. But when a knee injury sidelined him in late 2018, he lost his primary motivator to stay away. After his friend left a Juul in his car, he found himself hitting it every day, then multiple times a day, then constantly. He vaped Juul's nicotine e-juices mostly, but sometimes he and his friends used e-liquids containing THC, the psychoactive component of marijuana. Daniel swore he'd quit by the time school and cross-country practice started back up in the fall of 2019, and as the summer after his sophomore year came to a close, he took his last hit.

He didn't think much of it when he woke up on the second day of his junior year with a headache, back pain, fatigue, and a fever. He dragged himself to class anyway, afraid of falling behind so early in the semester. The next day, though, he woke up feeling just as bad and was forced to admit he shouldn't be at school. He went to see his pediatrician, who told him he probably had pneumonia and sent him home.

Back at home, he began struggling to breathe. By the time his mother drove him to the emergency room at Ascension St. John Hospital on September 4, 2019, it seemed like Daniel had something much worse than pneumonia. He spilled his secrets to the doctors in the ER: Juul, vaping, THC, all of it. The last thing he remembers is being taken upstairs to the hospital room where his lungs began to fail.

In a roundabout way, Daniel knew to mention his vaping habit only because of work done months earlier by Dr. Lynn D'Andrea, a pulmonologist at Children's Wisconsin, a hospital in Milwaukee. She'd been working the pediatric intensive care unit there over Independence Day weekend 2019. Hospitals typically brace for plenty of drunken injuries, yard game mishaps, and fireworks burns over the holiday weekend. But D'Andrea wasn't prepared for three different teenagers to come in with signs of strange lung damage.

"All of them came in with the same symptoms: fever, shortness of breath, this rather unusual bilateral pneumonia pattern on their chest x-ray,"

D'Andrea remembers. "And they weren't necessarily getting better with just antibiotics."

As she tried to figure out what was going on, D'Andrea thought back to a couple of strange cases her colleagues at the hospital had seen at the start of the summer. Their cases looked awfully similar to those of the three young people she was now treating. It was highly abnormal for a handful of previously healthy teenagers to come in with a severe pneumonia-like illness, and within roughly the same span of time during the summer. The fact that none of them was responding to standard treatment was even more unusual. D'Andrea decided to perform a bronchoscopy on each of her three patients, to get a better look at their lungs. "That was the aha moment," she says. Their lungs did not suggest they had pneumonia. Instead, "some were red and inflamed. Other had little burn marks in them." Their lungs didn't look like they'd been infected by a virus or bacteria; they looked like they'd been injured by inhaling something toxic.

D'Andrea knew she was onto something; she just wasn't quite sure what. After she got the bronchoscopy results, she rushed upstairs to find her colleague, pediatric ICU medical director Dr. Michael Meyer. He was on the unit's fourth floor, preparing to examine one of her young lung disease patients. D'Andrea stopped him before he went into the room. "I've got to tell you, this is not infectious," she said, her voice deadly serious. "I don't know what this is right now, but I'm willing to bet anything this is not an infection. We need to change how we're looking at this."

Meyer agreed. Nothing about these patients' conditions seemed like a typical infection. The chest x-rays and CT scans were all coming back abnormal, and the patients weren't doing well on antibiotics that would normally have wiped out something like pneumonia. If the two doctors were right, and these patients were sick because they'd been exposed to a dangerous substance, they knew the problem was probably bigger than just their hospital. There could be something out there sickening people across the whole city or state—maybe even the whole country.

D'Andrea worked the case reports up the chain of command to the hospital's chief medical officer, who reported the cluster of patients to the Wisconsin Department of Health Services. Once the department put out an alert to other medical centers in the area, a few other hospitals responded, saying they'd treated similar cases, mostly among younger adults and teenagers. And the patients just kept rolling in.

By the end of July 2019, Children's Wisconsin had treated ten young patients with mysterious lung damage. D'Andrea still didn't know exactly what she was dealing with, but with each patient who came through the door, she was learning more and more. Eventually, she took an educated guess and started treating her patients with steroids, which are used to fight many lung diseases stemming from exposure to toxic substances. The therapy seemed to be working, but it was a leap of faith. She still didn't know exactly what these patients had, and if they *were* sick with an infectious disease after all, steroids could actually make it worse.

"It was uncomfortable," D'Andrea admits. "You don't want to hurt someone while you're trying to help them." Still, the more kids who came through the doors at Children's Wisconsin, and the more doctors D'Andrea talked to in other parts of the state, the surer she got that these kids did not have pneumonia or any other infection. Over time, she and her colleagues were able to piece together a pattern: all the patients who were well enough to answer questions said they had vaped within the month prior to getting sick. It seemed to be the common thread among them. The question was: Which products were causing this severe damage, and why?

"The piece I wish we [had] jumped on," says D'Andrea's colleague Meyer, is that the disease looked similar to something he'd seen frequently as a medical fellow in the early 2000s: injuries from ingesting lamp oil. Back then, it was common for restaurants to decorate their tables with candles or lamps filled with oil in pretty colors. Sometimes kids would drink the oil, mistaking it for juice. They'd usually throw it up quickly, but even a tiny bit of exposure to the toxic oil could damage their lung tissue, making it difficult to breathe. "As this evolved, that's where my mind went to," Meyer says. But back in July 2019, he wasn't there yet.

In early August, Brian King, the deputy director of research translation for the CDC's Office on Smoking and Health, got a media inquiry from a reporter asking about a cluster of strange lung diseases at a Wisconsin pediatric hospital. King didn't know too much about it, so he referred the reporter to the Wisconsin Department of Health Services and went about his day. He was soon interrupted again.

"Within a matter of hours," King says, "we started to hear from the state [of Wisconsin] in terms of the potential cluster." Officials from Wisconsin's health department told King that people kept turning up at hospitals across the state with a strange form of lung injury. Nobody knew exactly what it was, but the working theory was that it was linked to vaping. Officials from Illinois reported something similar not long after. This made King sit up a little straighter. "Once you start getting into multiple states reporting the same thing that's out of the ordinary, that's really the clarion call when it comes to public health outbreaks," King says. The fact that vaping seemed to be at the root of things only added intrigue. "We've always known that e-cigarette aerosol is not harmless," King says, "but this seemed to be distinct" from the kind of long-term risks the CDC worried about.

On August 17, 2019, the CDC publicly announced that it was investigating "a cluster of pulmonary illnesses linked to e-cigarette product use." Children's Wisconsin had sounded the original alarm, but from late June to mid-August of that summer, a total of ninety-four people across the country had shown signs of this new and perplexing lung injury. (Eventually, the CDC named it "E-cigarette or Vaping Product Use–Associated Lung Injury," or EVALI.) Most of the patients were adolescents or young adults, according to the CDC, and although the exact cause of their illnesses remained under investigation, they all seemed to trace back to vaping.

The story was catnip for the media. It had everything: a dramatic, mysterious illness mostly affecting young people, apparently caused by an industry that many people already loved to hate. Between news reports and social media, many of the unlucky people who'd fallen ill with EVALI found themselves overnight online celebrities. In Florida, eighteen-year-old Chance Ammirata, who started juuling in 2017 in his high school culinary class, went viral for tweeting a photo of his diseased lungs after undergoing emergency surgery. In California, eighteen-year-old Simah Herman had her own viral moment at the end of August, racking up almost a million likes on an Instagram photo of herself, pale-faced in a hospital bed after days of intubation, holding a piece of loose-leaf paper scrawled with the words, "I want to start a no vaping campaign."

Plenty more stories like these were going untold, except in the CDC's ever-climbing tally of people who had suffered vaping-related lung injuries. On August 23, the agency said it had counted almost two hundred confirmed cases of EVALI. One person, an adult in Illinois, had died from the condition. "This tragic death in Illinois reinforces the serious risks associated with e-cigarette products. Vaping exposes users to many different substances for which we have little information about related harms," CDC director Dr. Robert Redfield said in a statement after the death was announced. "CDC has been warning about the identified and potential dangers of e-cigarettes and vaping since these devices first appeared."

Kevin Burns was skeptical, a former Juul employee remembers. The CDC was taking great pains to say it had no idea what could be causing these lung injuries, and its spokespeople emphasized over and over, in statements and press conferences, that any e-cigarette product could be dangerous. But to Burns, it seemed obvious that Juul's products weren't to blame. Millions of people had been using Juul e-cigarettes for years, and nothing like this had ever happened before. "If [Juul] was causing some 'death pneumonia,'" Burns apparently told his executive team during a staff meeting shortly after the EVALI news broke, "we would have seen mass deaths by now."

Still, just to be safe, Burns asked his science team to do a full workup of Juul's pods, quadruple-checking that the company's hands were clean. Juul's scientists ran analyses on Juul pods in every flavor and nicotine strength, looking for signs of tainted products or foreign substances that could have caused the lung injuries the CDC was describing. They found nothing, according to a former employee with knowledge of the testing. Next, they hired an outside laboratory to test Juul-compatible pods made by competitors and black-market brands, just in case people were getting sick from knockoff pods they thought had been legitimately made by Juul. "We found concerning things in these products," says a source with knowledge of the testing, "but nothing so concerning that it would cause death."

It seemed safe to say Juul pods and devices, and even illegal knockoff Juul products, were not to blame for the outbreak. After a few weeks of testing, the company's scientists summarized their findings in a letter to the CDC detailing the company's testing procedures and conclusions and offering to cooperate with the investigation.

Brian King acknowledges that the CDC received that letter, but he says the agency chose not to work with Juul. "There really wasn't much added benefit," King says. Plus, "early on . . . it became apparent that although a sizable portion of patients reported using nicotine-containing products, the percent of nicotine-only use was about 15 percent. [The lung condition] was clearly driven by THC-containing products, which aren't necessarily produced by major e-cigarette companies[,] including Juul."

Indeed, data from the CDC and the FDA showed as early as August 2019 that most people who got sick had vaped products containing THC, not those made by nicotine e-cigarette companies like Juul. Some people—like Michigan teenager Daniel Ament, who went on to recover after receiving a successful double-lung transplant—had also vaped nicotine, but very few of the patients had used *only* nicotine. The vast majority had used THC before they got sick. Still, federal investigators were hesitant to point the finger at THC specifically.

When the CDC held a press briefing on August 23 to confirm the first EVALI-related death, journalists asked over and over whether the problem likely traced back to THC cartridges, which were subject to even fewer regulations than nicotine vaping products and were more likely to be purchased illegally. Despite what seemed like fairly clear-cut data, the CDC refused to draw firm conclusions. "Investigators haven't identified any product or compound linked to all of the cases," the CDC's Ileana Arias said on the August 23 press call. Until its investigators could be sure, the CDC urged people to stay away from all vaping products. ("We are a data-driven agency, so we follow the data to inform our decision making,"

King says now, adding that there wasn't enough data at that point to make an assessment.)

With the CDC refusing to clear its name, Juul was in trouble. The lung disease panic was getting through to people, especially young people, in ways that boring health warnings from the CDC and the FDA hadn't been able to. People were panicking, afraid of developing lung injuries like the ones they'd seen splashed across the evening news. During the EVALI crisis, Google searches for terms like "quit vaping" spiked almost fourfold, a study later found. Teenagers like Chance Ammirata, who had posted online about his own experience, were flooded with Instagram messages from people vowing never to vape again. "I got tens of thousands of messages. It was absolutely insane," Ammirata says. "I tried to reply to as many as I could. I was scrolling through my phone, and the list didn't end. Most of the people that were sending me those messages were quitting their vaping devices."

Juul was seeing all this play out in its balance sheet. "You just saw the numbers tank week to week," remembers a high-level former staffer. Kevin Burns and his executives usually lived for Monday mornings, when they got the new Nielsen Consumer Insights data tracking cigarette and vaping product sales. For years, they'd watched cigarette sales steadily go down as Juul's sales continued to grow, an indication that people were indeed switching from cigarettes to e-cigarettes. "Then when [the lung outbreak] hit," the former staffer says, "the cigarette number starts going back up, and the Juul growth number goes negative." People seemed to be giving up their e-cigarette habits. The question was whether they were recreational e-cigarette users quitting outright, former smokers going back to combustible cigarettes, or some combination of the two.

In late August 2019, Burns agreed to an on-camera interview with *CBS This Morning*'s Tony Dokoupil. Wearing a pale purple button-down shirt and a serious expression, Burns tried to defend Juul and redirect the conversation about EVALI to THC products. "Most [cases] that have any specifics have said they're related to THC," Burns told Dokoupil. "We don't have the details on all those reports. If there was any indication that there was an adverse health condition related to our product, I think we'd take very swift action associated with it." Dokoupil was clearly unconvinced. "I don't know about *most*" cases being linked to THC, he responded skeptically. But Burns was right: most cases at that point *had* been linked to THC. Still, there wasn't much else he could say without looking defensive or combative. His hands were tied.

Juul, at that moment, was persona non grata; nearly everything the company did—school visits, grant funding, advisory groups, lobbying campaigns—had blown up in its face, held up as an example of an evil empire out to addict kids and fool parents. Some of the criticism was well deserved, but it was also relentless enough that it colored the way people perceived of anything the company did, well intended or not. Over time, Juul's executives had learned that the best way to make headlines go away was to ignore them. But this time, the headlines weren't going away.

19

ILLICIT PRODUCTS (JUNE–SEPTEMBER 2019)

Tyler Huffhines had developed quite the reputation around his hometown of Paddock Lake, Wisconsin. His mother was a realtor, which gave the family a certain amount of name recognition, and Tyler was a hotshot football player over at Westosha Central High School. But Tyler was really making a name for himself as a businessman. In the spring of 2018, when he was an eighteen-year-old high school senior, a journalist at the local paper wrote a glowing piece on his entrepreneurial abilities—specifically, buying and reselling luxury sneakers. "But his business model is not just shoes," the reporter wrote. "He is willing to buy and sell anything, if there's a profit to be had."

That line turned out to be somewhat prophetic. By the summer of 2019, selling THC was allegedly a family affair for the Huffhines. Based on what investigators later pieced together, Tyler and his older brother, Jacob, had put together one of the largest THC rings in all of Wisconsin. Their mother was apparently even in on the business. She'd allegedly used someone else's name to rent out a condo in Bristol Bay, Wisconsin, so Tyler could use it as home base for his drug operation. Tyler, according to law enforcement officials, would hire runners to drive out to California (where marijuana is legal), so they could pick up jars of THC distillate and drive it back to Wisconsin (where it is not). He apparently used the condo his mother had rented as a combination laboratory and factory. Tyler retained a staff of roughly a dozen people, who'd clock in and out with actual time cards. For twenty dollars an hour each, they'd heat and liquify the THC, then use syringes to inject the oil into plastic cartridges people could use in their vape pens. These cartridges were then allegedly distributed to Tyler's fleet of dealers, who'd sell the cartridges all over Kenosha County and beyond.

In June 2019, one of those dealers got busted. His parents found a collection of THC cartridges and cash in his bedroom and turned them over to the Waukesha Police Department. Investigators convinced him to give up the person providing him with the drugs to sell, which set them off on a chain of interviews that eventually led to Tyler Huffhines. Justin Rowe, a Waukesha detective working the case, trailed Tyler until he had a pretty good idea of where he was running his operation. He found a real estate listing for the address online and cross-referenced photos of the property with posts on Tyler's Snapchat account. The name on the condo's lease wasn't familiar, but the rental agreement had been handled by Courtney Huffhines, Tyler's mother.

On September 5, 2019, Waukesha officers raided the condo and found more than thirty thousand cartridges filled with THC vaping oil, more than fifty one-liter mason jars full of THC distillate, and hundreds of boxes in which the e-liquid cartridges would eventually be sold. The packages were stamped with dozens of flavors and brand names, but two came up most often: "Dank Vapes" and "Cookie." By Rowe's estimation, the street value of everything his team found in the condo easily topped $2 million. When Rowe arrested Jacob and Tyler Huffhines at their home, he found another $48,000 in cash on Tyler's bedroom nightstand and $11,000 and a loaded AR-15 rifle on Jacob's. Days after the raid, police obtained a shipping container rented in Tyler Huffhines's name filled with even more cartridges and packaging.

All three Huffhines pled not guilty to the charges against them when they were arraigned in October 2019. They each subsequently rejected plea bargains in the summer of 2020; their cases had not been tried as of January 2021.

The sheer magnitude of the Huffhineses' alleged vaping ring made it impossible to ignore, but Rowe had extra motivation for pursuing the case. He'd gotten a few tips from informants who said they used THC cartridges from the Huffhineses' operation and then landed in the hospital, a claim Huffhines's lawyer said was baseless. With a vaping-related lung disease out-break tearing through the United States, Rowe had a hunch that getting these products out of circulation could be potentially lifesaving. He didn't know why people were getting sick after vaping, or how, but he knew it was scary. "You can do so much more than putting some [marijuana] flower in a bowl and smoking it. There are so many different ways to consume this stuff," Rowe says. "You don't know what's being put in it."

When news of the lung disease crisis broke, Juul was pulled into the media fray. To many people, "juuling" had become virtually synonymous with "vaping," so it was logical enough to wonder whether its products might be involved in the outbreak. After all, the CDC had included the word *e-cig-arettes* in the official name assigned to the new lung disease: "E-cigarette or Vaping Product Use–Associated Lung Injury." To most people knowl-edgeable about vaping, the word *e-cigarette* specifically connoted a cigarette alternative product containing nicotine, rather than a vaporizer used for marijuana. By naming the disease EVALI, the CDC seemed to be implying that e-cigarette manufacturers like Juul were potentially to blame.

But as Rowe's informants told him during the summer of 2019, and as the CDC's own data showed, many of the people getting sick weren't juuling or using other nicotine e-cigarettes. They were vaping THC, often purchased from illicit sources. And as Rowe rightly pointed out, it was extremely diffi-cult to know if dealers and distributors were adding dangerous ingredients to their THC liquids. Juul's executives had been concerned about the burgeoning market of counterfeit and illicit vaping liquids for some time—in part because cheap knockoff products were stealing their market share and in part because vaping products without safety and manufacturing standards could get people sick and make the whole industry look bad. "When you talk about brand protection, you talk about health and safety as part of that," says a former member of Juul's legal team whose duties included cracking down on illegal producers. The lung disease crisis seemed to be dragging Juul's name through the mud and fulfilling executives' worst brand-protection nightmares.

By the summer of 2019, one substance seemed to be turning up increasingly often in bootleg THC products: vitamin E acetate, an oily, synthetic form of vitamin E that's frequently used in beauty and food products. While reputable cannabis vaping companies like Juul's sister organization, Pax, didn't touch the stuff, some distributors were making frequent use of it. They'd buy vitamin E acetate solution by the gallon, mix it with a small amount of THC distillate, and then apportion the concoction into pods. If the vitamin E acetate was good, it would pay for itself very quickly. Producers could sell THC cartridges watered down with vitamin E acetate while duping users into paying full price—but only if the stuff was good.

A pure THC liquid is thick enough that when a user flips over a pod, they can see air bubbles moving slowly through the solution as if pushing through molasses. When a cartridge has been diluted with a cutting agent, it often thins the liquid enough that the air bubbles move faster, exposing the mixture's poor quality. Knowledgeable THC vapers won't buy products that fail this "bubble test." But some vitamin E acetate solutions were so thick they could fool even expert vapers. Honey Cut, reportedly one of the leading vitamin E acetate suppliers in 2019, advertised on its (now-defunct) website that the solution could be used "as a thickener to eliminate bubble movement and leakage." Honey Cut had plenty of competitors, too. But what these enterprising businesses either ignored or overlooked is that vitamin E acetate, while typically harmless when ingested or applied topically, is not meant to be inhaled. Nobody actually knew if vitamin E acetate was safe to breathe into your lungs dozens of times per day.

On September 5—the same day Wisconsin police raided Tyler Huffhines's condo—the New York State Department of Health released new data on the vaping lung disease outbreak. Its testing strongly suggested that tainted THC pods were involved. According to the department's testing, thirty-four New Yorkers had gotten sick after vaping THC cartridges laced with vitamin E acetate.

"Vitamin E acetate is now a key focus of the Department's investigation of potential causes of vaping-associated pulmonary illnesses," the health department declared in a press statement. It seemed like a big break in the case, but the day after New York State released its data, the CDC specifically noted in a press release that vitamin E acetate had *not* been found in some product samples. "It is too early to pinpoint a single product or substance common to all cases," the agency emphasized. New York's results were compelling, but for the CDC to come out strongly against vitamin E acetate, it would first need effectively to rule out every other possible cause. "We don't base our recommendations on anecdotes," King says.

As September continued, there were dozens of new EVALI diagnoses reported each week in the United States, enough that the CDC activated its Emergency Operations Center to deal with the outbreak. Almost five hundred agency employees were working on the investigation, routinely pulling sixteen-to-eighteen-hour days as they continued to search for answers.

Meanwhile, several more high-profile THC busts hit the news cycle. In mid-September, Arizona police caught two Phoenix men with more than one thousand bootleg THC cartridges. The following week, Minnesota's Northwest Metro Drug Task Force seized almost 77,000 illegal THC cartridges from a home in Coon Rapids. Days after that, Virginia police raided a Waynesboro home that was hiding, among other drugs, more than 1,000 THC pods. Law enforcement and health officials were waking up to a reality that Juul and its competitors had known for years: black-market and knock-off vaping products were everywhere, and they were a big problem. "It's scary to me, from a public health standpoint," says Brian Marquart, an officer for Minnesota's Department of Public Safety, which had led the massive Coon Rapids raid. "It's difficult to know what's in them."

It was also difficult to know where they were coming from, investigators were quickly learning. The country's patchwork of marijuana laws was one obstacle. By the summer of 2019, about a dozen states had legalized recreational marijuana, and even more had decriminalized possession or allowed medicinal use of the drug. As the market for legal marijuana grew larger, the so-called "gray market" expanded exponentially. Now that THC oil could be produced legally in states across the country, from Massachusetts to California, it wasn't too difficult for an aspiring dealer to find somebody who would quietly "funnel it out the back door," to a buyer in a state like Minnesota or Wisconsin, where the stuff was still illegal for recreational use, Marquart says. After that point, there was no telling what someone had added to the batch before taking it to the streets for sale.

Even in states where marijuana is legal, regulation is complex. The FDA does not regulate marijuana vaping products, though it does regulate some cannabis-derived products. The Drug Enforcement Agency also makes it difficult for independent scientists to study THC products on their own. Marijuana is considered a Schedule I drug—the same class as LSD and heroin—so researchers need special permission to work with it. Even when that permission is granted, scientists are limited to studying products from DEA-sanctioned sources. That list is limited to a single facility: the University of Mississippi. That means academic researchers are all but blocked from studying commercially available derivative products like THC oils and concentrates—which means there's hardly any independent research on these products' safety. Some states do have manufacturing and safety standards that THC companies are expected to meet, but the chaotic regulatory system means that this process is often followed essentially on the honor code. A company can stamp "lab-tested" on its label and put a product on the market, and chances are good no one will double-check its claims unless there's a problem. Even in states where marijuana is legally sold in dispensaries with safety standards, there's often a thriving black market of products packaged to *look* like they've gone through extensive testing, even though they haven't. Forget law enforcement. Even consumers often have no idea what's in the product they're using.

This convoluted supply chain made it extremely difficult for the CDC to zero in on which specific products or brands could be causing the lung injuries, King says. CDC investigators asked each patient who met the agency's criteria for an EVALI diagnosis which product or products they had used in the thirty days before they got sick. Many said they'd used products from Dank Vapes, one of the names that had allegedly shown up on packaging in Tyler Huffhines's condo. But as King as his team dug deeper, they learned that Dank Vapes wasn't a single brand so much as "a series of illicit brands that use that label." Dealers sold their goods in Dank Vapes boxes, which looked professional enough to trick customers into thinking they were buying something at least semi-legitimate. Each black box came stamped with the Dank Vapes logo and a photo illustrating whatever flavor of THC was purportedly inside. The packages looked like they came from one common manufacturer, which presumably had some sort of quality-control procedure in place. The boxes even promised that the contents were "all organic." In reality, though, it was impossible to tell what was actually in each box. That was up to the individual supplier who had bought the packaging and filled it with its own goods, "which makes it very difficult to isolate a single source" of tainted product, King explains.

But to many observers, not only in the vaping industry but also in the research community, the CDC's silence on the source of the EVALI outbreak seemed to extend beyond typical scientific caution. Federal agencies move slowly by nature, and they're understandably risk-averse, particularly during high-stakes investigations. But to some, it seemed unusual that no one at the CDC was sounding the alarm about vitamin E acetate, or THC products as a whole, when there were increasingly strong data to suggest these products were the problem. The FDA had started warning consumers specifically about THC products in September, so why wasn't the CDC? Even if the public health agency couldn't point the finger at one specific supplier or brand, many people wondered why it wasn't asking consumers to be extra cautious about using THC products in general, and why it wasn't coming forward to say that nicotine e-cigarette companies like Juul did not seem to be at fault. "I love CDC. I worked with them forever," says Tom Glynn, the former National Cancer Institute official. "But I think it took them too long to acknowledge that [THC products were likely to blame]. They spent too long demonizing [nicotine] vaping in the process."

King, from the CDC, argues that the agency was simply doing its due diligence, waiting until studies confirmed with a high degree of confidence that vitamin E acetate actually was to blame. "It's very easy to spew out hypotheses and potential causes," King says, "but you have to be able to back it up with the data, because if you do something or say something that's not consistent with the data, then you lose credibility." But many in the vaping world saw it differently. To them, it looked like the CDC was capitalizing on the lung disease outbreak as if it had been handed to them on a silver platter. The CDC had been trying for years to get people, especially teenagers, to quit nicotine e-cigarettes, particularly Juuls. If a lung disease outbreak was the thing that finally did it, wasn't that a silver lining to a horrible situation? Why let a good crisis go to waste?

King vehemently denies this characterization, but the trickle-down effect is hard to deny. By mid-September 2019, surveys showed that 63 percent of Americans thought vaping was at least as dangerous as smoking. Whether the CDC meant it to or not, the EVALI investigation was finally getting people to quit vaping.

20

WAKE ME UP WHEN SEPTEMBER ENDS (SEPTEMBER 2019)

August 2019 was an inflection point for the e-cigarette industry. According to CDC data, e-cigarette product sales had increased by roughly 300 percent from November 2016 to August 2019—from 5.6 million products sold each month in the United States to 22 million. But starting in August 2019, as the EVALI crisis kicked into gear, sales started dropping for the first time in years, eventually falling back down to less than 15 million products sold per month. Eighty percent of vape shops experienced some decline in sales during the EVALI crisis, with an average 18 percent drop in sales, a survey later found. Juul, as the category's dominant brand, was hit hard by this sudden change, too. Even though its products had not been directly implicated in the lung disease outbreak, the industry-wide bad PR brought on by the crisis was enough to help sink its bottom line, along with the continuing scrutiny from regulators and the financial hit of removing some flavors from stores. Juul's revenue fell to $607 million in the financial quarter ending September 2019, down from $745 million the quarter before.

But the consequences of the EVALI crisis weren't only financial. The outbreak also unleashed a new antivaping fervor among lawmakers—one that would make September 2019 arguably Juul's worst month ever. Michigan governor Gretchen Whitmer kicked things off on September 4, 2019, with the announcement that her administration planned to ban all flavored nicotine vaping products. "As governor, my number one priority is keeping our kids safe," Whitmer said in a statement. "And right now, companies selling vaping products are using candy flavors to hook children on nicotine and misleading claims to promote the belief that these products are safe. That ends today." It was like the San Francisco vaping ban all over again, but this time it extended across an entire state. Juul could handle losing much of its revenue in Michigan, but that wasn't the company's biggest problem. Bans, as they'd already seen, beget more bans.

On September 9, just days after Whitmer's announcement, the FDA sent Juul a warning letter. Warning letters are among the worst things a regulated company can receive from the FDA. They signify, according to the FDA's website, that a company has "significantly violated FDA regulations." In Juul's case, after reviewing testimony from the congressional hearing earlier that summer, FDA regulators were pretty convinced that Juul was implicitly marketing its products as safer than cigarettes—something tobacco companies are forbidden from doing without applying for and earning approval from the FDA. Among other violations, the agency cited a Juul representative's dubious comments during a school visit (that its products were "totally safe," for one) and a public letter from Kevin Burns that promised Juul could offer nicotine "without the combustion and the harm associated with" smoking. If Burns didn't produce a detailed plan for correcting the company's marketing violations within fifteen business days, the FDA's letter warned, Juul risked "civil money penalties, seizure, and/or injunction."

The letter would have been a big enough scare on its own, but just two days later, President Donald Trump piled on. On September 11, he addressed the nation from the Oval Office. He said that his wife, Melania, was deeply concerned about the toll vaping was taking on the nation's young people. The couple's son, Barron, was then thirteen years old. Kids younger than he were already vaping, and with hundreds of people seriously ill from the habit, the First Family said they were taking the problem very seriously. "We can't allow people to get sick," Trump said from the White House. "And we can't have our kids be so affected."

His solution was a drastic one. Alex Azar, Trump's secretary of health and human services, announced that his department (which includes the FDA) was finalizing a policy that would pull vaping products in any flavor except tobacco off the market until they went through the FDA review process. At Trump's direction, the FDA had essentially decided to ban flavored vaping products until they got the agency's rubber stamp, a process that could take a year or more. Juul had already stopped selling its flavors in stores, but with online sales still in the picture, Mango and Mint remained by far its best-selling flavors; Tobacco was toward the bottom of the list. If flavored cartridges were taken off the market entirely, more than 80 percent of Juul's pod sales, totaling millions and millions of dollars each year, would be gone in a puff of smoke. Brands like Vuse and NJOY, which still sold flavors in stores, would also be forced to pull most pods off the market. Hundreds of smaller e-juice makers would have to halt production almost entirely until they could get FDA approval—a goal many knew they'd never reach.

Trump's vow to ban flavors opened the floodgates. On September 15, New York joined Michigan in banning flavored nicotine vaping products. On September 19, a bipartisan group of lawmakers working with PAVE, CTFK, and other groups introduced federal legislation that would ban flavored e-cigarettes and place new taxes on vaping products. Massachusetts came next, on September 24, with a ban on all flavored vaping products, both nicotine and cannabis. Rhode Island, Montana, Washington, Oregon, and California soon took similar action. The lung disease outbreak had lit a fire under state lawmakers. It was no longer enough for health departments to issue some concerned statements about youth vaping rates. They wanted this stuff gone.

But the industry, which relied on sales of flavored products, wasn't going down without a fight. Across the country, from Montana to Rhode Island, independent vape shop owners and patrons were coming together under a single rallying cry: "We vape. We vote." They were trying to send a message to the White House and state lawmakers—a reminder that adult vapers were out there, that they were passionate, and that they were angry. "What you saw with 'We vape, we vote' harkened back to that early community spirit," says Julie Woessner from Consumer Advocates for Smoke-free Alternatives, recalling the days when vapers would compare notes on internet message boards. "It was [spurred by] the smaller businesses that are very much the lifeblood of the community. They serve so many people." Several vape shops and advocacy groups even sued states that had banned flavored products, arguing that the policies placed an undue burden on businesses and would force many shops to close. The vaping voting bloc was real, and it was loud.

Juul mostly sat these protests out. There was enough going on back at its San Francisco headquarters; each day seemed to bring a new crisis. "It seemed like mass hysteria, to be honest," says a customer service employee from this era. "You'd come in to work, and it'd be like, 'Oh God, what happened today, who got banned today?'" Each new state ban meant more work for Juul's employees, who had to move lightning fast to update the website, the e-commerce platform, customer service policies, and directions for Juul vendors—all just to avoid breaking new policies. It was exhausting, especially when it felt like everything was constantly going wrong in spite of all that work. "Just think of the shitstorm that we were in in September of 2019," says another former employee. "Raja Krishnamoorthi had made us his personal cause. There's no trust in society. There is a vaping epidemic. We were at a nadir."

There were even more problems brewing overseas. Burns was convinced that overseas markets were the company's future. In an interview just months earlier, in July 2019, he'd insisted that "in three, four years, fifty percent of the revenue of this company should be outside the U.S. Just look at the numbers, in terms of where the smokers are," he'd urged, leaping up to sketch out projections on the conference room whiteboard. "We're not creating an industry; we're migrating one."

Except, the migration wasn't going well. Burns was quickly learning that what worked in the United States didn't always work overseas—and the EVALI crisis was only making things worse. After months of panicked headlines and gruesome stories about teenagers like Daniel Ament nearly dying from EVALI, e-cigarette sales were down all over the world. "When the U.S. sneezes," says Juul's former marketing director Kurt Sonderegger, "the world catches a cold."

Europe and the Asia-Pacific region were supposed to be the future of Juul, but it felt like every market the company entered had a problem. Even before EVALI, many countries simply didn't have a vaping culture that came anywhere close to rivaling that in the United States. "It's an uphill battle with consumer attitudes, because a lot of people in Europe don't see any problem with smoking," says a former employee with knowledge of Juul's overseas marketing. In countries like France and Spain, where smoking was more socially acceptable than it was in the United States, people weren't exactly flocking to e-cigarettes.

In other areas, like China, Juul simply couldn't find a way around local regulations. Burns and his team knew that getting Juul products into China would be hugely lucrative, given that almost a third of the world's smokers lived there. But it would also be a formidable challenge: state-run China National Tobacco Corporation quashes nearly all competition. Still, Burns and his team were determined. "Kevin talked about entering China like it was Normandy in June 1944," quips a company source. Some members of his finance team thought he was crazy. "I used to say, 'It's a pipe dream. You're not going to be able to enter China. Nobody can,'" remembers a high-ranking former staffer who used to work for Altria.

But Juul's Asia-Pacific team thought they'd found a back door. They worked out of an an independent company in China and used this business both to list Juul products on a site run by e-commerce giant Alibaba and to sell them online directly to consumers. The platform was up and running by early September. For a moment, it really looked like Juul had done it.

Then, abruptly, everything went dark. Within days of launching, Juul products were no longer for sale on Alibaba, and its shell company's domain was down. From what employees could glean, Chinese officials found out Juul was for sale online in China and shut the whole thing down.

"As soon as Alibaba took it down, all the other e-commerce sites in China followed suit," says the finance staffer. "What China wants is a Chinese Juul, so they don't want Juul to come in and be successful." (Incidentally, Juul's former chemist Chenyue Xing went on to create a vaping product that's popular in China, called Myst.) Juul staffers couldn't believe it. Company executives had hired extra people and told existing employees to work over-time just to get the China launch ready. It had all been for nothing. After a month of bans and protests and lawsuits and late nights, employees were fed up. Juul has "this weird start-up vibe where it's like, 'We're just going to do things and ask for forgiveness later,'" says a former employee who was with the company during the China fiasco. "Juul, as a company, forgets that you can't do that with tobacco."

Juul was also still struggling to stoke its lackluster sales in the United Kingdom, about a year after launch there. The company had estimated that Juul would make up to $180 million in its first year in the United Kingdom—a country so friendly toward e-cigarettes that they were sold in some hospitals. It made only about $30 million, in part because of the United Kingdom's policy of limiting nicotine to 1.7 percent of an e-liquid solution. That's where Turbo, the pod designed to deliver a denser vapor, was supposed to have come into the picture. The Juul management team "believed this would be the savior for the company's business in Europe," says a company source, and they poured millions of dollars into its development. So, no one could understand why, after Turbo hit shelves in the United Kingdom, as well as countries including Germany, in 2019, sales were still much lower than projected.

The answer as to why was as simple as it was infuriating. According to a company source, nobody had bothered to thoroughly test whether Turbo was more satisfying than the original Juul pod before it went to market. They'd done the testing required by regulators, and Juul employees had done some self-testing and market research to assess appeal, but they hadn't rigorously tested the pod's major selling point: that it could deliver lower-strengh nic-otine solutions in a more satisfying way than the original Juul pod could. If they had, they would have seen what Juul's science team learned in 2019, when they conducted a new study on the new pod.

Juul's scientists recruited more than two hundred people to test the new pod, the original pod, and a cigarette in a controlled clinical study. With the participants given specific instructions about how many puffs they should take on each product and how often, the research team monitored their blood nicotine concentrations to find the peak nicotine level achieved by each product, as well as how long it took to get to that point. Under these controlled test conditions, Juul's scientists could see that the experience of using Turbo closely mirrored that of the original Juul pod.

If somebody drew on an original Juul pod after not using it for a while, the first few puffs on it were particularly strong, but then they mellowed out. The Turbo pod, meanwhile, had a more uniform nicotine delivery, without those first few potent "boost" drags. The pod's consistency was seen within the company as a good thing—but the fact that its nicotine satisfaction ended up so similar to the original pod's was not. Swapping out the pod's wick—not to mention sinking roughly ten million dollars into product development—hadn't done what the company thought it would. Juul's scientists couldn't believe it.

"Not a single person had checked the box and said, 'Have we *really* studied this? Do we *really* know it's better?'" recalls a company source with knowledge of the testing. It was just one more disappointment in a historically bad month—and the month wasn't over yet.

On the morning of September 25, 2019, an email landed in in-boxes across Juul Labs. It explained that Kevin Burns was no longer Juul Labs's CEO. After just shy of two years with the company, he was moving on. K. C. Crosthwaite, a longtime Altria executive until now serving as the company's chief growth officer, would be taking his place. The message came as a shock.

"Everyone was really unsettled because they didn't really know much about the Altria guy," says an employee from that time. And if people hadn't been happy that Juul was taking an investment from a Big Tobacco firm, they sure didn't love the idea of their company being run by a career Big Tobacco executive. But by the time anyone knew what was happening, it was too late. Hours after employees woke up to the email bearing the news, Juul released an official statement announcing Burns's resignation and Crosthwaite's hiring.

"I have worked nonstop, helping turn a small firm into a worldwide business," Burns said in the statement, "so a few weeks ago I decided that now was the right time for me to step down." Many employees read between the lines. "When a CEO leaves," says a company source, "there's never a willing transition." Such was the case with Burns, many people believed.

September had been for Juul a singularly bad month in a supremely bad year, and Burns had the misfortune of being the one in charge during all of it. There was the China incident; the mishap with the Turbo pod in Europe; the lung disease outbreak; vaping bans; and, of course, the continuing youth vaping epidemic. Burns may have chosen to resign, but by that point, the writing was on the wall.

"It is not uncommon at all that a company will outgrow the CEO," says early Juul investor Ralph Eschenbach. "They're perfectly matched [when they come on], and then a year or two later they're going to be way under what the company needs at that point in time." Burns had pushed Juul's growth into hyperdrive, increasing annual revenue from $200 million to $1.3 billion and more than doubling the company's valuation in less than two years; nobody could deny that. But he was volatile; he had a temper; he could be shortsighted, losing focus on all but the goal in front of him; and, under his leadership, the company had seriously angered regulators. Companies like Juul and Altria, companies that live under a harsh, constant spotlight, need stability in a CEO. That's what K. C. Crosthwaite offered.

If you had to draw a picture of the stereotypical American businessman, it would look an awful lot like K. C. Crosthwaite. The career Altria executive looked at home in a crisp suit, and he kept his brown hair cropped short. In his midforties, with wrinkles just starting to appear around his piercing blue eyes, he spoke as if reading straight from a media training document, rarely saying anything controversial. He was the polar opposite of colorful, casual, cursing Kevin Burns, who had frequently walked around Juul headquarters in jeans and soccer jackets. "K.C. is fundamentally a boring person," says one former Juul employee—and that seemed to be exactly the point. "You don't want to have any personality about any of these people, and you don't want them to be in the news at all." Crosthwaite would be the adult in the room, helping Juul right itself and win back the trust of regulators and the American public.

It didn't hurt, of course, that he'd picked up a great deal of regulatory knowledge in his two decades with Altria. After years of Juul Labs acting more like a tech company than a tobacco company, its board seemed finally to recognize that to survive the regulatory shark tank, it would need someone with institutional knowledge from Big Tobacco. With the FDA's PMTA filing deadline bearing down, the company couldn't afford to keep making screwups. About a week after Burns's replacement, the company doubled down and brought on Joe Murillo, another top Altria executive, to become Juul's chief of regulatory affairs. "Everything changed after that. The whole direction changed," says one staffer who left not long after Burns. "It went completely to Altria protecting its investment. At that point, I knew it wasn't Juul anymore."

21

THE TAKEOVER (SEPTEMBER 2019–MARCH 2020)

In the tobacco world, people sometimes joke that Altria is so overrun with lawyers that it's really just a law firm that happens to make cigarettes. Not long after K. C. Crosthwaite took over, Juul started feeling like that, too.

Within weeks of taking over, he made several dramatic business decisions in rapid succession. First, he halted almost all Juul product advertising and publicly committed not to lobby the White House on anything related to FDA guidance. Next, he pulled Juul's support from the campaign to reverse the vaping ban in San Francisco, even though the company had by then poured $18 million into lobbying to overturn that ban. And in mid-October, he pre-emptively decided to stop selling Juul's fruit and dessert flavors online to get ahead of the FDA's looming ban on flavored products, a decision that left only Mint, Tobacco, and Menthol pods for sale. Mango alone had accounted for about a third of Juul's pod sales at one point, so the decision sent a message: Crosthwaite was willing to do whatever it took, and to lose as much revenue as necessary, to win back the FDA's trust and repair Juul's reputation.

Employees were stunned by how fast Crosthwaite was moving to build a squeaky-clean image for the new-and-improved Juul. The litmus test for every decision Crosthwaite made seemed to be whether it would rock the boat in Washington or at the FDA. The result was cultural whiplash. "Dust hasn't settled from changes in management," one Juul employee wrote in mid-October on Blind, an anonymous messaging app for people who work at technology companies. "It's kind of 'plug your nose' and get through the next year or so." Juul's culture hadn't always been the most cautious, but Crosthwaite seemed like a purely by-the-book kind of guy. With him in charge, it was clear a lot was about to change.

Not long after Crosthwaite and regulatory director Murillo joined the company, they began pausing long-standing projects and systems within the company, seemingly shutting down anything that so much as risked drawing rebukes from regulators. There would be regulations on self-testing of Juul products, no juvenile *Teenage Mutant Ninja Turtle* product nicknames, and, at least for the moment, no more connected device app, despite the years of time and effort that had gone into it. "The belief from Joe and K.C. and the team was [the app] is something that's super complicated from a regulatory standpoint, and we just needed a lot more time and resources and conversations with regulators before it could properly be explored," a company source explains.

James seemed to be struggling with this transformation, some onlookers say. The app had been his pet project for years, despite the warnings about how a nicotine usage monitor and "perfect puff" feature could be perceived as manufacturing addiction, and the *Teenage Mutant Ninja Turtles* nicknames were a vestige of the company's early days. These changes may have seemed like a sign of something bigger—a signal that Crosthwaite and his staff now held more sway than either James or the handful of Ploom-era employees who'd stayed on this long. "Altria wanted—and they still do want—to put their own people in at Juul and run it," says a former employee who'd worked at both companies. That can't have been easy on a cofounder's ego. "James didn't want the company's cultural legacy to get wiped," remembers another former employee.

By then, it was hard to remember the days when James and Adam had stood around a pool table drinking beers with their employees—in part because the founders' friendship had atrophied to the point that they looked like "a couple that was about ready to get divorced every time you were with them," as one former hire put it. Many of the thousands of people who now worked at Juul had never had a real conversation with the founders.

Both founders were becoming increasingly withdrawn, former employees say, but Crosthwaite accelerated this trend.

In October 2019, Crosthwaite moved James and Adam—previously, the company's chief product officer and chief technology officer—out of the C-suite and into a "Founders' Office," from which they'd theoretically advise him and his team. The message wasn't terribly subtle. It was (another) demotion, albeit one dressed up with a fancy name. "They may have called it the Founders' Office, but that was a joke," says a company source. "It was like, 'You're gone, see you.'" James, company sources say, took the news harder than Adam, who had been even less engaged in day-to-day life at Juul since the Altria deal closed. "He was ready to go anyway," says a company insider of Adam. "He has less ego behind him."

Some company sources maintain the transition was smooth, but other people who knew James guessed the decision stung. It was one thing for him to pull back of his own accord and another to have it done forcefully. "James had very strong opinions about how his company should be run," says a company source. He was used to pulling rank over most Juul executives, even if he wasn't in every single meeting anymore. He might not have been the one actually making day-to-day decisions, but he was still the cofounder, still on the board, still the man whose idea had launched a multibillion-dollar company. "Finally, you have K.C. there, an adult in the room, and I'm sure James didn't like that one bit," muses a former employee.

Other Juul executives were even worse off than Adam and James. Chief Administrative Officer Ashley Gould, Chief Financial Officer Tim Danaher, and Chief Marketing Officer Craig Brommers all left the company by the end of October 2019, as the new Altria-fronted management team continued cleaning house. Around the same time, Juul announced that it would cut five hundred jobs by the end of the year as part of what Crosthwaite called a "necessary reset." Rather than expansion at all costs, as had been the modus operandi under Kevin Burns, the company's singular focus, Crosthwaite said, would be "earning a license to operate in the U.S. and around the world." The company had no other priority. Everything it did from there on out would be about righting the ship and saving what was left of Juul's reputation.

But even the most carefully laid plans can fall apart. That's exactly what happened at the end of October 2019—all thanks to a man named Siddharth Breja, who'd joined Juul as its senior vice president of global finance in 2018. He was fired in March 2019 for reasons that varied depending on whom you asked. According to Juul's HR department and Breja's boss, Breja's job performance simply didn't live up to expectation.

Breja had another story. In a lawsuit he filed on October 29, he argued that he'd been unjustly fired for speaking out about the quality of Juul's pods. The legal complaint painted Juul as a lawless company operating with no regard for public safety, under the authority of Kevin Burns, a foul-mouthed, foul-tempered CEO who proclaimed himself the "king" of Juul. In the world described in Breja's lawsuit, Burns ruled with fear. "Tell that motherfucker that I'll take him out of the room and shoot him with a shotgun if he challenges my decisions," Burns once barked during an executive meeting, according to the complaint.

Even within that culture, Breja claimed that he had stood up to Burns and, on two separate occasions, voiced his concerns about Juul's products. First, he said he learned during a February 2019 executive meeting that a distributor had returned a batch of unsold pods to the company. The pods were now about a year old, potentially old enough for their quality and flavor to be compromised, but Burns allegedly authorized their resale anyway. Breja claimed that he pushed back, arguing that the pods should not be resold and that all future batches should be marked with a "best by" or expiration date—to which Burns, according to the complaint, shot back, "Half our customers are drunk and vaping like mo-fos, who the fuck is going to notice the quality of our pods?"

Only a month after this incident, Breja allegedly learned of another problem: an entire batch of about one million Mint-flavored Juul pods had been contaminated, but executives didn't want to recall them. When Breja voiced his concern about leaving the contaminated pods on the market, his boss allegedly told him to "remember his loyalty to Juul" and claimed that recalling the pods would cause financial and public relations headaches the company couldn't afford. Breja was fired a week later, according to the complaint.

A Juul spokesperson called Breja's allegations "baseless" and "meritless," and Burns, through a spokesperson, denied the quotes attributed to him. Unsurprisingly, the bombshell lawsuit still ripped through the headlines as soon as it was filed. By this point, journalists had been covering the intensifying lung disease outbreak for months, and the CDC was still tight-lipped about its cause. Could Breja's lawsuit explain why, seemingly out of nowhere, more than fifteen hundred Americans had gotten sick after vaping?

But there were problems with Breja's complaint. (In December 2019, two months after the lawsuit was first filed, his lawyer submitted a motion to stop representing him; as of January 2021, the case is still moving toward arbitration.) The complaint never specified how the pods had supposedly been contaminated, or by what—and a former Juul employee with knowledge of the situation says that this omission misconstrued what had actually happened. There had been a problem with some of Juul's Mint pods, according to the employee, but nothing like what Breja had described.

In the spring of 2019, "there was a batch of Mint [e-liquid] that had separated. It wasn't a homogenous mixture," the employee says. The pods looked like something out of a middle school science class, with liquids of different densities sitting in layers, one on top of the other. "Everybody was perplexed, like, 'Has this gone bad; did something happen to it?'" remembers the employee. But "it went out for a full [toxicology] panel and came back normal." Indeed, according to documents first obtained by Buzz-Feed.News, months before Breja filed his lawsuit, Broughton Laboratories in the United Kingdom tested the pods and concluded that the issue was purely visual and "was not expected to impact any potential hazard associated with the intended use of the product." Only 143 customers reported complaints related to the million-pod batch, and none reported serious injury or death, according to Juul's records.

Based on those results, it was highly unlikely that the batch had any-thing to do with the EVALI outbreak—but Breja's claims were already out there, splashed across the pages of newspapers all over the country. Fair or not, the lawsuit encapsulated the reputation that Crosthwaite wanted to leave in the past: the idea that Juul was a lawless, reckless company concerned only with profit. There would be no such scandals under Crosthwaite's watch.

In the wake of Breja's complaint, the CDC was finally getting close to an explanation for EVALI. Its researcher Brian King was in the Ottawa, Canada, airport on the early November day when he got the call. Local health depart-ments had been collecting lung fluid samples from EVALI patients since the outbreak began, with the hope of testing them to look for foreign substances that could have caused the lung injuries. Twenty-nine of those samples had been passed along to the CDC for further analysis. The agency tested the samples for more than a half dozen toxicants, and as King learned that day in the Ottawa airport, the CDC investigators had found one substance in every single sample: vitamin E acetate, the dangerous additive found in many illicit THC products. "That was really the turning point in the investigation," King says. Overnight, CDC scientists wrote a report on their findings and, the very next day, submitted it for publication to the agency's in-house medical journal. It was posted online on November 8, 2019. "It was so critical that we got that information out to the public and didn't sit on it," King says.

But by that point, the public had been hearing for months that any e-cigarette product could be unsafe. They'd read about Juul's alleged tainted pods. They'd heard that President Donald Trump wanted to ban flavored vaping products. Maybe they knew that both India and China had banned or severely restricted the sale of e-cigarette products, in large part due to the EVALI scare. The damage had already been done. "You can't unsee those pictures of a sixteen-year-old with tubes coming out everywhere and the headline says, 'Teen Hospitalized for Vaping,'" says Kurt Sonderegger, Juul's former marketing director.

For people inside Juul, it felt like everybody had been perfectly happy to lump its products in with the bad stuff when the EVALI investigation began, but nobody was circling back to explicitly clear the company's name now that the evidence was pointing more and more strongly toward illicit THC products. They could shout it from the rooftops and, still, no one would hear. The CDC continued to warn consumers that other products could be to blame for lung illnesses, and it was still reminding them that some people had vaped nicotine products before they got sick. And it felt like the press wasn't running nearly as many stories on vitamin E acetate as it had when the EVALI outbreak was new and mysterious. "We were waiting on the news. The news never came back around and said it wasn't from Juul," says a company sales employee from that era. "And then Trump was threatening to remove all e-cigarettes at that time. . . . All that was really affecting our business as the sales team. It was a very frustrating place to be, and the culture felt like it was dying, for sure."

By that point, "Juul didn't really have a culture," says a former customer service employee who joined the company in 2019. "They used to, when it was a small office and they were hand-filling pods. People talk about that [period] all romantically." But that era was clearly over. By the time K. C. Crosthwaite took over, the average tenure at Juul was about six months, in part due to turnover and in part because the company had gone on such an aggressive hiring spree earlier in the year, with four thousand employees on the payroll at its height. The old guard from the Ploom and Pax days had mostly moved on, either by choice or by force. And as they left, they took pieces of the old culture—the innovative start-up out to disrupt the cigarette industry—with them, leaving behind Altria suits and PMTA regulations. If there was any culture left, the customer service rep says, it was "people getting trashed on the weekends or doing whatever they had to do to release steam, because they're getting worked to the bone."

K. C. Crosthwaite's antiseptic leadership style wasn't exactly helping. In early November, as Trump's Department of Health and Human Services continued to weigh the possibility of a flavored vape ban, Crosthwaite decided to pull Juul's Mint pods from the market preemptively, just as he'd done the prior month with fruity and sweet flavors. At the time, Mint reportedly accounted for 70 percent of Juul's pod sales, as most people who had once used Mango or other sweet pods had migrated to Mint when the other flavors were discontinued. Falling on this revenue sword was another way for Crosthwaite to signal his seriousness to the FDA. Not only would Juul comply with stricter regulations on flavors, but it would institute such policies itself, before they were required.

The layoffs Crosthwaite promised began in November, too. A pall fell over the office as employees tried to guess who might get the ax. Everyone at the company was on edge, and no one felt safe. Managers were getting fired, and so were *their* managers. "If you got an email the night before to show up at a certain time at a [certain] location, it's like, 'Well, that's it,'" says an employee who was let go at this time. More than six hundred employees were fired over the course of a couple weeks in November, called into meetings with a department head and an HR manager, who would walk them through their separation agreement, ask them to sign a nondisclosure agreement, and escort them off the premises. "It was brutal," the former employee says. "A lot of people were crying, in shock, upset."

As hundreds of his employees faced layoffs, Adam made a decision of his own. It was time to go. He'd had one foot out the door long before he and James were relegated to the Founders' Office, a company source says. Adam never had a taste for the limelight, and Juul was now at the center of a drama unfolding every single day in the news. Building a company had once seemed like it would be "easy and fun," and it didn't feel that way anymore.

Every day felt like it brought a new crisis. Despite the CDC's stronger conviction that tainted THC products were likely behind most cases of EVALI, lawmakers were still painting the vaping industry with a broad brush, instituting sweeping flavored product bans for the entire category. The attorneys general from California and New York had recently filed lawsuits against Juul, arguing that it had manufactured addiction to its potent pods and purposely hooked young people on nicotine. (Juul has largely denied the allegations in both complaints, and as of January 2021, both suits were moving toward trials.) Several school districts, fed up with the burden of teen vaping on campus, had also brought suits against the company, some of which were eventually rolled into multi-district litigation. That fall, Altria had written down its investment by $4.5 billion, citing unexpected challenges like flavor bans and the lung disease outbreak. It was a significant enough ding that, less

than a year after they'd gotten into the exclusive club, Adam and James were
no longer billionaires.

They were also a far cry from the grad school buddies they'd once been,
their friendship squeezed out by the constant pressures brought on by running one of America's most controversial start-ups. James was still hanging
onto his role at Juul, fighting to retain a piece of what he'd built by hand all
those years ago in grad school. But Adam was ready. He still had plenty of
money, and he could take it and leave at any time. It was time to say good-bye.

With Crosthwaite and his team now in charge of the company, it was
easy enough to slip out mostly undetected. In November 2019, Adam left for
a prolonged trip to Argentina, where his wife had grown up. He wanted his
children to see their mother's home—and it didn't hurt that it was thousands
of miles away from San Francisco. He packed some bags, took his family, and
left. True to form, he told only the people who absolutely needed to know.
Adam "had been tip-toeing out, and then he evaporated," the coworker says.
He had vaporized without a trace.

In the months since President Trump's Oval Office promise to wipe flavored
vaping products from the market, nothing had happened. To Raja Krishnamoorthi, the Illinois congressman who led the congressional hearing on Juul
in July, the whole thing looked like an elaborate filibuster. After such a long
wait for the FDA to step in and regulate e-cigarettes, the delay felt like déjà-vu.

Krishnamoorthi was pretty sure he knew what was going on: All
those "We vape, we vote" protests and visits from tobacco lobbyists had
rattled Trump. The president was afraid of losing supporters from the
vaping world, especially heading into a reelection campaign in 2020, so
he was looking for any way out of the flavor ban that, only a few months
earlier, he himself had proposed. The whole process, in Krishnamoorthi's
view, had become "Trumpified." The congressman was furious. "I think
the voting bloc that opposes the youth vaping epidemic is much more
powerful, but it's silent," he says. He believed most Americans truly cared
about protecting children from nicotine addiction, and he felt they were
being overshadowed by a very loud and very angry minority passionate

about vaping. In early December 2019, Krishnamoorthi decided to hold another hearing to find out how that vocal minority had swayed the FDA so effectively. But this time, it wouldn't be James Monsees in the hot seat. It would be Mitch Zeller, the director of the FDA's Center for Tobacco Products.

When Zeller was hauled before Krishnamoorthi's subcommittee on December 4, 2019, his statements seemed to confirm Krishnamoorthi's worst fears. Wearing a gray suit that matched his salt-and-pepper hair, Zeller confirmed that the FDA had written a policy that would clear the market of flavored e-cigarette products and that, in October, it had submitted it to federal authorities for review. Since then, however, the policy's progress had stalled due to what Zeller repeatedly called "parallel" policy discussions involving the FDA and the White House—discussions in which Zeller, despite directing the FDA's Center for Tobacco Products, was only "tangentially" involved. "I can't give a definitive answer [on when a policy might come out], other [than] to say that discussions that have been taking place continue," he told the subcommittee. Zeller wouldn't say who at the White House was leading these parallel discussions, but Krishnamoorthi had a hunch. It looked an awful lot like the president wanted to bury the policy he had specifically asked for in September and was sidelining his own FDA in the process. Zeller "more or less said it's out of his hands," Krishnamoorthi says. "That was extremely frustrating, and it signaled to me [that] this has become a political issue more than a public health and scientific issue." ("There were discussions that took place that I was not a party to," Zeller said when asked if Krishnamoorthi's sense was accurate.)

Just before Christmas 2019, President Trump gave the e-cigarette industry his gift. Instead of pulling flavors off the market, as he had promised to do just months earlier, he raised the legal age of tobacco purchase to twenty-one—not just for e-cigarettes, but for all tobacco products. Politically, it was about the safest decision the administration could have made. It at least partially pleased health groups, who had backed Tobacco 21 policy for years. They were upset about losing out on the vaping flavor ban, but keeping cigarettes, cigars, and e-cigarettes out of the hands of teenagers softened the blow. E-cigarette industry groups were fairly happy, too, given that they'd lobbied long and hard for Tobacco 21 instead of flavor bans. And perhaps most important for Trump, Tobacco 21 placated the "We vape, we vote" crowd, which viewed a flavor ban as the absolute worst-case scenario, both for businesses and for adult smokers.

Shortly after the New Year, the FDA added to the Trump administration's Tobacco 21 policy: "Amid the epidemic levels of youth use of e-cigarettes and the popularity of certain products among children," the agency announced that it would be banning all fruity, minty, and sweet e-juice flavors for cartridge-based e-cigarette products like Juul. These e-cigarette companies could now legally sell only tobacco- and menthol-flavored liquids. Clunkier, refillable, open-system products, which had never taken off among young people in quite the same way, would be exempted from the policy, as would disposable products. After years of scrutiny, the FDA was cracking down squarely on products like Juul.

Things weren't looking great for K. C. Crosthwaite's new company. Without fruit-flavored or Mint pods on the market, and in the aftermath of EVALI and numerous state vaping bans, Juul's revenue for the last quarter of 2019 came in at around $157 million, far below the $745 million it had brought in during the second quarter of that year, before the EVALI crisis peaked. In January 2020, Altria wrote down its investment by another $4 billion, citing continued losses from the EVALI outbreak and scrutiny on the vaping industry as a whole. In only a year, Juul's valuation had plummeted from $38 billion to $12 billion—a staggering loss for a company that had once looked primed for unstoppable growth.

Altria's executives were plainly upset by the situation. "I'm highly disappointed in the financial performance of the Juul investment," Altria CEO Howard Willard told the *Wall Street Journal* in late January, adding that under a new agreement, Altria would no longer help Juul with marketing or retail distribution and would instead focus all its energy on preparing Juul's PMTA for the FDA. The emergency brake was thrown on international expansion plans, with Juul pulling back from such countries as South Korea and New Zealand. The subtext was clear: getting a PMTA authorization in the United States was the company's first and only priority. Without the FDA's green light, the whole Juul experiment could go up in smoke. Everything Adam and James had built seemed to be crumbling, and Adam wasn't even there to see it. Only James.

Slowly but surely over the years, Juul had been wrenched from James's grip. First, he'd been removed as CEO. Then the board had taken over. Then he'd had to answer first to Tyler Goldman, and then to Kevin Burns. Now he was sequestered in the "Founders' Office," contributing more in a symbolic than a substantive way. His app project was dead, and whatever shreds of the Juul culture that remained were dying with it. The company he'd built was no longer his.

On a Thursday in March 2020, James Monsees sent a companywide memo to the staff at Juul Labs. "After 15 years on this tremendous journey, it is with a great deal of thought and consideration that I have decided it is time for me to move on from JUUL Labs and step down from our Board," he wrote. "These many years have been incredible, and I did not make this decision lightly." He added that he was looking forward to spending more time with his family and pursuing new interests. Most of all, he wrote, he would treasure the legacy Juul had built. "I am most proud when I hear from an adult smoker who has transitioned away from combustible cigarettes about how grateful he or she is for our product."

From the outside, James's departure may have looked like yet another Silicon Valley entrepreneur taking his payout and walking, looking for the next pain point to solve or industry to disrupt. But for those who'd watched the company transform over the last handful of years, it seemed that James's decision was inevitable. Altria, and the ex-Altria executives who now ran Juul, wanted him out so they could run the company the way they saw fit. The company James had built with his grad school buddy didn't exist anymore; like Adam and James's own friendship, it had slowly eroded under years of pressure from investors and journalists and regulators. Now it was something corporate, controlled by men in suits with legal degrees. Adam—always more reserved, never getting too close to anyone or anything—had been ready to admit this earlier than James, who had clung on long enough that he never really got around to admitting it at all. "James did not decide to leave. He was marginalized," says a former high-level employee. "The path that he ended up walking down was an inevitable path that had been laid the moment he was removed as CEO."

The news of James's departure broke fairly quietly. The day before he made his announcement, the World Health Organization declared the spread of COVID-19, a novel coronavirus sweeping the globe, a pandemic. As news of James's exit from Juul trickled out to newspapers and wire services, San Francisco and New York City were gearing up to implement sweeping, unprecedented shelter-in-place orders to keep the virus at bay. The coronavirus pandemic felt like all anyone could talk about and virtually all that most news outlets were covering. The country was captivated, paralyzed by a potent cocktail of stress, fear, and fascination. And so, the headlines about James Monsees leaving the company he had built from the ground up were mostly lost in the sea of news about COVID-19, remarked upon mostly by the closest watchers of Juul Labs and Big Tobacco.

With James gone only a few months after Adam had packed his bags, Juul's transformation was complete. A company built on grad school ambition to change what it meant to consume nicotine had become enmeshed with that which it had sought to disrupt. The men who innovated their way out of a smoking habit had been replaced by the executives who had sold the products that hooked them in the first place. Two friends who succeeded in crafting a device that could tempt people away from one of the deadliest consumer products in history would be remembered not as public health saviors, but as merchants of addiction. Five years after Juul began its incendiary rise, James Monsees and Adam Bowen abandoned ship, taking their money and their notoriety and leaving the world to wonder if their company's mistakes sank what could have been one of the most revolutionary public health tools of all time—or if it had all been smoke and mirrors from the start.

EPILOGUE

James Monsees and Adam Bowen designed arguably the best e-cigarette the world had ever seen. Beautifully constructed, eminently usable, and scientifically sophisticated, the Juul was perhaps the first e-cigarette that actually stood a chance of dethroning combustible cigarettes. It cracked the code of delivering "smoke" without fire, and it did so in a way that people found irresistible. As soon as they saw it, smokers noticed the difference between Juul and the low-tech e-cigarettes that came before it.

"When I saw the Juul product, I was blown away," says a former Juul employee who used to smoke. With a buzz that rivaled a cigarette, just the right throat hit, and a sleek look, "Juul is exponentially better than anything the Big Tobacco companies have come up with," the former employee says. Juul-funded research estimates that about half of adult smokers switch completely to vaping within ninety days of picking up a Juul, a number that, if confirmed by independent research, would put the product's efficacy considerably higher than that for nicotine gum, nicotine patches, and even many other e-cigarettes.

In laboratories not run by Juul, scientific debate over e-cigarettes is as lively as ever. There still isn't agreement on whether e-cigarettes actually help smokers quit for good, or how they affect the body over years or decades.

A Cochrane analysis of fifty prior studies on vaping, published in October 2020, concluded that if one hundred people used e-cigarettes to quit smoking, ten might do so successfully. That's not a massive number, but it is significantly higher than the six who could be expected to quit using other nicotine-replacement therapies, or than the four who could be expected to quit using behavioral support only, Cochrane concluded. And at scale, that could make a sizable difference for public health. As of the latest estimate, there are 34 million adult smokers in the United States alone, at least half of whom will try to quit in a given year. If Cochrane's analysis is right, 1.7 million of them could find success with e-cigarettes. Recent CDC data also suggest that about a quarter of U.S. adults who quit smoking in the past year used e-cigarettes.

But there's still reason for reservation. Even if e-cigarettes are safer than cigarettes, that does not mean they are safe. Small, preliminary studies have found concerning links between vaping and DNA changes that could indicate cancer, though nothing has been concretely proven yet. Observational research has shown that vaping may increase users' risks of heart attacks, but one of the most prominent papers on that subject, cowritten by UCSF's Stanton Glantz, was retracted in February 2020 due to reviewers' concerns that the data didn't back up Glantz's conclusions. Meanwhile, another 2019 study, also coauthored by Glantz (who retired in the summer of 2020), found that while vaping isn't good for the lungs, it does produce less damage than smoking. Most experts—even those who have devoted their careers to battling youth vaping—agree that e-cigarettes are less dangerous than traditional cigarettes, especially when used for only a short time, though there's not yet a consensus on how much less dangerous they are, or for how long they can be used without health consequences. Some experts even believe that Juul has the potential to be particularly effective.

"The product has many features and many characteristics that seem to be really important for smokers who try to quit smoking," says Maciej Goniewicz, an e-cigarette researcher from Roswell Park Comprehensive Cancer Center in New York. "The primary factor is the nicotine delivery. It's fast, and it contains a high dose of nicotine. It's convenient to use." The device's temperature-control settings also help minimize the production of dangerous by-products. The potent e-liquid cuts down on the overall amount of vapor (and thus, on the toxins and chemicals) smokers need to inhale into their lungs to feel satisfied. All these design elements, though subtle to the user, matter to scientists. "If we look at it from the population perspective, it's likely that Juul and other e-cigarettes could be lifesaving," says Andy Tan, who teaches health communication at the University of Pennsylvania and has researched Juul and other e-cigarettes.

But James, Adam, and, later, their successors at Ploom, Pax, and Juul made mistakes from the start. They marketed Juul as an object of desire rather than as a potentially lifesaving public health intervention. They didn't act decisively enough as concerns about youth use began to mount. They let history repeat itself, walking the path laid by Big Tobacco as they pushed out flashy advertisements, sent their representatives into schools, and, finally, accepted billions of dollars from the largest cigarette maker in the country. They tried to build sway and power in Washington while angering the regulators who held Juul's fate in their hands. They got lost in the pursuit of success and fortune, never pumping the brakes hard enough to slow the train as it skidded off the tracks. Their shortsightedness contributed to an epidemic not just of youth addiction but also of public scrutiny, from which it's not clear Juul will ever recover.

As of this writing in January 2021, a group of thirty-nine state attorneys general are investigating Juul's sales and marketing practices. More than one hundred school districts have sued the company for sparking youth addiction, and many of those lawsuits are still working their way through the court system. Hundreds of lawsuits alleging addiction and personal injuries related to Juul use have been consolidated and brought before a U.S. district court in California, which is set to begin hearing arguments in 2022. The Federal Trade Commission has brought an administrative complaint alleging that Altria agreed to shut down its own e-cigarette brand as a condition for buying a 35% stake in Juul Labs and thereby violated antitrust laws, which Juul and Altria deny; a hearing was scheduled for some time in 2021. Meanwhile, the Securities and Exchange Commission is evaluating whether Altria accurately warned its shareholders about the risks of investing in Juul. Altria has repeatedly written down its investment such that it now values its 35 percent stake in Juul at $1.6 billion—a far cry from the $12.8 billion it paid in late 2018. If that number dips below $1.28 billion, Altria will be released from its non-compete agreement.

Altria's blockbuster investment may have hastened Juul's demise, tying Juul's already dubious reputation to one of the most despised industries in the world. And the same thing that made Juul attractive to Altria in the first place (its massive popularity and superior product) made the tobacco company's investment a ticking time bomb. Once Juul shot to the top of the e-cigarette market, it became the face of the industry, scandals and all. "Ultimately, any product that was going to be good enough that it would rapidly increase the number of adults trying the product to quit smoking, that product was going to attract some amount of youth use," says Greg Conley, the president of the American Vaping Association. "You're not going to have a perfect harm-reduction product that isn't in some form attractive to some youth."

Juul was the first product good enough to become a sensation, and this made it the first product big enough for teenagers to try in droves. And with its flashy advertising and missteps around school visits and youth prevention, "Juul [Labs] made the job of the antivaping activists much easier than other companies would have," Conley says, but its fate was in many ways dictated by its own success.

Juul Labs's competitors weren't perfect, but they didn't attract the same level of scrutiny. Vuse, Blu, and NJOY sold flavored pods. They advertised on television and on social media. They made small, sleek vaporizers that kids could use in class. Vuse and Blu were backed by Big Tobacco companies. And yet, the FDA, Congress, public health advocates, researchers, and the public had latched on to Juul and made it Public Health Enemy Number One.

Politics can't be removed from Juul's story, either. Lobbying and political agendas, both from Juul and the public health groups that oppose it, shaped the public's understanding of vaping. Youth nicotine addiction—rightfully and understandably—became a rallying cry against Juul, to the extent that it became easy to forget many adults actually did use its products to stop smoking cigarettes. Things might have been different if adult smokers had as many allies on Capitol Hill as did the groups fervently protecting children.

The question now is whether Juul's reputation will sink its chances of securing the FDA approval it needs to keep selling its products in the United States. By the end of September 2020, the month by which manufacturers had to file their PMTAs given coronavirus-related delays, the FDA had received thousands of applications. Juul filed its long-awaited application in July 2020. The application, which covered the Juul device as well as its Menthol and Tobacco pods in 3 percent and 5 percent nicotine strengths, totaled 125,000 pages and included 110 studies. The culmination of years of scientific work carried out by 120 Juul employees across seven departments, it had cost millions of dollars to produce.

The FDA has a year from the application deadline of September 9, 2020, to decide whether Juul vaporizers are "appropriate for the protection of public health"—that is, whether they do more harm or good. As of January 2021, no decision had been reached. Depending on whom you ask, e-cigarettes will either save millions of lives and help make traditional cigarettes obsolete or they will doom an entire generation to a future of nicotine addiction and as-yet-unknown health consequences. The truth is probably somewhere in the middle, obscured by political sniping and inflated rhetoric on both sides. It's anyone's guess what the FDA will decide.

"If Juul gets a PMTA, it will survive by the skin of its teeth," says a former Juul employee involved in assembling the application. The company is confident in its product and premise, the source says, but the data around youth vaping—and perhaps even more damaging, the years of public debate and outrage around youth vaping—may turn out to be Juul's Achilles' heel. Approval could come down to whether the FDA is willing to overlook the youth epidemic it has battled for years in favor of the potential benefit Juul holds for adult smokers.

There are signs that the youth epidemic is waning. CDC data released shortly after Juul submitted its PMTA showed that almost two million fewer middle and high school students in the United States vaped in 2020 compared to 2019, probably due to a mixture of flavor bans, fear left over from the EVALI outbreak, and decreased access to nicotine sellers during the coronavirus pandemic. These data also showed that the whims of American teenagers are shifting. Only about 2 percent of high school vapers used single-use, disposable e-cigarettes in 2019. In 2020, more than a quarter said they did—an eye-popping 1,000 percent increase in a single year.

As with all trendy things, Juul's moment seems to be ending. In high school bathrooms across America, kids are reportedly now using disposable vaporizers made by brands like Puff Bar. Like Juul vaporizers, the Puff Bar has a slim, sleek rectangular body reminiscent of a flash drive, but it comes in an array of colors and flavors that would have made the tobacco control advocates of 2015 blush—from a "Blue Razz" flavor to a sunny yellow "Banana Ice." At 5 percent nicotine, the Puff Bar offers a hit that rivals that of a Juul, but each four-hundred-puff vape costs only twelve dollars, well within the reach of many teenagers. As Meredith Berkman from PAVE told NPR in early 2020, "Juul is almost old school. It's no longer the teen favorite."

The Juul Labs that exists today is not the Juul Labs that could have been. In some alternate reality, maybe Adam, James, and their team never greenlit the Vaporized ad campaign. Maybe they never advertised on Instagram or seduced influencers. Maybe they worked harder to stop teenagers from buying their products and posting about them online. Maybe they stayed away from schools and Native American tribes. Maybe they didn't make an enemy of the FDA's Scott Gottlieb. Maybe they hung up the phone when Altria came calling. Maybe they had people around them who pushed back a little harder, people who knew the regulatory landscape and the world of trouble they could fall into if they erred. Maybe they listened to what the experts told them. Maybe they convinced the world they had made Juul for the right reasons.

But in this reality, Juul is just a promising product that was mismanaged at every turn, a brilliant innovation that's now partially controlled by a Big Tobacco company whose first priority is and always has been making money for its shareholders. The people who made Juul what it is aren't there to see it across the FDA finish line.

James Monsees still lives in San Francisco. Adam Bowen is mostly off the grid, working for Juul only in a vague "consulting" capacity. Richard Mumby lives in New York City. Kevin Burns is the president and chief operating officer of a pharmacy company. Ashley Gould advises the CEO of a sustainable food start-up. Youth prevention director Julie Henderson has almost no public internet footprint. Howard Willard, the Altria CEO who so desperately wanted a piece of Juul, retired after recovering from COVID-19 in the spring of 2020. Even Juul itself looks different. In the spring of 2020, the San Francisco born and bred company packed up and moved its headquarters to Washington, DC, a move meant to distance Juul, both physically and figuratively, from the Bay Area culture known for moving fast and breaking things.

All that Juul's creators can do now is watch as K. C. Crosthwaite and his team from Altria continue whittling down Juul's workforce, shrinking from the media spotlight, and promising over and over again to regain the public's trust. In 2020, the company pulled back from international markets, including France, Spain, Austria, Portugal, Belgium, and South Korea, with plans to exit even more. In September 2020, Crosthwaite laid off another one thousand employees—about half of Juul's workforce. At its height, Juul employed about four thousand people. As of December 2020, that number had fallen to around eleven hundred. Those who remain are hanging by a thread. "Popping anxiety pills like tic tacs," one employee wrote on the anonymous messaging app Blind.

At this point, there are just as many questions about vaping's safety and efficacy as there are answers. But one thing is clear: Faced with numerous decisions over the years, Juul's team so often made the wrong one. There were times, certainly, when Juul would have been hard-pressed to change minds already made up, no matter what it did. But Adam, at least, seems to recognize that things could have gone differently. During an interview in 2019, he admitted that the Vaporized ad campaign was a mistake, and he acknowledged that skepticism about the Altria investment is reasonable. "There are a lot of things I'd do differently," he said. Thinking of them all, he said, was like "opening Pandora's box. It's too long a list. You can always do things better, every step of the way."

Whether his and James's intentions for Juul were good is no longer the point. Time and time again, Juul executives' actions, or inaction, outweighed their intentions, leaving the world's best e-cigarette with a reputation that precedes it—and that precludes it from making the kind of impact on public health its founders and employees always claimed to want. Hated by parents, teachers, regulators, lawmakers, activists, and smaller vaping companies alike, Juul faces a future doomed to be a reflection of its past. Smokers are the ones who will lose out.

"It was a colossal missed opportunity, starting from the board to the management team to the early science into what's now going to be a lesser product line for Altria," says a high-ranking former employee. "If you could have asked for a worse outcome, aside from bankruptcy, I'd love to hear it. That's a tragedy."

NOTES

1   "My name is": *Examining Juul's Role in the Youth Nicotine Epidemic: Part II, Hearings Before the Subcommittee on Economic and Consumer Policy of the Committee on Oversight and Reform*, 116th Cong., 5 (2019) [hereafter: *Examining Juul's Role in the Youth Nicotine Epidemic: Part II*] (testimony of James Monsees).

1   James wore a: *Examining Juul's Role in the Youth Nicotine Epidemic: Part II*.

2   staff of twenty: CNBC, "How Juul Became a $15 Billion Giant," video, YouTube, September 11, 2018, https://www.youtube.com/watch?v=3odfavdF07g&list=LL2BWlbMnIWq3F1ZdymJcqZA&index=299.

2   a $10 billion valuation: Zack Guzman, "Juul Surpasses Facebook as Fastest Startup to Reach Decacorn Status," Yahoo Finance, October 9, 2018, https://finance.yahoo.com/news/juul-surpasses-facebook-fastest-startup-reach-decacorn-status-153728892.html.

2    $38 billion empire: Angelica LaVito, "Tobacco Giant Altria Takes 35% Stake in Juul, Valuing E-cigarette Company at $38 Billion," CNBC, December 20, 2018, https://www.cnbc.com/2018/12/20/altria-takes-stake-in-juul-a-pivotal-moment-for-the-e-cigarette-maker.html.

2   rumpled graduate students: Sophie Alexander, "Juul Founders Are Crowned Billionaires as Altria Takes a Stake," Bloomberg, December

19, 2018, https://www.bloomberg.com/news/articles/2018-12-19/juul
-founders-poised-to-be-crowned-billionaires-with-altria-deal.

2   By the end: "2019 National Youth Tobacco Survey Shows Youth
E-cigarette Use at Alarming Levels," infographic, U.S. Food and Drug
Administration https://www.fda.gov/media/132299/download.

2   a narrative that: "Altria Makes $12.8 Billion Minority Investment in
JUUL to Accelerate Harm Reduction and Drive Growth," news release,
Altria Group, December 20, 2018, https://investor.altria.com/press
-releases/news-details/2018/Altria-Makes-128-Billion-Minority
-Investment-in-JUUL-to-Accelerate-Harm-Reduction-and-Drive-Growth
/default.aspx.

7   Standing outside Stanford: John Biggs, "Smoke Up: An Interview with
the Creator of the Ultracool Pax Vaporizer," *Tech Crunch*, June 18, 2012,
https://techcrunch.com/2012/06/17/an-interview-with-the-creator-of-the
-ultracool-pax-vaporizer/.

7   "We're relatively smart": Gabriel Montoya, "Pax Labs: Origins with
James Monsees," *Social Underground*, https://socialunderground.com
/2015/01/pax-ploom-origins-future-james-monsees/.

8   The quiet, cerebral: Laurie Collier Hillstrom, *The Vaping Controversy*
(ABC-CLIO, 2019), 102.

8   attracting the "smartest": "Pomona College Top Questions," Unigo,
https://www.unigo.com/colleges/pomona-college/reviews/what-is-the
-stereotype-of-students-at-your-school.

8   He'd spent his: Juul Labs, "Juul Labs Founders' Story," video, YouTube,
February 27, 2019, https://www.youtube.com/watch?v=J1pTToByIHE.

8   At Pomona, he: "Zero Gravity Plane on Final Flight," NASA, October 29, 2004, https://www.nasa.gov/vision/space/preparingtravel
/kc135onfinal.html.

8   the Sigma Xi: Adam Bowen, LinkedIn profile, https://www.linkedin.com
/in/abowen/.

8   James carried that: Juul Labs, "Juul Labs Founders' Story."

8   As a teenager: Juul Labs, "Juul Labs Founders' Story."

9   "I hated cigarettes": Juul Labs, "Juul Labs Founders' Story."

9   "James is a": James Monsees, LinkedIn profile.

9   After about a: James Monsees, LinkedIn profile.

9   Both men still: Pax Vapor (@PaxVapor), "Today is our 10 year anniver-
sary. It has been an amazing journey and we are so grateful to all of you

for supporting us through our evolution," Instagram post, March 15, 2017, https://www.instagram.com/p/BRrMWUKh0xZ/.

9   Both loved solving: "Big Vape," Season 1, Episode 2, *Broken*, directed by Sarah Holm Johansen, 2019, Netflix, https://www.netflix.com/title/81002391.

10   Previously, both men: David H. Freedman, "How Do You Sell a Product When You Can't Really Say What It Does?," *Inc.*, May 2014, https://www.inc.com/magazine/201405/david-freedman/james-monsees-ploom-ecigarette-company-marketing-dilemma.html.

10   people who wanted: J. R. Hughes et al., "A Meta-analysis of the Efficacy of Over-the-Counter Nicotine Replacement," *Tobacco Control* 12, no. 1 (March 2003): 21–27, http://dx.doi.org/10.1136/tc.12.1.21.

10   But they hated: Juul Labs, "Adam and James' Thesis Presentation," video, YouTube, February 27, 2019, https://www.youtube.com/watch?v=ZBDLqWCjsMM.

10   Adam and James began: Freedman, "How Do You Sell a Product?"

12   Glantz turned the: "Truth Tobacco Industry Documents: History," University of California, San Francisco (website), https://www.industrydocuments.ucsf.edu/tobacco/about/history/.

12   Master Settlement Agreement: "Master Settlement Agreement," Public Health Law Center, https://publichealthlawcenter.org/topics/commercial-tobacco-control/commercial-tobacco-control-litigation/master-settlement-agreement.

12   And significantly for: "Master Settlement Agreement."

13   "We had so": Montoya, "Pax Labs."

13   By the early: Naomi Oreskes and Erik M. Conway, "What's Bad Science? Who Decides?" in *Merchants of Doubt* (New York: Bloomsbury Press, 2010).

13   Their unease was: "History of the Surgeon General's Reports on Smoking and Health," Surgeon General's Reports on Smoking and Tobacco Use, Data and Statistics, U.S. Centers for Disease Control and Prevention (website), https://www.cdc.gov/tobacco/data_statistics/sgr/history/index.htm.

13   Combustion happens when: "Glossary: Combustion," Philip Morris International (website), https://www.pmi.com/glossary-section/glossary/combustion.

14   Why not get: Stanton A. Glantz, John Slade, Lisa A. Bero, Peter Hanauer, and Deborah E. Barnes, *The Cigarette Papers* (Berkeley:

University of California Press, 1996), 74–77, http://ark.cdlib.org/ark:
/13030/ft8489p25j/.

14   Ellis's team had: Stephan Risi, "On the Origins of the Electronic Cigarette: British American Tobacco's Project Ariel (1962–1967)," *American
Journal of Public Health* 107, vol. 7 (July 2017): 1060-67, https://ajph.apha-
publications.org/doi/10.2105/AJPH.2017.303806.

14   Soon after the: Lynn T. Kozlowski and David B. Abrams, "Obsolete
Tobacco Control Themes Can Be Hazardous to Public Health: The Need
for Updating Views on Absolute Risks and Harm Reduction," *BMC
Public Health* 16, no. 432 (May 2016), https://doi.org/10.1186/s12889-016
-3079-9.

15   Michael Russell: Michael Russell, "Low-Tar Medium-Nicotine Cigarettes: A New Approach to Safer Smoking," *British Medical Journal* 1,
no. 6023 (June 1976): 1430–34, https://www.bmj.com/content
/1/6023/1430.

15   Over the following: L. E. Rutqvist, B. Mattson, and T. Signomk-
lao, "Cancer Mortality Trends in Sweden 1960–1986," *Acta Onco-
logica* 28, no. 6 (August 1989): 771–75, https://doi.org/10.3109
/02841868909092306; Paolo Boffetta et al., "Smokeless Tobacco and
Cancer," *Lancet Oncology* 9, no. 7 (July 2008): 667–75, https://doi.org/10
.1016/S1470-2045(08)70173-6.

15   U.S. Public Health Service: Ronald Andersen and Ross Mullner, "Assess-
ing the Health Objectives of the Nation," *Health Affairs* 9, no. 2 (Summer
1990), https://doi.org/10.1377/hlthaff.9.2.152.

15   R.J. Reynolds, the: "Who We Are," R.J. Reynolds Tobacco (website),
https://rjrt.com/transforming-tobacco/.

15   the Premier: Robert K. Jackler et al., "Global Marketing of IQOS: The
Philip Morris Campaign to Popularize 'Heat Not Burn' Tobacco," Stanford Research into the Impact of Tobacco Advertising, February 21,
2020, http://tobacco.stanford.edu/tobacco_main/publications/IQOS
_Paper_2-21-2020F.pdf.

15   A burning charcoal: Glantz et al., *Cigarette Papers*, 76–77.

16   test groups: Douglas C. McGill, "'Smokeless' Cigarette's Hapless Start,"
New York Times, November 19, 1988, https://www.nytimes.com/1988/11
/19/business/smokeless-cigarette-s-hapless-start.html.

16   Many sources floating: Yoav Nir, *Game Changing Innovation* (N.p.:
Charte, 2018), https://www.google.com/books/edition/Game_changing

_innovation/wIJHDwAAQBAJ?hl=en&gbpv=1&dq=game+changing+in
novation&printsec=frontcover.

16   Philip Morris's Accord: Jackler et al., "Global Marketing of IQOS."

16   He quit with: "Big Vape."

17   In 2004: Barbara Demick, "A High-Tech Approach to Getting a Nico-
      tine Fix," *Los Angeles Times*, April 25, 2009, https://www.latimes.com
      /archives/la-xpm-2009-apr-25-fg-china-cigarettes25-story.html.

17   At $208: "Chinese 'E-cigarette' Helps You Stub Out the Habit,"
      Reuters Life!, May 9, 2007, https://www.reuters.com/article/us-china
      -cigarette/chinese-e-cigarette-helps-you-stub-out-the-habit
      -idUSSP23039020070509.

17   "A new brand": Seung Lee, "Juul Labs Co-founders Say They're Working
      Toward a World Without Smokers," *Mercury News*, September 12, 2018,
      https://www.mercurynews.com/2018/09/12/juul-labs-co-founders-say
      -theyre-working-toward-a-world-without-smokers/.

18   Throughout the eighteen-minute: Juul Labs, "Adam and James' Thesis
      Presentation."

21   Their buddies had: Biggs, "Smoke Up."

22   "We had thought": Freedman, "How Do You Sell a Product?"

22   James had accepted: Nathan Chan, interview with James Monsees,
      Foundr, podcast audio, September 24, 2015, https://foundr.com/james
      -monsees.

22   Hasso Plattner Institute: Biggs, "Smoke Up."

22   They set up: Allison Keeley, "Vice Made Nice?," *Stanford Magazine*,
      July/August 2012, https://stanfordmag.org/contents/vice-made-nice.

22   "The first time": Juul Labs, "Juul Founders' Story."

22   In February 2007: Email from Ploom cofounder Adam Bowen to Stan-
      ford alumni Listserv, subject line: "Investment opportunity: high volume
      consumer product company," sent February 20, 2007.

22   As they trolled: Keeley, "Vice Made Nice?"

22   Sand Hill Road: Davey Alba, "How Sand Hill Road Became the Main
      Street of Venture Capital," *Wired*, October 24, 2017.

23   Their first victory: "About Sand Hill Angels," Sand Hill Angels (website),
      https://www.sandhillangels.com/about.

23   They explained that: "Fast Facts," Data and Statistics, Smoking & Tobacco
      Use, U.S. Centers for Disease Control and Prevention (website), https://
      www.cdc.gov/tobacco/data_statistics/fact_sheets/fast_facts/index.htm.

23   gums and patches: Hughes et al., "A Meta-analysis of the Efficacy of Over-the-Counter Nicotine Replacement."

23   With one investor: "Global Asset Capital," Global Asset Capital (website), http://gacapital.com/.

24   Conwood chewing tobacco: "Reynolds American Will Buy Conwood for $3.5 billion," *Memphis Business Journal*, April 25, 2006, https://www.bizjournals.com/memphis/stories/2006/04/24/daily13.html.

25   "gets things done": James Monsees, "Adam gets things done," LinkedIn recommendation for Adam Bowen, February 7, 2007, https://www.linkedin.com/in/abowen/.

25   "James loves coffee": Adam Bowen, "James loves coffee," LinkedIn recommendation for James Monsees, February 7, 2007, https://www.linkedin.com/in/jamesmonsees/.

25   A sample Adam: Adam Bowen (@adambowenSF), "Having a muffin," tweet, November 13, 2008, https://twitter.com/adambowenSF/status/1004133520.

25   Weiss's father: Benjamin Wallace, "Smoke Without Fire," *New York*, April 26, 2013, https://nymag.com/news/features/e-cigarettes-2013-5/.

26   All users had: Delighted Robot, "NJOY Electronic Cigarette," video, YouTube, January 16, 2008, https://www.youtube.com/watch?v=9XUD9lwgQYQ&feature=emb_title.

26   flurry of press: Charlie Sorrel, "Smokes on a Plane: NJOY Electronic Cigarettes," *Wired*, June 5, 2008, https://www.wired.com/2008/06/smokes-on-a-pla/.

26   In April 2009: U.S. Customs and Border Protection, "The Tariff Classification of a Nicotine Inhaler and Part from China," Ruling NY M85579, August 22, 2006.

27   The Family Smoking: "Tobacco Control Act of 2009," Public Health Law Center (website), https://publichealthlawcenter.org/topics/special-collections/tobacco-control-act-2009.

27   The law also: "Tobacco Product Marketing Restrictions" (pdf), Tobacco Control Legal Consortium, July 2009, https://www.publichealthlawcenter.org/sites/default/files/fda-2007-3.pdf.

27   If the FDA: "A Deeming Regulation: What Is Possible Under the Law" (pdf), Tobacco Control Legal Consortium, April 2014, https://regulatorwatch.com/wp-content/uploads/2016/03/DEEMING-REGULATIONS-EXPLAINED-2014.pdf.

28   As vape industry legend: Michael Grothaus, "Trading Addictions: The
      Inside Story of the E-cig Modding Scene," *Engadget*, October 1, 2014,
      https://www.engadget.com/2014-10-01-inside-story-e-cig-modding-uk
      .htmlhttps://www.engadget.com/2014-10-01-inside-story-e-cig-modding
      -uk.html.

28   There was a: "Historical Timeline of Vaping & Electronic Cigarettes,"
      Consumer Advocates for Smoke-Free Alternatives Association (website),
      http://www.casaa.org/historical-timeline-of-electronic-cigarettes/.

28   They also passed: Murray Laugesen, "Safety Report on the Ruyan
      E-cigarette Cartridge and Inhaled Aerosol" (pdf), Health New Zealand Ltd.,
      October 30, 2008, https://www.researchgate.net/publication/237451220
      _Safety_Report_on_the_RuyanR_e-Cigarette_and_Inhaled_Aerosol.

28   In 2008, the: "Marketers of Electronic Cigarettes Should Halt
      Unproved Therapy Claims," news release, World Health Organization,
      September 19, 2008, https://www.who.int/mediacentre/news/releases/
      2008/pr34/en/.

28   By 2009, the: "FDA Warns of Health Risks Posed by E-cigarettes" (pdf),
      U.S. Food and Drug Administration Consumer Updates, Consumer
      Advocates for Smoke-Free Alternatives Association (website), https://
      www.casaa.org/wp-content/uploads/FDA-Press-Release-2009.pdf.

28   States including New Jersey: "Historical Timeline of Vaping & Electronic
      Cigarettes."

29   Top public health groups: Smoking Everywhere Inc. and Sottera Inc. v.
      Food and Drug Administration, case no. 10-5032, United States Court
      of appeals for the District of Columbia Circuit, brief of *Amici Curiae*
      from the American Academy of Pediatrics, American Cancer Society,
      American Cancer Society Cancer Action Network, et al., filed May 24,
      2010.

29   But in December: "Sottera Inc. v. U.S. Food and Drug Administration
      /Smoking Everywhere Inc. v. U.S. Food and Drug Administration
      (2009)," Public Health Law Center (website), https://www
      .publichealthlawcenter.org/content/sottera-inc-v-us-food-and-drug
      -administration.

29   There wasn't even: Dorie E. Apollonio and Stanton A. Glantz, "Mini-
      mum Ages of Legal Access for Tobacco in the United States From 1863 to
      2015," *American Journal of Public Health* 106, no. 7 (July 2016): 1200–207,
      https://doi.org/10.2105/AJPH.2016.303172.

30   They came in: Samara Lynn, "Blu E-cigs Review," *PCMag*, July 30, 2013, https://www.pcmag.com/reviews/blu-e-cigs.

30   one of five: Sparky, "Blu cigs Electronic Cigarette Review," Electronic Cigarette Review, http://www.electroniccigarettereview.com/blu-cigs -electronic-cigarette-review/.

30   He was right: "Activities of the E-cigarette Companies," in National Center for Chronic Disease Prevention and Health Promotion, Office on Smoking and Health, *E-cigarette Use Among Youth and Young Adults: A Report of the Surgeon General* (Atlanta, GA: Centers for Disease Control and Prevention, 2016), chap. 4, https://www.ncbi.nlm.nih .gov/books/NBK538679/.

30   Once things were: SmartPlanetCBS, "A Smarter Way to Smoke?" video, YouTube, November 5, 2010, https://www.youtube.com/watch?v =NI4d5NzK-HY.

32   ModelOne looked like: Daniel Terdiman, "Stanford Grads Hope to Change Smoking Forever," CNET, May 13, 2010, https://www.cnet.com /news/stanford-grads-hope-to-change-smoking-forever/.

32   Nobody wanted to: Alex Norcia, "JUUL Founders' First Marketing Boss Told Us the Vape Giant's Strange, Messy Origins," Vice, November 5, 2019, https://www.vice.com/en/article/43kmwm/juul-founders -first-marketing-boss-told-us-the-vape-giants-strange-messy-origins.

32   The whole thing: Freedman, "How Do You Sell a Product?"

33   Ultimately, the ModelOne: Freedman, "How Do You Sell a Product?"

33   "I remember when": Norcia, "JUUL Founders' First Marketing Boss Told Us."

35   Riaz Valani and: "Form D—Notice of Exempt Offering of Securities," issued by Ploom Inc. to the United States Securities and Exchange Commission, May 5, 2011, https://www.sec.gov/Archives/edgar /data/1520049/000152004911000001/xslFormDX01/primary_doc.xml.

35   In 2011, Japan: Japan Tobacco International, "Innovative Partnership for Ploom and Japan Tobacco International: JTI To Take Minority Share in Ploom," news release, December 8, 2011, https://www.jti.com/news -views/newsroom/innovative-partnership-ploom-and-japan-tobacco -international-jti-take-minority.

35   A publicly traded: Japan Tobacco Inc., *Annual Report 2011* (pdf), June 24, 2011, https://www.jti.com/sites/default/files/global-files/documents /jti-annual-reports/ar-2011annual-report-2011.pdf.

36   In interviews, James: Montoya, "Pax Labs."

36   has waxed poetic: Josh Mings, "Ploom ModelTwo Slays Smoking with Slick Design and Heated Tobacco Pods," *SolidSmack*, April 23, 2014, https://www .solidsmack.com/design/ploom-modeltwo-slick-design-tobacco-pods/.

36   While James and Adam: Japan Tobacco International, "Innovative Partnership."

37   The $250 device: Freedman, "How Do You Sell a Product?"

37   The company didn't: Freedman, "How Do You Sell a Product?"

38   "Unicorn Poop": "Unicorn Poop—Rainbow Sherbet E-Juice by Drip Star E-Liquid," Vapes.com, https://www.vapes.com/products/drip-star -unicorn-poop-eliquid.

38   Users also began: Caroline Chen, Yue-Lin Zhuang, and Shu-Hong Zhu, "E-cigarette Design Preference and Smoking Cessation," *American Journal of Preventive Medicine* 51, no. 3 (2016): 356–63, https://doi.org/10.1016 /j.amepre.2016.02.002.

38   "I get made": Katoo, "I get made fun of by smokers. I get made fun of by non-smokers. Why do they do that?," post on the E-Cigarette Forum, December 31, 2008, https://www.e-cigarette-forum.com/threads/why-do -people-make-fun-of-it.4865/#post-76268https://www.e-cigarette-forum .com/threads/why-do-people-make-fun-of-it.4865/.

39   A majority of: "56% Favor Legalizing, Regulating Marijuana," Rasmussen Reports, May 17, 2012, https://www.rasmussenreports.com/public _content/lifestyle/general_lifestyle/may_2012/56_favor_legalizing _regulating_marijuana.

39   Colorado and Washington: Aaron Smith, "Marijuana Legalization Passes in Colorado, Washington," CNN Business, November 8, 2012, https://money.cnn.com/2012/11/07/news/economy/marijuana -legalization-washington-colorado/index.html.

39   joining a group: "Legal Medical Marijuana States and DC," Britannica ProCon, https://medicalmarijuana.procon.org/legal-medical-marijuana -states-and-dc/.

39   Customers in Ploom's: "Medicinal Marijuana Law," Sacramento County Public Law Library, https://saclaw.org/articles/marijuana-laws-in -california-edl/.

39   Sarah Richardson, who: Chan, interview with James Monsees.

39   glasses of beer: Pax Vapor (@PaxVapor), "Happy Weekend. Love, Emerald," Instagram post, May 25, 2013, https://www.instagram.com/p/ZwMa6JxqIB/.

39 platters of nachos: Pax Vapor (@PaxVapor), "#Pax #beer #nachos. Have a great weekend!," Instagram post, September 6, 2013, https://www.instagram.com/p/d8DxMARqEC/.

39 in Times Square: Pax Vapor (@PaxVapor), "Hey Ploomers, it's contest time! Tag your best #PloomWithAView #Pax pic and we'll pick a winner Thursday morning. Creativity #FTW," Instagram post, June 11, 2013.

39 laptops streaming: Pax Vapor (@PaxVapor), "Jonesin' for the new Anchorman 2 trailer? Join us on Facebook.com/ploomroom for the link!" Instagram post, June 19, 2013, https://www.instagram.com/p/awEH5axqCG/.

39 in hashtags like: Pax Vapor (@PaxVapor), "#LadiesWhoPax #CultureCollide," Instagram post, October 11, 2013.

40 sponsored music festivals: Brad Stone, "Ploom's E-cigarettes, Vaporizers Use Real Tobacco," *Bloomberg Businessweek*, December 22, 2013, https://www.sfgate.com/business/article/Ploom-s-E-cigarettes-vaporizers-use-real-tobacco-5086773.php.

40 "Unlike most of": Stone, "Ploom's E-cigarettes, Vaporizers Use Real Tobacco."

40 "I consume a": Mario Schulzke, "James Monsees—Co-founder and CEO of Ploom," IdeaMensch, April 11, 2014, https://ideamensch.com/james-monsees/.

41 In an interview: "How Ploom Is Disrupting Big Tobacco," video, 20to30, July 24, 2014, http://20to30.com/video/james-monsees-how-ploom-and-pax-are-disrupting-big-tobacco/.

41 which was approaching: Stone, "Ploom's E-cigarettes."

43 It got some: Mings, "Ploom ModelTwo Slays Smoking."

43 Smoking rates in: "Adult Cigarette Smoking Rate Hits All-Time Low," news release, U.S. Centers for Disease Control and Prevention, November 26, 2014, https://www.cdc.gov/media/releases/2014/p1126-adult-smoking.html.

43 Cigarette sales, logically: U.S. Federal Trade Commission, *Federal Trade Commission Cigarette Report for 2018* (pdf), 2019, https://www.ftc.gov/system/files/documents/reports/federal-trade-commission-cigarette-report-2018-smokeless-tobacco-report-2018/p114508cigarettereport2018.pdf.

43 and when e-cigarettes: "Economic Trends in Tobacco," Fast Facts and Fact Sheets, Data & Statistics, U.S. Centers for Disease Control and

Prevention (website), https://www.cdc.gov/tobacco/data_statistics/fact
_sheets/economics/econ_facts/index.htm.

43   They looked like: "Breaking News: R.J. Reynolds Vapor Launches
'VUSE' Digital Vapor Cigarette," CStore Decisions, June 6, 2013, https://
cstore-decisions.com/2013/06/06/r-j-reynolds-vapor-launches-vuse
-digital-vapor-cigarette/.

44   That same year: Sonya Chudgar, "Altria to Launch MarkTen E-cigarette
in Indiana," *AdAge*, June 11, 2013, https://adage.com/article/news/altria
-launches-markten-e-cigarette-indiana/242043.

44   With multimillion-dollar: Jennifer Cantrell et al., "Rapid Increase in
E-cigarette Advertising Spending as Altria's MarkTen Enters the Marketplace," *Tobacco Control* 25 (2016): 16–18, http://dx.doi.org/10.1136
/tobaccocontrol-2015-052532.

44   Ploom's tobacco pods: Juul Labs, "Juul Founders' Story."

45   Perfetti eventually wrote: Thomas Perfetti, "Investigation of Nicotine
Transfer to Mainstream Smoke, I. Synthesis of Nicotine Salts," R.J. Reynolds Division of Chemical Research (1978), 1–17.

46   In the summer: Chenyue Xing (Chenyue X.), LinkedIn profile, https://
www.linkedin.com/in/chenyuexing/.

46   It was clear: Chris Kirkham, "Juul Disregarded Early Evidence It Was
Hooking Teens," Reuters, November 5, 2019, https://www.reuters.com
/investigates/special-report/juul-ecigarette/.

51   and propylene glycol: "Propylene Glycol in Food: Is This Additive
Safe?," Healthline, March 2, 2018, https://www.healthline.com/nutrition
/propylene-glycol#TOC_TITLE_HDR_3.

52   A representative from: In Re: Juul Labs Inc. Marketing, Sales Practices
and Products Liability Litigation, Plaintiffs' Amended Consolidated Master Complaint (Personal Injury), Case no. 19-md-02913-WHO, United
States District Court, Northern District of California, San Francisco
Division, filed June 18, 2020, [hereafter: In Re: Juul Labs Inc.], pp. 46–47.

52   Chenyue Xing, Adam's: Kirkham, "Juul Disregarded Early Evidence."

53   the patent application: Adam Bowen and Chenyue Xing, "Nicotine Salt
Formulations for Aerosol Devices and Methods Thereof," U.S. Patent
9,215,895 B2, filed October 10, 2014, and issued December 22, 2015.

53   "It has been": Bowen and Xing, "Nicotine Salt Formulations."

56   that they did: Jamie Brown, Emma Beard, Daniel Kotz et al., "Real-
World Effectiveness of E-cigarettes When Used to Aid Smoking

Cessation: A Cross-Sectional Population Study," Addiction 109, no. 9 (September 2014): 1531–40, https://onlinelibrary.wiley.com/doi /full/10.1111/add.12623.

56   didn't find them a: Jessica K. Pepper, Kurt M. Ribisl, Sherry L. Emery, and Noel T. Brewer, "Reasons for Starting and Stopping Electronic Cigarette Use," International Journal of Environmental Research and Public Health 11, no. 10 (September 2014): 10345–61, https://www.mdpi .com/1660-4601/11/10/10345.

56   didn't fully switch: Youn O. Lee, Christine J. Hebert, James M. Nonne-maker, and Annice E. Kim, "Multiple Tobacco Product Use Among Adults in the United States: Cigarettes, Cigars, Electronic Cigarettes, Hookah, Smokeless Tobacco, and Snus," Preventive Medicine 62 (May 2014): 14–19, https://doi.org/10.1016/j.ypmed.2014.01.014.

58   in appealing flavors: Matt Richtel, "E-cigarette Makers Are in an Arms Race for Exotic Vapor Flavors," New York Times, July 15, 2014, https:// www.nytimes.com/2014/07/16/business/e-cigarette-makers-are-in-an -arms-race-for-exotic-vapor-flavors.html.

58   In the federally: "Trump Administration Combating Epidemic of Youth E-cigarette Use with Plan to Clear Market of Unauthorized, Non-Tobacco-Flavored E-cigarette Products," news release, U.S. Department of Health and Human Services, September 11, 2019, https://www.hhs. gov/about/news/2019/09/11/trump-administration-combating-epidemic -youth-ecigarette-use-plan-clear-market.html.

58   Perhaps even more: Center for Tobacco Products, "Youth Tobacco Use: Results from the 2014 National Youth Tobacco Survey," infographic (pdf), U.S. Food and Drug Administration, http://www.smchd.org/wp -content/uploads/NYTS_YouthTobaccoUse_508.pdf.

58   Some research also: Natalia A. Goriounova and Huibert D. Mansvelder, "Short- and Long-Term Consequences of Nicotine Exposure During Adolescence for Prefontal Cortex Neuronal Network Function," Cold Spring Harbor Perspectives in Medicine 2, no. 12 (December 2012): https://www.ncbi.nlm.nih.gov/pmc/articles/PMC3543069/.

58   "It is critical": René A. Arrazola et al., "Tobacco Use Among Middle and High School Students—United States, 2011–2014," Morbidity and Mortality Weekly Report 64, no. 14 (2015): 381–85, https://www.cdc.gov /mmwr/preview/mmwrhtml/mm6414a3.htm.

58   Vaping is: Wendy Koch, "FDA Announces Rules Restricting E-cigarettes
      and Cigars," *USA Today*, April 24, 2014, https://www.usatoday.com/story
      /news/nation/2014/04/24/fda-e-cigarette-rules/8050875/.

59   NJOY purchased a flashy: Wallace, "Smoke Without Fire."

59   the company advertised: Mark J. Miller, "NJOY Takes Advantage of
      Non-Regulated E-cig Market with Super Bowl Activation," brand-
      channel, January 30, 2014, https://www.brandchannel.com/2014/01/30
      /njoy-takes-advantage-of-non-regulated-e-cig-market-with-super-bowl
      -activation/.

59   Blu was also: Regine Haardörfer et al., "The Advertising Strategies of
      Early E-cigarette Brand Leaders in the United States," *Tobacco Regula-
      tory Science* 3, no. 2 (2017): 222–31, https://doi.org/10.18001/TRS.3.2.10.

59   It even created: Joshua Brustein, "A Social Networking Device for Smok-
      ers," *New York Times*, May 10, 2011, https://www.nytimes.com/2011/05
      /11/technology/11smoke.html.

59   Senators berated executives: *Aggressive E-cigarette Marketing and Poten-
      tial Consequences for Youth, Hearings Before the Senate Committee on
      Commerce, Science and Transportation*, 113th Cong. (2014) (statement of
      Senator Richard J. Durbin).

59   "I don't know": *Aggressive E-cigarette Marketing and Potential Conse-
      quences for Youth, Hearings Before the Senate Committee on Commerce,
      Science and Transportation*, 113th Cong. (2014) (statement of Senator
      John D. Rockefeller IV).

60   FDA finally issued: "Deeming Tobacco Products to Be Subject to the
      Federal Food, Drug, and Cosmetic Act, as Amended by the Family Smok-
      ing Prevention and Tobacco Control Act; Regulations on the Sale and
      Distribution of Tobacco Products and Required Warning Statements for
      Tobacco Products," a proposed rule of the U.S. Food and Drug Adminis-
      tration, April 25, 2014.

60   The FDA pointed: Emily Baumgaertner, "The FDA Tried to Ban Flavors
      Years Before the Vaping Outbreak. Top Obama Officials Rejected the
      Plan," *Los Angeles Times*, October 1, 2019, https://www.latimes.com
      /politics/story/2019-10-01/vaping-flavors-obama-white-house-fda.

60   135,000 responses: "Deeming Tobacco Products to Be Subject to the
      Federal Food, Drug, and Cosmetic Act, as Amended by the Family
      Smoking Prevention and Tobacco Control Act; Restrictions on the Sale

and Distribution of Tobacco Products and Required Warning Statements for Tobacco Products," a rule of the U.S. Food and Drug Administration, May 10, 2016.

60   "I seriously feel": Ben Sims, "Hi, my name is Ben Sims, I'm 42, married, and finally after many failed attempts, a non-smoker . . . ," comment on U.S. Food and Drug Administration proposed rule, Regulations.gov, June 12, 2014.

61   Indeed, after winning: Thomas Burton, "Dick Durbin, Longtime Anti-Smoking Advocate, Turns Sights on Vaping," *Wall Street Journal*, September 23, 2019, https://www.wsj.com/articles/longtime-anti-smoking -advocate-durbin-turns-sights-on-vaping-11569237667.

61   In 2010, the: "Campaign for Tobacco-Free Kids Honors Sen. Richard Durbin for Three Decades of Leadership in Fighting Tobacco's Devastating Toll," news release, Campaign for Tobacco Free Kids, May 12, 2010, https://www.tobaccofreekids.org/press-releases/2010_05_12_champion.

61   Celebrities like: Emily Lowe, "10 More Celebrities Who Vape," *Ashtray Blog*, https://www.ecigarettedirect.co.uk/ashtray-blog/2014/08/10-more -celebrities-who-vape.html.

61   *Oxford English Dictionary*: Oxford University Press, "VAPE Is Named Oxford Dictionaries' Word of the Year 2014," news announcement, November 18, 2014, https://global.oup.com/academic/news/book -announcements/woty14?lang=en&cc=de.

63   He'd gotten an: Richard Mumby, LinkedIn profile, https://www.linke -din.com/in/rpmumby/.

64   "There's a lot": Nicola Fumo, "Pax Has Brilliantly Positioned Itself as Fashion's Vaporizer," *Racked*, October 13, 2015, https://www.racked.com /2015/10/13/9514363/pax-vaporizer.

64   In December 2014: Commonwealth of Massachusetts v. Juul Labs Inc. and Pax Labs Inc., Superior Court Department of the Trial Court, filed February 12, 2020, p. 8.

64   "JUUL is the": Cult Collective, "Creative Platform" (PowerPoint presentation, Cult Collective pitch meeting, Calgary, Canada, December 2014).

65   "Everything changes, eventually": Cult Collective, "Creative Platform."

65   He was a: "Photographer Steven Baillie 'The Purveyor': Learn More About 'The Model Hunter,'" *ISO 1200*, April 19, 2012, http://www .iso1200.com/2012/04/photographer-steven-baillie-purveyor.html.

66   and he'd worked: Steven Baillie, LinkedIn profile, https://www.linkedin
.com/in/steven-baillie-50b15a50/.

66   his portfolio filled: Steven Baillie, Tumblr profile, https://stevenbaillie
.tumblr.com/.

66   One photography website: "Photographer Steven Baillie: 'The Purveyor.'"

66   And in 2006: Baillie: John Bowe, "The Mail-Order Bride," *GQ*, April
2006.

66   The mood board: Steven Baillie, "The Vapors" (PowerPoint presentation
to Juul Labs and Pax Labs, 2015).

67   "New York trendsetters": The People of the State of California v. Juul
Labs Inc. and Pax Labs Inc., and Docs 1–100, Inclusive, Complaint for
Permanent Injunction, Abatement, Civil Penalties, and Other Equitable
Relief, Superior Court of the State of California, County of Alameda,
November 18, 2019, p. 18.

67   Baillie put together: Steven Baillie, "Thoughts on Casting . . ." (Power-
Point presentation to Pax Labs, 2015).

67   Smoking was far: Elyse Phillips et al., "Tobacco Product Use Among
Adults—United States, 2015," *Morbidity and Mortality Weekly Report*
66, no. 44 (2017): 1209–15, https://www.cdc.gov/mmwr/volumes/66/wr
/mm6644a2.htm.

68   A "key need": In Re: Juul Labs Inc., p. 107.

68   Outside the hard-core: In Re: Juul Labs Inc., p. 107.

68   *Wall Street Journal*: Holly Finn, "Vice's Lame New Devices," *Wall Street
Journal*, April 5, 2013, https://www.wsj.com/articles/SB100014241278873
23646604578400423620541936.

68   and Business Insider: Wallace, "Smoke Without Fire."

68   When the company pitched: In Re: Juul Labs Inc., p. 107.

69   Winge was dressed: Commonwealth of Massachusetts v. Juul Labs Inc.
and Pax Labs Inc., p. 15.

69   "There was some": In Re: Juul Labs Inc., p. 110.

71   The JTI deal: "JTI Acquires 'Ploom' Intellectual Property Rights from
Ploom, Inc.," news release, Japan Tobacco International, February 16,
2015, https://www.jti.com/our-views/newsroom/jti-acquires-ploom
-intellectual-property-rights-ploom-inc.

71   and by 2015: "In Debate Over Legalizing Marijuana, Disagreement
Over Drug's Dangers," U.S. Politics & Policy, Pew Research Center,

April 14, 2015, https://www.pewresearch.org/politics/2015/04/14/in-debate
-over-legalizing-marijuana-disagreement-over-drugs-dangers/.

73   In the year: U.S. Department of Health and Human Services, "Trump
      Administration Combating Epidemic."

73   "E-cigarette makers are": Letter from Senator Richard J. Durbin et al. to
      U.S. Department of Health and Human Services Secretary Sylvia Bur-
      well, March 11, 2015.

79   The party was: "Events with Jack," Jack Studios, https://www.jackstudios
      .com/events/.

80   guests could pose: "We Got #Vaporized: Inside the JUUL Launch Party,"
      Guest of a Guest, June 16, 2015, https://guestofaguest.com/new-york
      /events/we-got-vaporized-inside-the-juul-launch-party.

80   The events team: "We Got #Vaporized: Inside the JUUL Launch Party."

80   not to mention: *Examining Juul's Role in the Youth Nicotine Epidemic:
      Part II*, Exhibits 1–30, pp. 27–28.

80   *Vice*'s readers could: "Vice Digital Media Kit" (pdf), Vice (web-
      site), January 2016, https://upload-assets.vice.com/files/2016/01/15
      /1452894236compressed.pdf.

81   Sarah Richardson: Sarah Richardson (sarahinsf), LinkedIn profile,
      https://www.linkedin.com/in/sarahrinsf/.

81   Grit Creative Group: "We Don't Study Culture, We Live It," Grit Creative
      Group, http://gritcreativegroup.com/#/about.

81   twenty influencer guests: *Examining Juul's Role in the Youth Nicotine
      Epidemic, Part II*, Exhibits 1–30, pp. 27–28.

82   "Having way too": Erin Brodwin, "Silicon Valley E-cig Startup Juul
      'Threw a Really Great Launch Party' to Launch Its Devices, Which
      Experts Say Deliberately Targeted Youth," Business Insider, September
      4, 2018, https://www.businessinsider.com/juul-e-cig-startup-marketing
      -appealed-to-teens-2018-7.

82   "The party was": In Re: Juul Labs Inc., p. 107.

82   Outside major cities: Commonwealth of Pennsylvania v. Juul Labs,
      Inc., Notice to Defend, in the Court of Common Pleas of Philadelphia
      County, Pennsylvania, filed February 10, 2020, pp. 24–25.

82   Only 15 percent: Ahmed Jamal et al., "Current Cigarette Smoking Among
      Adults—United States, 2005–2015," *Morbidity and Mortality Weekly
      Report* 65, no. 44 (2016): 1205–11, https://www.cdc.gov/mmwr/volumes/65
      /wr/mm6544a2.htm.

82   In urban areas: *Examining Juul's Role in the Youth Nicotine Epidemic,*
      Part II, Exhibits 1–30, pp. 26–28.

83   often attractive young: The People of the State of New York by Letitia
      James v. Juul Labs Inc., Supreme Court of the State of New York, County
      of New York, submitted November 19, 2019, p. 15.

83   Sarah Richardson signed: *Examining Juul's Role in the Youth Nicotine*
      Epidemic, Part II, Exhibits 1–30, pp. 26–28.

83   "I would catch": Julie Creswell and Sheila Kaplan, "How Juul Hooked a
      Generation on Nicotine," *New York Times*, November 23, 2019, https://
      www.nytimes.com/2019/11/23/health/juul-vaping-crisis.html.

84   "@juulvapor is the": Paul (@ppthomps), "@juulvapor is the best,
      most satisfying #ecig I've tried. Great product! Only $50 too! #juul,"
      tweet on Twitter, June 10, 2015, https://twitter.com/ppthomps/status
      /608612624931131394.

84   "Juul has won": Aaron Souppouris, "Juul is the e-cig that will finally
      stop me from smoking (I hope)," *Engadget*, June 3, 2015, https://www
      .engadget.com/2015-06-03-pax-labs-juul-e-cigarette.html?ncid=rss
      _truncated.

84   A *Wired* profile: David Pierce, "This Might Just Be the First Great E-cig,"
      Wired, April 21, 2015, https://www.wired.com/2015/04/pax-juul-ecig/.

84   "We created ridiculous": "Launching a New Product to a Competitive
      Category," Cult Collective.

84   an *Ad Age* article: Declan Harty, "Juul Hopes to Reinvent E-cigarette Ads
      with 'Vaporized' Campaign," *Ad Age*, June 23, 2015, https://adage.com
      /article/cmo-strategy/juul-hopes-reinvent-e-cigarette-ads-campaign/299142.

85   In July 2015: State of Hawai'i v. Juul Labs Inc. et al., Complaint for Per-
      manent Injunction, Civil Penalties, Damages, and Other Equable Relief;
      Demand for Jury Trial; Summons, in the Circuit Court of the First Cir-
      cuit, dated June 29, 2020, p. 91.

85   It would "send": In Re: Juul Labs Inc., p. 126.

86   If parents had: Commonwealth of Massachusetts v. Juul Labs Inc. and
      Pax Labs Inc., pp. 16–18.

86   Besides, the eye: Commonwealth of Massachusetts v. Juul Labs Inc. and
      Pax Labs Inc., Complaint, p. 60.

86   When Juul launched: In Re: Juul Labs Inc., p. 136.

86   eighteen in most: Apollonio and Glantz, "Minimum Ages of Legal
      Access for Tobacco in the United States from 1863 to 2015."

87   And there were: The People of the State of California v. Juul Labs Inc.
      and Pax Labs Inc., and Docs 1–100, Inclusive, Complaint for Permanent
      Injunction, Abatement, Civil Penalties, and Other Equitable Relief,
      Superior Court of the State of California, County of Alameda, November
      18, 2019, p. 44.

87   Before too long: "Statement from FDA Commissioner Scott Gottlieb,
      M.D., on New Enforcement Actions and a Youth Tobacco Prevention
      Plan to Stop Youth Use of, and Access to, JUUL and Other E-cig-
      arettes," news release, U.S. Food and Drug Administration, April
      23, 2018, https://www.fda.gov/news-events/press-announcements/
      statement-fda-commissioner-scott-gottlieb-md-new-enforcement
      -actions-and-youth-tobacco-prevention.

87   Shortly after the: Kirkham, "Juul Disregarded Early Evidence."

88   comedian Stephen Colbert: *The Late Show with Stephen Colbert*, "Vaping
      Is So Hot Right Now," video, YouTube, October 7, 2015, https://www
      .youtube.com/watch?v=PMtGca_7leM.

88   the World Health Organization: Charlotta Pisinger, "A Systematic Review
      of Health Effects of Electronic Cigarettes" (pdf), Research Centre for
      Prevention and Health for the World Health Organization, Decem-
      ber 2015, https://www.who.int/tobacco/industry/product_regulation
      /BackgroundPapersENDS3_4November-.pdf.

89   Public Health England: A. McNeill et al., "E-cigarettes: An Evidence
      Update. A Report Commissioned by Public Health England," August
      2015, https://www.gov.uk/government/publications/e-cigarettes-an
      -evidence-update.

89   Michael Bloomberg: Eliana Dockterman, "A History of Bloomberg Bans:
      Smoking, Trans Fats, and Now Maybe Styrofoam," *Time*, November 24,
      2013, https://nation.time.com/2013/11/24/smoking-transfats-and-now
      -maybe-styrofoam-a-history-of-bloomberg-bans/.

92   Since before Juul: In Re: Juul Labs Inc., pp. 151–55.

92   But getting Juul: Kirkham, "Juul Disregarded Early Evidence."

92   The entire industry: Jidong Huang et al., "Vaping versus JUULing: How
      the Extraordinary Growth and Marketing of JUUL Transformed the US
      Retail E-cigarette Market," *Tobacco Control* 28 (2019): 146–51, http://dx
      .doi.org/10.1136/tobaccocontrol-2018-054382.

93   compared to the: Grand View Research, "U.S. Tobacco Market Size,

Share & Trends Analysis Report By Product Type (Cigarettes, Smoking Tobacco, Smokeless Tobacco, Cigars & Cigarillos), Competitive Landscape and Segment Forecasts, 2018–2025," April 2018, https://www .grandviewresearch.com/industry-analysis/us-tobacco-market.

93   fewer than 4 percent: Charlotte A. Schoenborn and Renee M. Gindi, "Electronic Cigarette Use Among Adults: United States, 2014," National Center for Health Statistics Data Brief, no. 217 (October 2015), https:// www.cdc.gov/nchs/products/databriefs/db217.htm.

93   If convenience stores: In Re: Juul Labs Inc., pp. 151–55.

93   They promised to: Kirkham, "Juul Disregarded Early Evidence."

93   When they showed: Kirkham, "Juul Disregarded Early Evidence."

94   Philip Morris USA: Matthew Bultman, "Philip Morris Settles Marlboro E-cig Trade Dress Suit," Law360, November 13, 2015.

95   That fall, Volkswagen: "Learn About Volkswagen Violations," Volkswagen Violations, United States Environmental Protection Agency (website), https://www.epa.gov/vw/learn-about-volkswagen-violations.

97   With Pax Labs: In Re: Juul Labs Inc., p. 16.

97   And after years: In Re: Juul Labs Inc., p. 130.

98   U.S. vaping industry: U.S. Department of Health and Human Services, *E-cigarette Use Among Youth and Young Adults.*

98   Even better, they: In Re: Juul Labs Inc., pp. 151–55.

98   Internal documents later: In Re: Juul Labs Inc., pp. 35–36.

100   By the middle: Pax Labs, "Pax Labs Hires CEO Tyler Goldman to Handle Rapid Growth," news release, August 22, 2016, https://www.prnewswire .com/news-releases/pax-labs-hires-ceo-tyler-goldman-to-handle-rapid -growth-300316084.html.

101   By early 2016: Robert K. Jackler, Cindy Chau, Brook D. Getachew et al., Stanford Research Into the Impact of Tobacco Advertising, "Juul Advertising Over Its First Three Years on the Market," January 31, 2019, http://tobacco.stanford.edu/tobacco_main/publications/JUUL_Marketing_Stanford.pdf.

101   "We heard some": Jamie Ducharme, "How Juul Hooked Kids and Ignited a Public Health Crisis," *Time*, September 19, https://time.com/5680988 /juul-vaping-health-crisis/ 2019.

101   the CDC released: "E-cigarette Ads Reach Nearly 7 in 10 Middle and High-School Students," news release, U.S. Centers for Disease Control and

Prevention, January 5, 2016, https://www.cdc.gov/media/releases/2016/p0105
-e-cigarettes.html.

101 Around the same: California Department of Public Health, "Protecting
the Youth of California from E-cigarettes" (pdf), January 2016, http://
www.safekidscalifornia.org/wp-content/uploads/2015/03/Protecting
-Youth-from-E-Cigarettes-slideshow-2-10-16.pdf.

101 In March 2016: In Re: Juul Labs Inc., p. 126.

102 Kids could hit: Tracie White, "Stealth Vaping Fad Hidden from Parents,
Teachers," *Scope* (published by Stanford Medicine), September 19, 2018,
https://scopeblog.stanford.edu/2018/09/19/stealth-vaping-fad-hidden
-from-parents-teachers/.

102 "Freshmen that juul": Meghan (@MeghanEdgerton), "Freshmen that
juul as they are leaving school," tweet on Twitter, March 31, 2016, https://
twitter.com/MeghanEdgerton/status/715649723353280513.

102 "[Shaking my head]": Mookie (@dudeguy420), "Smh when the juul pod
runs out @ school," tweet on Twitter, May 16, 2016, https://twitter.com
/dudeguy420/status/732296299697971200.

102 Someone else on: Jacob Staudenmaier (@upsettrout), "Movie idea dos:
Title—El Bano, Spanish language horror film about the underground
juul clubs that control most of the school bathrooms," tweet on Twitter,
May 19, 2016, https://twitter.com/upsettrout/status/733190735407677440.

102 New York City teenager: Lauren Levy, "New York Teens Created the
Biggest Vape Trend (and Now They're Over It)," The Cut, April 18, 2018,
https://www.thecut.com/2018/04/new-york-teens-explain-how-they
-created-vape-trend-juul.html.

102 The board chose: Pax Labs, "Pax Labs Hires CEO Tyler Goldman."

102 He'd gotten a: Tyler Goldman, LinkedIn profile, https://www.linkedin
.com/in/tylergoldman/.

103 the Food and Drug Administration published: "Deeming Tobacco
Products to Be Subject to the Federal Food, Drug, and Cosmetic Act,
as Amended by the Family Smoking Prevention and Tobacco Control
Act; Restrictions on the Sale and Distribution of Tobacco Products and
Required Warning Statements for Tobacco Products," final rule by the
U.S. Food and Drug Administration, *Federal Register* 81, no. 90 (May
10, 2016), https://www.federalregister.gov/documents/2016/05/10/2016
-10685/deeming-tobacco-products-to-be-subject-to-the-federal-food
-drug-and-cosmetic-act-as-amended-by-the.

103   The rule officially: "FDA Takes Significant Steps to Protect Americans from Dangers of Tobacco Through Regulation," news release, U.S. Food and Drug Administration, May 5, 2016, https://www.fda.gov/news-events/press-announcements/fda-takes-significant-steps-protect-americans-dangers-tobacco-through-new-regulation.

103   Manufacturers of products: "Premarket Tobacco Product Applications," U.S. Food and Drug Administration (website), https://www.fda.gov/tobacco-products/market-and-distribute-tobacco-product/premarket-tobacco-product-applications.

104   Cigarettes in all: "Family Smoking Prevention and Tobacco Control Act—An Overview," U.S. Food and Drug Administration, https://www.fda.gov/tobacco-products/rules-regulations-and-guidance/family-smoking-prevention-and-tobacco-control-act-overview.

104   A large study: Matthew E. Rossheim et al., "Cigarette Use Before and After the 2009 Flavored Cigarette Ban," *Journal of Adolescent Health* 67, no. 3 (September 2020): 432–37, https://doi.org/10.1016/j.jadohealth.2020.06.022.

105   A draft version: Baumgaertner, "The FDA Tried to Ban Flavors Years Before the Vaping Outbreak."

105   From the end: Baumgaertner, "The FDA Tried to Ban Flavors Years Before the Vaping Outbreak."

105   By the time: Natalie Hemmerich, Elizabeth Klein, and Micah Berman, "Evidentiary Support in Public Comments to the FDA's Center for Tobacco Products," *Journal of Health Politics, Policy and Law* 42, no. 4 (August 2017): 645–66, https://doi.org/10.1215/03616878-3856121.

105   Juul products were: Pax Labs, "Pax Labs Hires CEO Tyler Goldman."

108   Pax sold 2.2 million: "Sales of JUUL E-cigarettes Skyrocket, Posing Danger to Youth," news release, U.S. Centers for Disease Control and Prevention, October 2, 2018 https://www.cdc.gov/media/releases/2018/p1002-e-Cigarettes-sales-danger-youth.html.

108   By 2017, brands: In the Matter of Certain Electronic Nicotine Delivery Systems and Components Thereof, verified complaint, investigation no. 337-TA-1139, United States International Trade Commission, Washington, DC, submitted October 3, 2018, p. 12.

108   Many of these: "A Beginners [sic] Guide to EonSmoke, JUUL Compatible Pods," I Love ECigs (website), May 29, 2019, https://www.iloveecigs.com/blog/en/a-beginners-guide-to-eonsmoke-juul-compatible-pods/.

108   They weren't made: "Protecting Youth from Illegal, Unregulated, and

Harmful Counterfeit and Infringing Products," news release, Juul Labs, February 1, 2019, https://www.juullabs.com/juul-action-plan-update -protecting-youth-from-illegal-unregulated-and-harmful-counterfeit -and-infringing-products/.

108   As of 2017: "Tobacco Brand Preferences," Smoking & Tobacco Use, U.S. Centers for Disease Control and Prevention, https://www.cdc.gov/tobacco /data_statistics/fact_sheets/tobacco_industry/brand_preference/index.htm.

108   Altria's net revenue: Altria Group, *Altria Group Inc. 2017 Annual Report*, March 1, 2018.

108   Its slim, white: "Mark Ten XL Review: Mark Ten XL Cartridges and Amp," *Electric Tobacconist*, January 28, 2018, https://www .electrictobacconist.com/blog/2018/01/mark-10-xl-a-complete-guide-to -their-e-cigarette-flavors/.

108   Reviewers found them: "Mark Ten E-cig Review—An Easy Vaping."

108   Altria's top executives: Letter from Altria CEO Howard A. Willard III to Senators Richard J. Durbin, Patty Murray, Richard Blumenthal et al., October 14, 2019, https://www.altriacom/-mediaProject/Altria/Altria /about-altria/federal-regulation-of-tobacco/regulatory-filings/documents /Altria-Response-to-October-1-2019-Senate-Letter.pdf.

109   Throughout 2015 and 2016: Huang et al., "Vaping versus JUULing," pp. 146–51.

109   "Although Altria set": In the Matter of Altria Group, Inc. and Juul Labs, Inc., Before the Federal Trade Commission Office of Administrative Law Judges, docket no. 9393, Answer and Defenses of Defendant Altria Group, received July 27, 2020.

109   the executive team: Letter from Altria CEO Howard A. Willard III to Senators Richard J. Durbin, Patty Murray, Richard Blumenthal et al., October 14, 2019.

109   Adam and James: Ducharme, "How Juul Hooked Kids."

110   including Altria's rival: Jennifer Maloney and Dana Mattioli, "Why Marlboro Maker Bet on Juul, the Vaping Upstart Aiming to Kill Cig-arettes," *Wall Street Journal*, March 23, 2019, https://www.wsj.com /articles/why-marlboro-maker-bet-on-juul-the-vaping-upstart-aiming -to-kill-cigarettes-11553313678.

110   "Big tobacco is:" In Re: Juul Labs Inc., p. 37.

112   National Youth Tobacco Survey: Teresa Wang et al., "Tobacco Product Use Among Middle and High School Students—United States, 2011–2017," *Mor-*

bidity and Mortality Weekly Report 67, no. 22 (June 2018): 629–33, https://www.cdc.gov/mmwr/volumes/67/wr/mm6722a3.htm?s_cid=mm6722a3_w.

112   era of 2015: U.S. Department of Health and Human Services, "Trump Administration Combating Epidemic."

112   In May 2017: Maggie Lager, "Interview with a 15 Year Old Juul Addict," *Knight Life*, May 17, 2017, https://knightlifenews.com/15231/feature/interview-with-a-15-year-old-juul-addict/.

112   National data showed: U.S. Department of Health and Human Services, *E-cigarette Use Among Youth and Young Adults.*

112   from 2014 to 2017: Satomi Odani, Brian S. Armour, and Israel T. Agaku, "Racial/Ethnic Disparities in Tobacco Product Use Among Middle and High School Students—United States, 2014–2017," *Morbidity and Mortality Weekly Report* 67, no. 34 (August 2018): 952–57, https://www.cdc.gov/mmwr/volumes/67/wr/mm6734a3.htm?s_cid=mm6734a3_w.

113   Kids who got: Levy, "New York Teens Created the Biggest Vape Trend."

113   Teenagers were starting: Jia Tolentino, "The Promise of Vaping and the Rise of Juul," *New Yorker*, May 14, 2018, https://www.newyorker.com/magazine/2018/05/14/the-promise-of-vaping-and-the-rise-of-juul.

113   In May 2017: Allie Conti, "This 21-Year-Old Is Making Thousands a Month Vaping on YouTube," *Vice*, February 5, 2018, https://www.vice.com/en/article/8xvjmk/this-21-year-old-is-making-thousands-a-month-vaping-on-youtube.

113   While DonnySmokes was: Ainsley Harris, "How Juul, Founded on a Life-Saving Mission, Became the Most Embattled Startup of 2018," *Fast Company*, November 19, 2018, https://www.fastcompany.com/90262821/how-juul-founded-on-a-life-saving-mission-became-the-most-embattled-startup-of-2018.

113   including how to: In Re: Juul Labs Inc.

113   Next came Reddit: Yongcheng Zhan et al., "Underage JUUL Use Patterns: Content Analysis of Reddit Messages," *Journal of Medical Internet Research* 21, no. 9 (September 2019), https://www.jmir.org/2019/9/e13038/.

113   The best way: Zhan et al., "Underage JUUL Use Patterns."

114   In one instance: People of the State of California v. Juul Labs Inc. and Pax Labs Inc., p. 50.

114   The youth-use issue: People of the State of California v. Juul Labs Inc. and Pax Labs Inc., p. 40.

114 "I'm seeing kids": "Local Doctor Warns Parents of Dangers of Juul
     E-cigarettes," *Boston 25 News*, July 3, 2017, https://www.boston25news
     .com/news/local-doctor-warns-parents-of-dangers-of-juul-e-cigarettes
     /548847718/.

115 the Pax 3: Pax Labs, "PAX Introduces New Finishes, Colors and Prices
     for Iconic Vaporizer," news release, September 19, 2017, https://www
     .prnewswire.com/news-releases/pax-introduces-new-finishes-colors
     -and-prices-for-iconic-vaporizer-300522217.html.

115 the Pax Era: Melia Robinson, "The 'Apple of Vaping' Made an E-cigarette
     for Marijuana. Here's What It's Like," Business Insider, October 13, 2016,
     https://www.businessinsider.com/pax-era-vape-pen-review-2016-10.

115 Among those who: Melia Russell, "Marijuana Startup Spun Out of Juul
     Reaches New Highs," *San Francisco Chronicle*, February 24, 2019, https://
     www.sfchronicle.com/business/article/Marijuana-startup-spun-out-of
     -Juul-reaches-new-13638567.php.

115 Dr. Scott Gottlieb: "Scott Gottlieb, M.D., Commissioner of Food and
     Drugs," biography, U.S. Food and Drug Administration, February 21, 2020,
     https://www.fda.gov/about-fda/fda-leadership-1907-today/scott-gottlieb.

116 but he also: Jamie Ducharme, "'It Tortures Me That I'm Not There Help-
     ing': Former FDA Commissioner Scott Gottlieb on the Fight Against
     COVID-19," *Time*, April 9, 2020, https://time.com/5818226/scott-gottlieb
     -coronavirus-proposals/.

116 he had a: "Gottlieb Sees 'Watershed Opportunity' to Shape Future
     of FDA's Regulatory Process," Healio, November 16, 2017, https://
     www.healio.com/news/hematology-oncology/20171116/gottlieb-sees
     -watershed-opportunity-to-shape-future-of-fdas-regulatory-process.

116 Despite his medical: "Murray Questions President Trump's Nominee to
     Lead FDA About Potential Conflicts of Interest, Commitment to Pro-
     viding Independent Leadership," news release, U.S. Senate Committee
     on Health, Education, Labor and Pensions, April 5, 2017, https://www
     .help.senate.gov/ranking/newsroom/press/murray-questions-president
     -trumps-nominee-to-lead-fda-about-potential-conflicts-of-interest
     -commitment-to-providing-independent-leadership-.

116 The Senate approved: Senate Confirmation of U.S. Food and Drug
     Commissioner Scott Gottlieb, 115th Cong. (2017), https://www.congress
     .gov/nomination/115th-congress/118.

116 Antivaping advocates were: "FDA Nominee Scott Gottlieb Should

Recuse Himself from All Decisions Involving E-cigarettes Given His Financial Interests in a Vape Shop Company," news release, April 5, 2017, Campaign for Tobacco-Free Kids, https://www.tobaccofreekids.org/press -releases/2017_04_05_fda.

116   Gottlieb didn't quite: Jim McDonald, "Will Vaping Ties Hang Up FDA Nominee Gottlieb?" Vaping 360, April 26, 2017, https://vaping360.com /vape-news/47503/scott-gottlieb-fda/.

117   He proposed new: "FDA's Comprehensive Plan for Tobacco and Nicotine Regulation," U.S. Food and Drug Administration, https://www.fda.gov /tobacco-products/ctp-newsroom/fdas-comprehensive-plan-tobacco-and -nicotine-regulation.

117   In August 2017: Scott Gottlieb and Mitchell Zeller, "A Nicotine-Focused Framework for Public Health," *New England Journal of Medicine* 377 (September 2017): 1111–14, https://www.nejm.org/doi/full/10.1056 /NEJMp1707409.

118   *less* likely to quit: Sara Kalkhoran and Stanton Glantz, "E-cigarettes and Smoking Cessation in Real-World and Clinical Settings: A Systematic Review and Meta-analysis," *Lancet Respiratory Medicine* 4, no. 2 (February 2016): 116–28, https://doi.org/10.1016/S2213-2600(15)00521-4.

118   worrying side effects: Nardos Temesgen et al., "A Cross Sectional Study Reveals an Association Between Electronic Cigarette Use and Myo-cardial Infarction," poster presented at George Washington University Research Days, Washington, DC, 2017, https://hsrc.himmelfarb.gwu .edu/gw_research_days/2017/SMHS/85/.

118   thought to be: "Formaldehyde," What Causes Cancer?, Cancer A–Z, American Cancer Society, https://www.cancer.org/cancer/cancer -causes/formaldehyde.html.

118   when heated up: Skylar Klager et al., "Flavoring Chemicals and Alde-hydes in E-cigarette Emissions," *Environmental Science & Technology* 51, no. 18 (August 2017): 10806–13, https://doi.org/10.1021/acs.est.7b02205.

119   Sales had increased: U.S. Centers for Disease Control and Prevention, "Sales of JUUL E-cigarettes Skyrocket."

119   Sometimes it would: Melia Robinson, "How a Startup Behind the 'iPhone of Vaporizers' Reinvented the E-cigarette and Generated $224 Million in Sales in a Year," Business Insider, November 21, 2017, https://www .businessinsider.com/juul-e-cigarette-one-million-units-sold-2017-11.

119   "If we're not": Angelica LaVito, "JUUL E-cigs' Growth in Popularity

Strains Supply Chain," CNBC, October 30, 2017, https://www.cnbc.com /2017/10/30/juuls-popularity-exposes-the-challenges-of-making-a-mass -market-e-cig.html.

119   "'Juuling': The Most": Beth Teitell, "'Juuling': The Most Widespread Phe- nomenon You've Never Heard Of," *Boston Globe*, November 16, 2017, https://www.bostonglobe.com/metro/2017/11/15/where-teenagers-are-high -school-bathrooms-vaping/IJ6xYWWlOTKqsUGTTlw4UO/story.html.

119   "Teenagers Embrace JUUL": Angus Chen, "Teenagers Embrace JUUL, Saying It's Discreet Enough to Vape in Class," Your Health, NPR, December 4, 2017, https://www.npr.org/sections/health-shots/2017/12/04 /568273801/teenagers-embrace-juul-saying-its-discreet-enough-to-vape-in -class.

119   "Juuling Is Popular": Josh Hafner, "Juuling Is Popular with Teens, but Doctor Sees 'a Good Chance' That It Leads to Smoking," *USA Today*, October 31, 2017, https://www.usatoday.com/story/money/nation-now /2017/10/31/juul-e-cigs-controversial-vaping-device-popular-school -campuses/818325001/.

119   In October 2017: Shari Logan and Carl Campanile, "Schumer Pushes for Regulations on E-cigs as More Kids Vape," *New York Post*, October 15, 2017, https://nypost.com/2017/10/15/schumer-pushes-for-regulations-on -e-cigs-as-more-kids-vape/.

120   Buyers now needed: Jordan Crook, "The FDA Is Cracking Down on Juul E-cig Sales to Minors," Tech Crunch, April 25, 2018, https://techcrunch .com/2018/04/25/the-fda-is-cracking-down-on-juul-e-cig-sales-to-minors/.

120   In September 2017: Center for Environmental Health v. Totally Wicked E-Liquid et al., First Amended Complaint for Injunctive Relief and Civil Penalties, case no. RG 15-794036, Superior Court for the State of Califor- nia County of Alameda, filed December 8, 2015.

120   By the time: Center for Environmental Health v. Totally Wicked E-Liquid et al. [proposed] Consent Judgment to Pax Labs, Inc., case no. RG 15- 794036, Superior Court for the State California for the County of Alameda, filed September 6, 2017.

121   as part of: Center for Environmental Health v. Totally Wicked E-Liquid et al. [proposed] Consent Judgment.

121   A Lumanu representative: Email from Rachel Sebald to Christina Zayas, subject line: "Collaboration Opportunity with JUUL," sent October 26, 2017.

122   The company dabbled: "Establishment Inspection Report, JUUL Labs,

Inc.," signed by U.S. Food and Drug Administration inspectors on November 16, 2018.

122 Juul's influencer team: *Examining Juul's Role in the Youth Nicotine Epidemic: Part II*, Exhibits 1–30, p. 16.

122 Juul had stopped: "Establishment Inspection Report, Juul Labs, Inc."

122 The rapper and actress: *Examining Juul's Role in the Youth Nicotine Epidemic: Part II*, Exhibits 1–30, p. 42.

123 in November 2017: "Minutes of the Tobacco Education and Research Oversight Committee," Sacramento, CA, February 6, 2018.

123 During his nearly: Kimberly S. Wetzel, "Superintendent Gains West County Support," *East Bay Times*, May 14, 2007, https://www.eastbaytimes.com/2007/05/14/superintendent-gains-west-county-support-2/.

123 Most recently, he'd: Joyce Tsai, "Mixed Reaction to West Contra Costa School Superintendent's Announced Retirement," *Mercury News*, January 18, 2016, https://www.mercurynews.com/2016/01/18/mixed-reaction-to-west-contra-costa-school-superintendents-announced-retirement/.

123 In late 2017: "Monitoring the Future 2017 Survey Results," National Institute on Drug Abuse, December 12, 2017, https://www.drugabuse.gov/drug-topics/trends-statistics/infographics/monitoring-future-2017-survey-results.

123 This prompted an outcry: "New Survey Shows Youth Cigarette Smoking Continues to Fall, but Raises Fresh Concerns About E-cigarettes and Cigars," news release, Campaign for Tobacco-Free Kids, December 14, 2017, https://www.tobaccofreekids.org/press-releases/2017_12_14_monitoringthefuture.

125 its sales were: Huang et al, "Vaping versus JUULing."

125 the company still: LaVito, "JUUL E-cigs' Growth in Popularity Strains Supply Chain."

126 Burns had most: "JUUL Labs, Inc., Appoints Kevin Burns, Previously President & Chief Operating Officer of Chobani, as Its Chief Executive Officer," news release, Juul Labs, Inc., December 11, 2017, https://www.prnewswire.com/news-releases/juul-labs-inc-appoints-kevin-burns-previously-president--chief-operating-officer-of-chobani-as-its-chief-executive-officer-300569620.html.

126 It also got: Lisa Baertlein and Ankush Sharma, "Yogurt Maker Chobani Says May Tap Turnaround Expert to Replace Founder as CEO," Reuters, January 6, 2015, https://www.reuters.com/article/us-hobani-ceo/yogurt

-maker-chobani-says-may-tap-turnaround-expert-to-replace-founder-as
-ceo-idUSKBN0KF1PO20150106.

126   Chobani's founder had reportedly: Ryan Grim and Ben Walsh, "Private
        Equity Exec Brags About Sealing Chobani Deal at Easter Mass," *Huff-
        Post*, January 7, 2015, https://www.huffpost.com/entry/private-equity
        -chobani_n_6431786.

127   The company would sell: U.S. Centers for Disease Control and Preven-
        tion, "Sales of JUUL E-cigarettes Skyrocket."

127   Juul Labs was in: Ari Levy, "E-cigarette Maker Juul Is Raising $150 Mil-
        lion After Spinning Out of Vaping Company," CNBC, December 19,
        2017, https://www.cnbc.com/2017/12/19/juul-labs-raising-150-million-in
        -debt-after-spinning-out-of-pax.html.

127   there'd been whispers: Brian Sozzi, "A Chobani IPO Is Looming, and
        Here Is Why It Has to Happen," *TheStreet*, June 19, 2014, https://www
        .thestreet.com/video/a-chobani-ipo-is-looming-and-here-is-why-it-has
        -to-happen-12750748.

128   "I have a lot": Ducharme, "How Juul Hooked Kids."

128   In December 2017: "Tyler Goldman Out as JUUL Labs CEO; Kevin
        Burns Steps In," *Tobacco Business*, December 11, 2017, https://
        tobaccobusiness.com/tyler-goldman-juul-labs-ceo-kevin-burns-steps/2/.

128   but the majority: Hannah Ritchie and Max Roser, "Smoking," Our World
        in Data, revised November 2019, https://ourworldindata.org/smoking.

129   pods still leaked: Lauren Etter, "Juul Quietly Revamped Its E-cigarette,
        Risking the FDA's Rebuke," *Bloomberg Businessweek*, July 23, 2020,
        https://www.bloombergquint.com/businessweek/could-juul-face
        -penalty-after-modifying-vaping-product.

129   Juul had received: "Establishment Inspection Report, Juul Labs, Inc."

130   *Bloomberg* reporting: Etter, "Juul Quietly Revamped Its E-cigarette."

131   "Shit happens": Ducharme, "How Juul Hooked Kids."

132   It reportedly wanted to: Maloney and Mattioli, "Why Marlboro Maker
        Bet on Juul."

132   it acquired from: In the Matter of Altria Group, Inc. and Juul Labs,
        Inc., Before the Federal Trade Commission Office of Administrative
        Law Judges, docket no. 9393, Answer and Defenses of Defendant Altria
        Group Inc., received July 27, 2020.

132   By this time: In the Matter of Certain Electronic Nicotine Delivery Sys-
        tems and Components Thereof, p. 12.

132   Juul's sales jumped: U.S. Center for Disease Control and Prevention, "JUUL E-cigarette Sales Skyrocket."

132   "The previously flat": Letter from Altria CEO Howard A. Willard III to Senators Richard J. Durbin et al.

133   With plans for: Robinson, "How a Startup Behind the 'iPhone of Vaporizers' Reinvented the E-cigarette."

135   an unusual proposal: Memorandum of Agreement Between Tamalpais Union High School District and Juul Labs Inc., signed by Bruce Harter, January 29, 2018.

136   About a week: Bonnie Halpern-Felsher, "Comparison of JUUL Labs, Inc Prevention Curriculum with Stanford Tobacco Prevention Toolkit," Report presented to Congress on July 20, 2019.

136   That work was: Halpern-Felsher, "Comparison of JUUL Labs, Inc Prevention Curriculum."

137   Juul denied doing: Halpern-Felsher, "Comparison of JUUL Labs, Inc Prevention Curriculum."

137   In 1998: Anne Landman, Pamela M. Ling, and Stanton A. Glantz, "Tobacco Industry Youth Smoking Prevention Programs: Protecting the Industry and Hurting Tobacco Control," *American Journal of Public Health* 92, no. 6 (June 2002): 917–30, https://doi.org/10.2105/AJPH.92.6.917.

137   special book covers: Katherine Clegg Smith and Melanie Wakefield, "USA: The Name of Philip Morris to Sit on 28 Million School Desks," *Tobacco Control* 10, no. 6 (2001), http://dx.doi.org/10.1136/tc.10.1.6f.

137   The discovery that: Matthew C. Farrelly et al., "Getting to the Truth: Evaluating National Tobacco Countermarketing Campaigns," *American Journal of Public Health* 92, no. 6 (June 2002): 901–7, https://doi.org/10.2105/AJPH.92.6.901.

137   Philip Morris scrapped: "Philip Morris' Termination of Ineffective 'Anti-Smoking' Ads Is Positive Step, but Tobacco Companies Should Stop Opposing Prevention Programs That Work," news release, Campaign for Tobacco-Free Kids, September 17, 2002, https://www.tobaccofreekids.org /press-releases/id_0542.

138   Juul was prepared: *Examining Juul's Role in the Youth Nicotine Epidemic: Part II*, Exhibits 1–30, pp. 54–58.

140   Equally apoplectic: *Examining Juul's Role in the Youth Nicotine Epidemic: Part II* (testimony of Meredith Berkman, Parents Against Vaping E-cigarettes).

141 "Just spoke w/": *Examining Juul's Role in the Youth Nicotine Epidemic: Part II*, Exhibits 1–30, p. 70.

142 The company gave: *Examining Juul's Role in the Youth Nicotine Epidemic: Part II*, Exhibits 1–30, pp. 60–67.

142 That kind of: Olivia Zaleski, "E-cigarette Maker Juul Labs Is Raising $1.2 Billion," *Bloomberg*, June 29, 2018, https://www.bloomberg.com/news /articles/2018-06-29/e-cigarette-maker-juul-labs-is-raising-1-2-billion.

142 Not long after: *Examining Juul's Role in the Youth Nicotine Epidemic: Part II*, Exhibits 1–30, pp. 101–2.

142 In June, he: *Examining Juul's Role in the Youth Nicotine Epidemic: Part II*, Exhibits 1–30, pp. 79–85.

143 In a BuzzFeed.News story: Stephanie M. Lee, "A Stanford Professor Says Juul Stole Her Anti-vaping PowerPoint Slides," BuzzFeed.News, December 23, 2019, https://www.buzzfeednews.com/article/stephaniemlee /stanford-juul-vaping-curriculum.

143 According to a commentary: Jessica Liu and Bonnie Halpern-Felsher, "The Juul Curriculum Is Not the Jewel of Tobacco Prevention Education," *Journal of Adolescent Health* 63, no. 5 (November 2018): 527–28, https://doi.org10.1016/j.jadohealth.2018.08.005.

143 Multiple studies have shown: Karma McKelvey and Bonnie Halpern-Felsher, "How and Why California Young Adults Are Using Different Brands of Pod-Type Electronic Cigarettes in 2019: Implications for Researchers and Regulators," *Journal of Adolescent Health* 67, no. 1 (July 2020): 46–52, https://doi.org/10.1016/j.jadohealth.2020.01.017.

144 The company was: Angelica LaVito, "Leading E-cig Maker Juul to Sell Lower-Nicotine Pods as Scrutiny Ratchets Higher," CNBC, July 12, 2018, https://www.cnbc.com/2018/07/11/juul-to-introduce-lower-nicotine -pods-for-some-of-its-flavors.html.

144 Juul product packaging: "Labeling and Warning Statements for Tobacco Products," U.S. Food and Drug Administration, https://www.fda.gov /tobacco-products/products-guidance-regulations/labeling-and-warning -statements-tobacco-products.

144 Biggest of all: "Juul Labs Announces Comprehensive Strategy to Combat Underage Use," news release, April 25, 2018, Juul Labs Inc., https://www .juullabs.com/juul-strategy-to-combat-underage-use/.

144 In the 1950s: Conal Walsh, "Big Tobacco's Last Battle," *Guardian*,

September 25, 2004, https://www.theguardian.com/society/2004/sep/26
/smoking.publichealth.

146   "My 20 year": Email from Katherine Snedaker to Juul, subject line: "My
son is addicted to Juul," sent May 3, 2018.

146   The lawyer sent: Email from Mark Jones to Katherine Snedaker, subject
line: "Re: My son is addicted to Juul," sent May 6, 2018.

147   Gottlieb could see: "Youth Tobacco Use Drops During 2011–2017," news
release, U.S. Centers for Disease Control and Prevention, June 7, 2018,
https://www.cdc.gov/media/releases/2018/p0607-youth-tobacco-use.html.

147   troubling new headline: Anna B. Ibarra, "The Juul's So Cool, Kids Smoke
It in School," Kaiser Health News via *Washington Post*, March 26, 2018,
https://www.washingtonpost.com/national/health-science/the-juuls-so
-cool-kids-smoke-it-in-school/2018/03/26/32bb7d80-30d6-11e8-b6bd
-0084a1666987_story.html.

147   disguising their habit: "Why 'Juuling' Has Become a Nightmare for
School Administrators," Kaiser Health News via NBC News, March 26,
2018, https://www.nbcnews.com/health/kids-health/why-juuling-has
-become-nightmare-school-administrators-n860106.

148   Agency investigators went: "Statement from FDA Commissioner Scott
Gottlieb, M.D., on New Enforcement Actions and a Youth Tobacco
Prevention Plan to Stop Youth Use of, and Access to, JUUL and Other
E-cigarettes," news release, U.S. Food and Drug Administration,
April 23, 2018, https://www.fda.gov/news-events/press-announcements
/statement-fda-commissioner-scott-gottlieb-md-new-enforcement
-actions-and-youth-tobacco-prevention.

148   Gottlieb's Center for: Letter from Matthew R. Holman, U.S. Food and
Drug Administration Center for Tobacco Products, to Ziad Rouag, Juul
Labs, dated April 24, 2018, https://www.fda.gov/media/112339/download.

148   A group of: Juul CEO Kevin Burns's letter to Senators Richard J. Durbin,
Sherrod Brown, Richard Blumenthal et al., dated April 27, 2018.

148   "Your company's product": "Durbin & Senators Press JUUL Labs, Inc. for
Answers on Marketing Addictive Vaping Products to Teens, Urge FDA
to Take Swift Action," news release, Office of Senator Dick Durbin, April
18, 2018, https://www.durbin.senate.gov/newsroom/press-releases/durbin
-and-senators-press-juul-labs-inc-for-answers-on-marketing-addictive-e
-cigarette-vaping-product-to-teens-urge-fda-to-take-swift-action-.

149   had recently sued: Nitasha Tiku, "Users Sue Juul for Addicting Them to
       Nicotine," *Wired*, July 23, 2018, https://www.wired.com/story/users-sue
       -juul-for-addicting-them-to-nicotine/.

149    $1.6 million on lobbying: "Client Profile: Juul Labs," Influence &
       Lobbying, OpenSecrets.org, https://www.opensecrets.org/federal
       -lobbying/clients/summary?cycle=2018&id =D000070920.

149   Tevi Troy: "Biography," Tevi Troy (website), https://www.tevitroy.org/about/.

149   Jim Esquea: Jim Esquea, LinkedIn profile, https://www.linkedin.com
       /in/jim-esquea/.

149   Tobacco had long been: Lan Liang, Frank J. Chaloupka, and Kathryn
       Ierulli, "Measuring the Impact of Tobacco on State Economies," Mono-
       graph 17, p. 176, https://cancercontrol.cancer.gov/brp/tcrb/monographs
       /17/m17_6.pdf.

150   Campaign for Tobacco-Free: "Client Profile: Campaign for Tobacco-Free
       Kids," Influence & Lobbying, OpenSecrets.org, https://www.opensecrets
       .org/federal-lobbying/clients/summary?cycle=2018&id=D000048229.

150   American Lung Association: "Client Profile: American Lung Assn," Influ-
       ence & Lobbying, last accessed December 31, 2020, https://www.opensecrets
       .org/federal-lobbying/clients/summary?cycle=2018&id=D000046976.

150   American Cancer Society: "Client Profile: American Cancer Society,"
       Lobbying & Influence, OpenSecrets.org, last accessed December 31,
       2020, https://www.opensecrets.org/federal-lobbying/clients/summary
       ?cycle=2018&id=D000031468.

150   Needham, Massachusetts: Jonathan P. Winickoff, Mark Gottlieb, and
       Michelle M. Mello, "Tobacco 21—An Idea Whose Time Has Come," *New
       England Journal of Medicine* 370 (2014): 295–97, https://www.nejm.org
       /doi/full/10.1056/NEJMp1314626.

150   including California: Xueying Zhang et al., "Evaluation of California's
       'Tobacco 21' Law," *Tobacco Control* 27, no. 6 (2018): 656–62, https://
       tobaccocontrol.bmj.com/content/27/6/656.

152   Miller recruited several: "JUUL Advisory Group organizational meeting
       summary," Office of Iowa Attorney General Tom Miller, June 26, 2018.

152   He also reached: "JUUL Advisory Group organizational meeting summary."

152   NYU's David Abrams: Professor David Abrams email to Lisa Wit-
       tmus, Iowa Attorney General's Office, subject line: "Fwd: Webinar
       Confirmation—FDA's New Tobacco Flavors Initiative—November 30,"
       sent December 2, 2018.

153   Mango pods, which: Letter from Willard to Durbin et al.

153   recommending that Juul: "Recommendations for JUUL and Other
       E-cigarette Companies to Reduce Youth Vaping," report of advisory
       group led by Tom Miller.

154   Members of the: "Recommendations for JUUL and Other E-cigarette
       Companies to Reduce Youth Vaping."

154   Juul paid outside: In Re: Juul Labs Inc., p. 60.

154   As 2018 pressed: Matthew Perrone and Richard Lardner, "As Teen Vap-
       ing Surged, Juul Labs Invited Former Massachusetts Attorney General
       Martha Coakley to Join Ranks, Lobby State Officials," Associated Press via
       MassLive, https://www.masslive.com/news/2020/03/as-teen-vaping-surged
       -juul-labs-invited-former-massachusetts-attorney-general-martha-coakley
       -to-join-ranks-lobby-state-officials.html.

155   Some attorneys general: Perrone and Lardner, "As Teen Vaping Surged."

155   In May 2018: Etter, "Juul Quietly Revamped Its E-cigarette."

156   on the heels: Jennifer Maloney, "Juul Raises $650 Million in Funding
       That Values E-cig Startup at $15 Billion," *Wall Street Journal*, July 10,
       2018, https://www.wsj.com/articles/juul-raises-650-million-in-funding
       -that-values-e-cig-startup-at-15-billion-1531260832.

156   Juul Labs was widely: Angelica LaVito, "Popular E-cigarette Juul's Sales
       Have Surged Almost 800 Percent over the Past Year," CNBC, July 2,
       2018, https://www.cnbc.com/2018/07/02/juul-e-cigarette-sales-have
       -surged-over-the-past-year.html.

156   to account for: In the Matter of Certain Electronic Nicotine Delivery
       Systems and Components Thereof, p. 6.

156   A June 2018: Pamela Kaufman, "Is JUUL Hype Overblown?," Morgan
       Stanley Research Report, June 26, 2018.

157   Juul Labs now occupied: "Form D—Notice of Exempt Offerings of
       Securities."

157   Pier 70: "Historic Pier 70," Orton Development, Inc. (website), http://
       www.ortondevelopment.com/project/pier-70/.

157   a neon sign: Angelica LaVito, "Juul Co-founder Defends E-cigarette
       Start-Up in Congressional Hearing over Its Alleged Role in Teen Vaping
       'Epidemic,'" CNBC, July 25, 2019, https://www.cnbc.com/2019/07/25/juul
       -hearing-scrutinizes-start-ups-role-teen-vaping-epidemic.html.

158   first international office: Erin Brodwin, "A $15 billion E-cig Startup
       That's Taking over the US Is Moving into London," Business Insider,

July 16, 2018, https://www.businessinsider.com/juul-e-cig-vape-startup
-growing-london-international-2018-7.

158   Public Health England: McNeill et al., "E-cigarettes: An Evidence Update."

158   Nonetheless, Juul introduced: Angelica LaVito, "Juul E-cigarette
Expands to England and Scotland, Eyes Asia," CNBC, July 16, 2018,
https://www.cnbc.com/2018/07/16/juul-e-cigarette-expands-to-england
-scotland-eyes-asia.html.

158   Before spreading out: LaVito, "Juul E-cigarette Expands to England and
Scotland."

159   Company executives devised: Sheila Kaplan, "Juul's New Product: Less
Nicotine, More Intense Vapor," *New York Times*, November 27, 2018,
https://www.nytimes.com/2018/11/27/health/juul-ecigarettes-nicotine
.html.

161   next-generation Juul: Jane Stevenson, "Privacy Expert Wary over
New JUUL 'Connected' Vape," *Toronto Sun*, August 5, 2019, https://
torontosun.com/news/local-news/privacy-expert-wary-over-new-juul
-connected-vape.

161   "If a consumer": Sarah Perez, "Juul Says It Will Use Technology to
Help You Quit E-cigarettes, Too," *TechCrunch*, September 5, 2018,
https://techcrunch.com/2018/09/05/juul-says-it-will-use-technology-to
-help-you-quit-e-cigarettes-too/.

162   The company's website: "Get Started," Juul Labs (website), https://www
.juul.com/learn/getstarted.

163   When Juul employees: The People of the State of California v. Juul Labs,
Inc. et al., pp. 62.

163   On July 31: Email from Professor Robert Jackler to Juul Youth Prevention Director Julie Henderson, sent July 31, 2018.

163   Earlier in 2018: The People of the State of California v. Juul Labs, Inc.
et al., pp. 55–56.

164   Kennedy's note suggested: The People of the State of California v. Juul
Labs, Inc. et al., pp. 55–56.

164   But Matt David: The People of the State of California v. Juul Labs, Inc.
et al., p. 62.

165   About half of: Annice E. Kim, Robert Chew, and Michael Wenger, "Estimated Ages of JUUL Twitter Followers," *JAMA Pediatrics* 173, no. 7
(May 2019): 690–92, https://jamanetwork.com/journals/jamapediatrics
/fullarticle/2733855.

165   On Instagram: Robert K. Jackler, "Stanford Research into the Impact of Tobacco Advertising: The JUUL Phenomenon" (PowerPoint presentation).

165   One popular YouTube: Nate420, "Juul Challenge," video, YouTube, April 22, 2018, https://www.youtube.com/watch?v=gnM8hqW_2oo&t=3s.

166   doctor smoked Camels: "More Doctors Smoke Camels," Doctors Smoking, Cigarette Advertising Themes, Stanford Research into the Impact of Tobacco Advertising (website), http://tobacco.stanford.edu/tobacco_main/images.php?token2=fm_st001.php&token1=fm_img0002.php&theme_file=fm_mt001.php&theme_name=Doctors%20Smoking&subtheme_name=More%20Doctors%20Smoke%20Camels.

166   "You're so smart": "You're So Smart," Targeting Women, Cigarette Advertising Themes, Stanford Research into the Impact of Tobacco Advertising (website), http://tobacco.stanford.edu/tobacco_main/images.php?token2=fm_st027.php&token1=fm_img0619.php&theme_file=fm_mt012.php&theme_name=Targeting%20Women&subtheme_name=You%27re%20So%20Smart.

166   that sold sex: "Objectifying Women," Targeting Women, Cigarette Advertising Themes, Stanford Research into the Impact of Tobacco Advertising (website), http://tobacco.stanford.edu/tobacco_main/images.php?token2=fm_st031.php&token1=fm_img0739.php&theme_file=fm_mt012.php&theme_name=Targeting%20Women&subtheme_name=Objectifying%20Women.

167   "fresh": "Freshness," Fresh, Pure Natural, Cigarette Advertising Themes, Stanford Research into the Impact of Tobacco Advertising (website), last accessed December 31, 2020, http://tobacco.stanford.edu/tobacco_main/images.php?token2=fm_st119.php&token1=fm_img3503.php&theme_file=fm_mt010.php&theme_name=Fresh,%20Pure,%20Natural%20&%20Toasted&subtheme_name=Freshness.

167   "pure": "Pure & Clean," Fresh, Pure, Natural, Cigarette Advertising Themes, Stanford Research into the Impact of Tobacco Advertising (website), http://tobacco.stanford.edu/tobacco_main/images.php?token2=fm_st122.php&token1=fm_img3572.php&theme_file=fm_mt010.php&theme_name=Fresh,%20Pure,%20Natural%20&%20Toasted&subtheme_name=Pure%20&%20Clean.

167   "relaxing": "Calms Your Nerves," Psychological Exploits, Cigarette Advertising Themes, Stanford Research into the Impact of Tobacco Advertising (website), http://tobacco.stanford.edu/tobacco_main/images

.php?token2=fm_st126.php&token1=fm_img3628.php&theme_file=fm
_mt011.php&theme_name=Psychological%20Exploits&subtheme_name
=Calms%20your%20Nerves.

167   fresh-faced cheerleaders: "School Days," Targeting Teens, Cigarette
Advertising Themes, Stanford Research into the Impact of Tobacco
Advertising (website), http://tobacco.stanford.edu/tobacco_main/images
.php?token2=fm_st132.php&token1=fm_img3834.php&theme_file
=fm_mt015.php&theme_name=Targeting%20Teens&subtheme_name
=School%20Days.

167   teenage rebellion: "Be the Rebel," Targeting Teens, Cigarette Advertising Themes, Stanford Research into the Impact of Tobacco Advertising
(website), last accessed December 31, 2020, http://tobacco.stanford
.edu/tobacco_main/images.php?token2=fm_st348.php&token1
=fm_img17124.php&theme_file=fm_mt015.php&theme_name
=Targeting%20Teens&subtheme_name=Be%20a%20Rebel.

167   Jackler had heard: Jackler et al., "Juul Advertising."

170   On September 24: "Establishment Inspection Report, JUUL Labs, Inc."

172   conveniently glossed over: Etter, "Juul Quietly Revamped Its E-cigarette."

172   "We thanked the": "Establishment Inspection Report, JUUL Labs, Inc."

172   *Bloomberg* in 2020: Etter, "Juul Quietly Revamped Its E-cigarette."

173   It all started: "2018 NYTS Data: A Startling Rise in Youth E-cigarette
Use," U.S. Food and Drug Administration, May 4, 2020, https://www.fda
.gov/tobacco-products/youth-and-tobacco/2018-nyts-data-startling-rise
-youth-e-cigarette-use.

173   The survey showed: "Results from 2018 National Youth Tobacco Survey
Show Dramatic Increase in E-cigarette Use Among Youth over Past Year,"
news release, U.S. Food and Drug Administration, November 15, 2018,
https://www.fda.gov/news-events/press-announcements/results-2018
-national-youth-tobacco-survey-show-dramatic-increase-e-cigarette-use
-among-youth-over.

173   school in Philadelphia: "School District Bans Flash Drives over Confu-
sion with E-cigarette Brand," Fox 29 Philadelphia, February 23, 2018,
https://www.fox29.com/news/school-district-bans-flash-drives-over
-confusion-with-e-cigarette-brand.

173   delivered a speech: "Statement from FDA Commissioner Scott Gottlieb,
M.D., on New Steps to Address Epidemic of Youth E-cigarette Use,"
news release, U.S. Food and Drug Administration, September 11, 2018,

https://www.fda.gov/news-events/press-announcements/statement-fda
-commissioner-scott-gottlieb-md-new-steps-address-epidemic-youth
-e-cigarette-use.

175   A few weeks: "Statement from FDA Commissioner Scott Gottlieb, M.D.,
      on Meetings with Industry Related to the Agency's Ongoing Policy
      Commitment to Firmly Address Rising Rates in Youth E-cigarette
      Use," news release, U.S. Food and Drug Administration, October 31,
      2018, https://web.archive.org/web/20190415150831/https://www.fda.gov
      /NewsEvents/Newsroom/PressAnnouncements/ucm624657.htm.

175   James Monsees would: *Examining Juul's Role in the Youth Nicotine
      Epidemic: Part II* (testimony of James Monsees), p. 9.

175   company's political arm: Lorraine Woellert and Sarah Owermohle,
      "Juul Tries to Make Friends in Washington as Regulators Circle," Politico,
      December 8, 2018, https://www.politico.com/story/2018/12/08/juul
      -lobbying-washington-1052219. "Issues Lobbied by JUUL Labs, 2018," in
      Client Profile: Juul Labs, Influence & Lobbying.

176   A deal was: Maloney and Mattioli, "Why Marlboro Maker Bet on Juul."

176   "Although we do not": Letter from Altria CEO Howard A. Willard III to
      FDA Commissioner Scott Gottlieb, dated October 25, 2018.

177   to large numbers: "Back to School Statistics," Fast Facts, National Center
      for Education Statistics (website), https://nces.ed.gov/fastfacts/display.asp
      ?id=372.

178   A late 2018: Donna M. Vallone et al., "Prevalence and Correlates of
      JUUL Use Among a National Sample of Youth and Young Adults,"
      Tobacco Control 28, no. 6 (2019): 603-609, http://dx.doi.org/10.1136
      /tobaccocontrol-2018-054693.

178   Truth Initiative: "Behind the Explosive Growth of Juul," Truth Initiative
      report, December 2018, https://truthinitiative.org/sites/default/files
      /media/files/2019/03/Behind-the-explosive-growth-of-JUUL.pdf.

178   By contrast: "United States 2017 Results," High School YRBS, U.S.
      Centers for Disease Control and Prevention (website), https://nccd.cdc
      .gov/Youthonline/App/Results.aspx?TT=A&OUT=0&SID=HS&QID
      =QQ&LID=XX&YID=2017&LID2=&YID2=&COL=S&ROW1
      =N&ROW2=N&HT=QQ&LCT=LL&FS=S1&FR=R1&FG=G1&FA
      =A1&FI=I1&FP=P1&FSL=S1&FRL=R1&FGL=G1&FAL=A1&FIL
      =I1&FPL=P1&PV=&TST=False&C1=&C2=&QP=G&DP=1&VA=CI&CS
      =Y&SYID=&EYID=&SC=DEFAULT&SO=ASC.

178 An analysis of : Allison M. Glasser et al., "Youth Vaping and Tobacco Use in Context in the United States: Results from the 2018 National Youth Tobacco Survey," *Nicotine & Tobacco Research* 23, no. 14 (January 2020), https://doi.org/10.1093/ntr/ntaa010.

178 "We must close": "Results from 2018 National Youth Tobacco Survey Shows Dramatic Increase in E-cigarette Use among Youth over Past Year," news release, U.S. Food and Drug Administration, November 15, 2018, https://www.fda.gov/news-events/press-announcements/results-2018 -national-youth-tobacco-survey-show-dramatic-increase-e-cigarette-use -among-youth-over.

179 Gottlieb was even: U.S. FDA, "Statement from FDA Commissioner Scott Gottlieb."

179 Youth vaping was: Jamie Ducharme, "Are E-cigarettes Safe? Here's What the Science Says," *Time*, November 2, 2018, https://time.com/5442252/are -e-cigarettes-safe/.

179 Altria also agreed: Letter from Altria CEO Howard A. Willard III to Senator Richard J. Durbin et al.

179 On November 28: Dana Mattioli and Jennifer Maloney, "Altria in Talks to Take Significant Minority Stake in Juul Labs," *Wall Street Journal*, November 28, 2018, https://www.wsj.com/articles/altria-in-talks-to-take -significant-minority-stake-in-juul-labs-sources-1543438776?mod=hp _lead_pos3.

179 chaos erupted: Dan Primack, "Exclusive: Juul Employees Upset over Possible Altria Deal," Axios, November 30, 2018, https://www.axios.com /juul-employee-resistance-altria-marlboro-cigarette-11981f0e-0038-44d1 -a487-7b5c1b6d6321.html.

180 "We remain committed": Angelica LaVito, "Altria Shutters Its E-cigarette Brands as It Eyes Juul, Awaits Iqos Decision," CNBC, December 7, 2018, https://www.cnbc.com/2018/12/07/altria-closes-e-cigarette-brands-as-it -eyes-juul-awaits-iqos-decision.html.

181 Under the terms: Letter from Altria CEO Howard A. Willard III to Senator Richard J. Durbin et al.

185 staggering $2 billion: Angelica LaVito and David Faber, "Juul Employees Get a Special $2 Billion Bonus from Tobacco Giant Altria—to Be Split Among Its 1,500 Employees," CNBC, December 20, 2018, https://www .cnbc.com/2018/12/20/juul-to-pay-2-billion-dividend-to-its-employees -after-altria-deal.html.

186 The payouts reportedly: LaVito and Faber, "Juul Employees Get a Special $2 Billion Bonus."

186 to become billionaires: "#1941 James Monsees," Billionaires 2019, Forbes.com, https://www.forbes.com/profile/james-monsees/?sh =44e0ef20526b; and "#1941 Adam Bowen," Billionaires 2019, Forbes .com, https://www.forbes.com/profile/adam-bowen/?sh=4d51b9363dd2.

186 Major investors: Theodore Schleifer, "In an Extraordinary Move, Juul Is Trying to Make Peace with Its Investors and Employees by Paying Them More Than $4 Billion," Vox Recode via Tech News Tube, December 20, 2018, https://technewstube.com/recode/1063389/in-an-extraordinary-move-juul -is-trying-to-make-peace-with-its-investors-and-employees-by-paying-th/.

187 "#Juul: How Social": Michael Nedelman, Roni Selig, and Arman Azad, "#Juul: How Social Media Hyped Nicotine for a New Generation," CNN Health, December 19, 2018, https://www.cnn.com/2018/12/17/health/juul -social-media-influencers/index.html.

187 On the same: "New Research Continues to Provide Data Regarding the Impact Juul Products Have on Smokers Trying to Switch from Combus-tible Cigarettes," news release, Juul Labs Inc., December 20, 2018, https:// www.juullabs.com/new-research-continues-to-provide-data-regarding -the-impact-juul-products-have-on-smokers-trying-to-switch-from -combustible-cigarettes/.

188 Juul "has lost": "Altria-Juul Deal Is Alarming Development for Pub-lic Health and Shows Need for Strong FDA Regulation," news release, Campaign for Tobacco-Free Kids, December 20, 2018, https://www .tobaccofreekids.org/press-releases/2018_12_20_altria_juul.

188 Burns admitted in: "JUUL Labs Issues Statement About Altria Minority Investment and Service Agreements," news release, December 20, 2018, Juul Labs Inc., https://www.prnewswire.com/news-releases/juul -labs-issues-statement-about-altria-minority-investment-and-service -agreements-300769518.html.

188 In an interview: Sheila Kaplan, "F.D.A. Accuses Juul and Altria of Back-ing Off Plan to Stop Youth Vaping," *New York Times*, January 4, 2019, https://www.nytimes.com/2019/01/04/health/fda-juul-altria-youth -vaping.html.

189 Juul's executives periodically: Email from Joanna Engelke, chief quality and regulatory officer at Juul Labs, to Lauren Roth, associate commis-sioner for policy at the U.S. Food and Drug Administration, subject line:

"Follow-up to JUUL November 13, 2018 Youth Action Plan: Restricted Distribution System Criteria," sent December 21, 2018.

189 the "worst offenders": Lauren Hirsch (@LaurenSHirsch), ".@ScottGott-liebMD says that Altria and Juul were the 'worst offenders' of going around FDA...," tweet on August 15, 2019, https://twitter.com/Lauren-SHirsch/status/1162107553280606209.

189 "I have never": Lachlan Markay and Sam Stein, "Juul Spins Vaping as 'Criminal Justice' Issue for Black Lawmakers," *Daily Beast*, June 10, 2019, https://www.thedailybeast.com/juuls-latest-play-to-survive-washington-dc-win-over-black-lawmakers.

191 eighty-seven thousand: "Sen. Richard Burr—North Carolina," Congress, OpenSecrets.org, https://www.opensecrets.org/members-of-congress/richard-burr/contributors?cid=N00002221&cycle=2018&type=C.

191 "If you believe": Steven T. Dennis, "GOP Senator Lights Up Trump's FDA Chief on Menthol Cigarette Ban," Bloomberg, January 31, 2019, https://www.bloomberg.com/news/articles/2019-01-31/gop-senator-lights-up-trump-s-fda-chief-on-menthol-cigarette-ban?sref=Qe05mWTE.

192 "the best job": Angelica LaVito, "Outgoing FDA Chief Scott Gottlieb Gets Personal About Leaving 'the Best Job' He's Ever Had," CNBC, March 31, 2019, https://www.cnbc.com/2019/03/31/outgoing-fda-chief-gottlieb-gets-personal-about-leaving-the-best-job.html.

192 "It was getting": Ducharme, "'It Tortures Me That I'm Not There Helping.'"

192 On March 13: Calendar invitation from Ann Simoneau, director of the Office of Compliance and Enforcement at the U.S. Food and Drug Administration's Center for Tobacco Products, subject line: "Commissioner Meeting with Altria and JUUL Labs."

192 White Oak campus: U.S. Food and Drug Administration, "Welcome to FDA's White Oak Campus," video, YouTube, April 19, 2017, https://www.youtube.com/watch?v=DqimZYtaqHw.

193 In a press statement: "Statement from FDA Commissioner Scott Gottlieb, M.D., on Advancing New Policies Aimed at Preventing Youth Access to, and Appeal of, Flavored Tobacco Products, Including E-cigarettes and Cigars," news release, U.S. Food and Drug Administration, March 13, 2019.

194 Morning Consult poll: Yusra Murad, "Juul Takes a Hit After a Long

Year," Morning Consult, September 16, 2019, https://morningconsult.
com/2019/09/16/juul-takes-a-hit-after-a-long-year/.

195 San Francisco residents: Rebekah Moan, "Dogpatch and Potrero Hill
Residents Unhappy About JUUL's Presence at Pier 70," *Potrero View*,
January 2019, https://www.potreroview.net/dogpatch-and-potrero-hill
-residents-unhappy-about-juuls-presence-at-pier-70/.

195 "We demand that": Moan, "Dogpatch and Potrero Hill Residents Unhappy."

195 At the time: Andrew Sheeler, "Vaping Could Be Snuffed Out in California if These Bills Become Law in 2019," *Sacramento Bee*, December 20,
2018, https://www.sacbee.com/news/politics-government/capitol-alert
/article222819750.html.

196 "San Francisco has": "Herrera, Walton Introduce Package of Legislation
to Protect Youth from E-cigarettes," news release, Office of the City
Attorney of San Francisco, March 19, 2019, https://www.sfcityattorney
.org/2019/03/19/herrera-walton-introduce-package-of-legislation-to
-protect-youth-from-e-cigarettes/.

196 In March 2019: Office of the City Attorney of San Francisco, "Herrera,
Walton Introduce Package of Legislation."

196 to heart disease: "E-cigarettes Linked to Heart Attacks, Coronary Artery
Disease and Depression: Data Reveal Toll of Vaping; Researchers Say
Switching to E-cigarettes Doesn't Eliminate Health Risks," news release,
American College of Cardiology, March 7, 2019, www.sciencedaily.com
/releases/2019/03/190307103111.htm.

196 respiratory issues: M. F. Perez et al., "E-cigarette Use Is Associated with
Emphysema, Chronic Bronchitis and COPD," presentation at American
Thoracic Society International Conference 2018, San Diego, CA, May 23,
2018, https://www.abstractsonline.com/pp8/#!/4499/presentation/19432).

196 and DNA damage: "E-cigarettes Can Damage DNA," news release,
American Chemical Society, August 20, 2018, https://www.acs.org
/content/acs/en/pressroom/newsreleases/2018/august/e-cigarettes-can
-damage-dna.html.

196 "It just absolutely": Ducharme, "How Juul Hooked Kids."

198 Juul-backed policy: "An Act to Prevent Youth Use of Vapor Products,"
initiative measure to be submitted directly to the voter, filed in San
Francisco, CA, on May 14, 2019, https://sfelections.sfgov.org/sites/default
/files/Documents/candidates/Nov2019_YouthVaporUse_LegalText.pdf.

198 ban became final: Laura Klivans, "San Francisco Bans Sales of
E-cigarettes," Public Health, NPR, June 25, 2019, https://www.npr.org
/sections/health-shots/2019/06/25/735714009/san-francisco-poised-to
-ban-sales-of-e-cigarettes.

199 In May 2019: American Academy of Pediatrics v. Food and Drug
Administration, case no. PWG-18-883, Memorandum Opinion and
Order, filed July 12, 2019.

199 The same month: "Attorney General Josh Stein Takes E-cigarette Maker
JUUL to Court," news release, Office of Attorney General Josh Stein,
May 15, 2019, https://ncdoj.gov/attorney-general-josh-stein-takes
-e-cigarette-make/.

199 twenty-eight-story: Catherine Ho, "Fast-Growing Juul Buys San Francisco
Office Tower," *San Francisco Chronicle*, June 19, 2019, https://www
.sfchronicle.com/business/article/Fast-growing-Juul-buys-San-Francisco
-office-tower-14015422.php.

199 a marketing makeover: Erik Oster, "Juul Halts Most U.S. Advertising
After Spending $104 Million in First Half of 2019," *AdWeek*, September
25, 2019, https://www.adweek.com/brand-marketing/juul-halts-mosts-u
-s-advertising-after-spending-104-million-in-first-half-of-2019/.

199 "I was a": E. J. Schultz, "Omnicom Cuts Ties with Embattled E-cigarette
Maker Juul," *AdAge*, September 27, 2019, https://adage.com/article/cmo
-strategy/omnicom-cuts-ties-embattled-e-cigarette-maker-juul/2202471.

200 the "existential threat": Ducharme, "How Juul Hooked Kids."

200 "We're more than": Jamie Ducharme, "Pulling Flavored E-cigs Hurt Sales in
a 'Very Meaningful Way,' Juul Founders Say," *Time*, April 24, 2019, https://
time.com/5574084/juul-adam-bowen-james-monsees-time-100-gala/.

200 multimillion-dollar machine: "Altria Group," Organizations, Influence &
Lobbying, OpenSecrets.org, https://www.opensecrets.org/orgs/summary
?id=D000000067.

200 Juul spent $4.3 million: "Juul Labs," Organizations, Influence &
Lobbying, OpenSecrets.org, https://www.opensecrets.org/orgs/summary
?lobcycle=2018&topnumcycle=2020&toprecipcycle=2020&contribcycle
=2020&outspendcycle=2020&id=D000070920.

200 more than $10.4 million: "Client Profile: Altria Group," Clients, Lobbying,
OpenSecrets.org, last accessed January 1, 2021, https://www.opensecrets
.org/federal-lobbying/clients/summary?cycle=2019&id=d000000067.

200 doubled down on: Angelica LaVito, "Campaign to Raise Minimum

Smoking Age to 21 Finds Unlikely Supporter: Big Tobacco," CNBC, May 12, 2019, https://www.cnbc.com/2019/05/11/juul-altria-british-american -tobacco-push-t21-laws-amid-teen-vaping-epidemic.html.

200   criminal justice issue: Markay and Stein, "Juul Spins Vaping."

200   In the 1950s: Phillip S. Gardiner, "The African Americanization of Men- thol Cigarette Use in the United States," *Nicotine & Tobacco Research* 6, no. 1 (February 2004): 55-65, http://www.acbhcs.org /wp-content/uploads/2017/11/African_Americanization.pdf.

201   70 percent: "African Americans and Tobacco Use," Tobacco-Related Disparities, U.S. Centers for Disease Control and Prevention (website), https://www.cdc.gov/tobacco/disparities/african-americans/index.htm.

201   In a statement: Markay and Stein, "Juul Spins Vaping."

201   "Juul doesn't have": Sheila Kaplan, "Black Leaders Denounce Juul's $7.5 Million Gift to Medical School," *New York Times*, June 19, 2019, https:// www.nytimes.com/2019/06/19/science/juul-meharry-grant-vaping.html.

201   health groups began: Liz Essley Whyte and Dianna Náñez, "Big Tobac- co's Surprising New Campaign to Raise the Smoking Age," Center for Public Integrity, May 23, 2019, https://publicintegrity.org/state-politics /copy-paste-legislate/big-tobaccos-surprising-new-campaign-to-raise -the-smoking-age/.

201   Sometimes they exempted: Whyte and Náñez, "Big Tobacco's Surprising New Campaign."

202   "The tobacco companies": Whyte and Náñez, "Big Tobacco's Surprising New Campaign."

202   In 2018: Stephanie M. Lee, "Juul Employees Say 'Morale Is at an All- Time Low' After Its Worst Year Ever," BuzzFeed.News, February 5, 2020, https://www.buzzfeednews.com/article/stephaniemlee/juul-low-morale.

205   Raja Krishnamoorthi never: Jamie Ducharme, "The D.C. Lawmaker Going Toe to Toe with Big Vape Never Planned to Be in This Fight," *Time*, December 10, 2019, https://time.com/5731818/raja-krishnamoorthi -juul/.

206   In June 2019: "Chairman Krishnamoorthi of the Subcommittee on Eco- nomic and Consumer Policy Opens Investigation into JUUL's Role in the Youth E-cigarette Epidemic," news release, Office of United States Con- gressman Raja Krishnamoorthi, June 10, 2019, https://krishnamoorthi .house.gov/media/press-releases/chairman-krishnamoorthi -subcommittee-economic-and-consumer-policy-opens.

206 Much of what: Ducharme, "The D.C. Lawmaker."

206 "one of the": Ducharme, "Pulling Flavored E-cigs."

207 Dr. Jonathan Winickoff: *Examining Juul's Role in the Youth Nicotine Epidemic: Part I, Hearings Before the Subcommittee on Economic and Consumer Policy*, 116th Cong. (2019) [hereafter *Examining Juul's Role in the Youth Nicotine Epidemic: Part I*] (testimony of Dr. Jonathan Winickoff), pp. 8–9.

207 Robert Jackler: *Examining Juul's Role in the Youth Nicotine Epidemic: Part I* (testimony of Dr. Robert Jackler), pp. 9–11.

208 Meredith Berkman: *Examining Juul's Role in the Youth Nicotine Epidemic: Part I* (testimony of Meredith Berkman), pp. 4–6.

208 American Indians smoke: "American Indians/Alaska Natives and Tobacco Use," Tobacco-Related Disparities, U.S. Centers for Disease Control and Prevention (website), https://www.cdc.gov/tobacco/disparities/american -indians/index.htm.

208 as sovereign nations: "Tribal Commercial Tobacco Control," Public Health Law Center (website), https://publichealthlawcenter.org/topics /commercial-tobacco-control/tribal-commercial-tobacco-control.

208 Testifying before Congress: *Examining Juul's Role in the Youth Nicotine Epidemic: Part I* (testimony of Rae O'Leary), pp. 6–8.

208 They were midway: Video taken by Rae O'Leary, January 2019.

208 company later described: Memorandum from Staff of the Subcommittee on Economic and Consumer Policy to Democratic Members of the Subcommittee, "Update on the Subcommittee's E-cigarette Investigation," dated February 5, 2020.

209 "The CRST may": *Examining Juul's Role in the Youth Nicotine Epidemic: Part I* (testimony of Rae O'Leary), pp. 6–8.

209 echoes of Big Tobacco: Lauren K. Lempert and Stanton A. Glantz, "Tobacco Industry Promotional Strategies Targeting American Indians/ Alaska Natives and Exploiting Tribal Sovereignty," *Nicotine & Tobacco Research* 21, no. 7 (July 2019): 940–48, https://doi.org/10.1093/ntr/nty048.

209 Cigarette companies had: Lempert and Glantz, "Tobacco Industry Promotional Strategies Targeting American Indians/Alaska Natives."

209 "It's a little": Jamie Ducharme, "'It's Insidious': How Juul Pitched E-cigs to Native American Tribes," *Time*, February 6, 2020, https://time.com /5778534/juul-native-american-tribes/.

209 A few months: Memorandum from Staff of the Subcommittee on Eco-

nomic and Consumer Policy to Democratic Members of the Subcommittee, "Update on the Subcommittee's E-cigarette Investigation," dated February 5, 2020.

209 "Make no mistake": *Examining Juul's Role in the Youth Nicotine Epidemic: Part I* (testimony of Richard Durbin), p.32.

210 James was up: *Examining Juul's Role in the Youth Nicotine Epidemic: Part II* (testimony and questioning of James Monsees).

213 when Ashley Gould: *Examining Juul's Role in the Youth Nicotine Epidemic: Part II* (testimony and questioning of Ashley Gould).

214 Daniel Ament: Jamie Ducharme, "The Teenager Who Needed a Double Lung Transplant Because He Vaped Has Something to Say," *Time*, January 31, 2020, https://time.com/5771181/double-lung-transplant-vaping/.

218 a cluster of: "CDC, States Investigating Severe Pulmonary Disease Among People Who Use E-cigarettes," news release, U.S. Centers for Disease Control and Prevention, August 17, 2019, https://www.cdc.gov/media/releases/2019/s0817-pulmonary-disease-ecigarettes.html.

218 Chance Ammirata: Chance Ammirata (@Chanceammirata), "PLEASE RETWEET THIS IS EFFECTING THE WORLD AND WE ARE THE ONES WHO CAN EFFECT CHANGE. DO NOT STOP SHARING TO SAVE LIVES. I WILL BE THE EXAMPLE IF IT MEANS NO ONE ELSE NEEDS TO BE!," tweet on Twitter, August 4, 2019, https://twitter.com/Chanceammirata/status/1158204231989571590.

218 Simah Herman: Simah Herman (@simahherman), private Instagram post, August 2019.

219 On August 23: U.S. Centers for Disease Control and Prevention, "Transcript of August 23, 2019, Telebriefing on Severe Pulmonary Disease Associated with Use of E-cigarettes," transcript, August 23, 2019, https://www.cdc.gov/media/releases/2019/t0823-telebriefing-severe-pulmonary-disease-e-cigarettes.html.

219 "This tragic death": "CDC Director's Statement on the First Death Related to the Outbreak of Severe Lung Disease in People Who Use E-cigarette or 'Vaping' Devices," news release, U.S. Centers for Disease Control and Prevention, August 23, 2019, https://www.cdc.gov/media/releases/2019/s0823-vaping-related-death.html.

220 When the CDC: U.S. Centers for Disease Control and Prevention, "Transcript of August 23, 2019 Telebriefing."

221 Google searches for: Sara Kalkhoran, Yuchiao Chang, and Nancy

Rigotti, "Online Searches for Quitting Vaping During the 2019 Outbreak of E-cigarette or Vaping Product Use-Associated Lung Injury," *Journal of Internal Medicine* 36 (February 2020): 559–60, https://doi.org/10.1007/s11606-020-05686-5.

221 an on-camera interview: Tony Dokoupil, "Juul CEO: Breathing Illness Cases Are 'Worrisome,'" *CBS This Morning*, August 28, 2019, https://www.cbsnews.com/news/juul-ceo-kevin-burns-breathing-illness-cases-are-worrisome/.

223 a glowing piece: Melinda Tichelaar, "Who Wants to Be a Millionaire? Busy Westosha Student Already on His Way," *Kenosha News*, April 26, 2018, https://www.kenoshanews.com/news/local/who-wants-to-be-a-millionaire-busy-westosha-student-already-on-his-way/article_90eaa3ef-30af-5b0d-8c9b-91b97e598c20.html.

223 She'd allegedly used: Stephen S. Hall, "Who Thought Sucking on a Battery Was a Good Idea?," *New York* (Intelligencer), February 4, 2020, https://nymag.com/intelligencer/2020/02/vaping-health-crisis.html.

225 Juul was pulled: Sheila Kaplan and Matt Richtel, "The Mysterious Vaping Illness that's 'Becoming an Epidemic,'" *New York Times*, August 31, 2019, https://www.nytimes.com/2019/08/31/health/vaping-marijuana-ecigarettes-sickness.html.

226 vitamin E acetate: "New York State Department of Health Announces Update on Investigation into Vaping-Associated Pulmonary Illnesses," news release, New York State Department of Health, September 5, 2019, https://www.health.ny.gov/press/releases/2019/2019-09-05_vaping.htm.

226 sister organization, Pax: "PAX Statement on Product Safety," news release, Pax Labs Inc., September 11, 2019, https://www.pax.com/blogs/press/pax-statement-on-product-safety.

226 Producers could sell: Marissa Wenzke and David Downs, "From 'Veronica Mars' to Toxic Vapes: The Rise and Fall of Honey Cut," *Leafly*, November 8, 2019, https://www.leafly.com/news/health/toxic-vaping-vapi-evali-lung-injury-rise-and-fall-of-vitamin-e-oil-honey-cut.

226 vitamin E acetate solutions: Wenzke and Downs, "From 'Veronica Mars' to Toxic Vapes."

226 while typically harmless: "Outbreak of Lung Injury Associated with the Use of E-Cigarette, or Vaping, Products," Electronic Cigarettes, Basic Information, U.S. Centers for Disease Control and Prevention (website), https://www.cdc.gov/tobacco/basic_information/e-cigarettes/severe-lung-disease.html.

226   On September 5: New York State Department of Health, "New York State
      Department of Health Announces Update."

227   the CDC specifically: "Initial State Findings Point to Clinical Similarities
      in Illnesses Among People Who Use E-cigarettes or 'Vape,'" news release,
      U.S. Centers for Disease Control and Prevention, September 6, 2019, https://
      www.cdc.gov/media/releases/2019/p0906-vaping-related-illness.html.

227   In mid-September: "Sheriff's Office Busts Illegal THC Vape Cartridge
      Operation in North Phoenix," azfamily.com, September 18, 2019, https://
      www.azfamily.com/news/sheriff-s-office-busts-illegal-thc-vape-cartridge
      -operation-in-north-phoenix/article_16d9501a-da44-11e9-bcad
      -472669780f57.html.

227   The following week: Estefan Saucedo and Jennifer Austin, "Nearly 77,000
      Illegal THC Vaping Cartridges Seized in Record Drug Bust," Kare 11,
      September 24, 2019, https://www.kare11.com/article/news/crime/75000
      -thc-vaping-cartridges-seized-in-record-drug-bust/89-88b92c27-cd4e
      -4fca-91c5-ad44dd49d2ff.

227   Days after that: Brad Zinn, "1,000 THC Vaping Cartridges Seized in
      Waynesboro Drug Bust," *News Leader*, September 25, 2019, https://
      www.newsleader.com/story/news/local/2019/09/25/1-000-thc-vaping
      -cartridges-seized-waynesboro-drug-bust/2442664001/.

227   By the summer: Michael Maciag, "State Marijuana Laws in 2019 Map,"
      Governing, June 25, 2019, https://www.governing.com/gov-data/safety
      -justice/state-marijuana-laws-map-medical-recreational.html.

228   The FDA does not: Sharon Lindan Mayl and Douglas C. Throckmorton,
      "FDA Role in Regulation of Cannabis Products," PowerPoint presenta-
      tion delivered at the National Institute on Drug Abuse, Bethesda, MD,
      February 2019, https://www.fda.gov/media/128156/download.

228   Some states do: Jamie Ducharme, "Is Vaping Marijuana Safe? Deaths and
      Lung Disease Linked to E-cigs Call That into Question," *Time*, September
      6, 2019, https://time.com/5670147/vaping-marijuana-lung-disease/.

229   Dank Vapes boxes: Emma Betuel, "Dank Vapes Is the 'Biggest Con-
      spiracy' in Pot That Can Put You in a Coma," *Inverse*, August 19, 2019,
      https://www.inverse.com/mind-body/58581-dank-vapes.

229   The FDA had: Kelly Young, "FDA Cautions People to Avoid Vaping
      Products with THC Oil, Vitamin E Acetate," *NEJM Journal Watch*,
      September 10, 2019, https://www.jwatch.org/fw115806/2019/09/10/fda
      -cautions-people-avoid-vaping-products-with-thc-oil.

230   By mid-September 2019: Chris Kahn, "More Americans Say Vaping Is as Dangerous as Smoking Cigarette: Reuters Poll," Reuters, September 24, 2019, https://www.reuters.com/article/us-health-vaping-poll/more-americans-say-vaping-is-as-dangerous-as-smoking-cigarettes-reuters-poll-idUSKBN1W9136.

231   e-cigarette product sales: Fatma Romeh M. Ali et al., "E-cigarette Unit Sales, by Product and Flavor Type—United States, 2014–2020," *Morbidity and Mortality Weekly Report* 69, no. 37 (September 2020): 1313–18, https://www.cdc.gov/mmwr/volumes/69/wr/mm6937e2.htm.

231   Eighty percent: Jim McDonald, "Vape Shops Blame Sales Decline More on 'EVALI' than COVID-19," Vaping360, November 30, 2020, https://vaping360.com/vape-news/107279/vape-shops-blame-sales-decline-more-on-evali-than-covid-19/.

231   Even though its products: Jasmine Wu, "E-cigarette Sales Slowing, Led by JUUL, Amid Negative Headlines," CNBC, October 1, 2019, https://www.cnbc.com/2019/10/01/e-cigarette-sales-slowing-led-by-juul-amid-negative-headlines.html.

231   Michigan governor: "Governor Whitmer Takes Bold Action to Protect Michigan Kids from Harmful Effects of Vaping," news release, Office of Governor Gretchen Whitmer, September 4, 2019, https://www.michigan.gov/whitmer/0,9309,7-387-90499_90640-506450--,00.html.

232   On September 9: Warning letter from Ann Simoneau, director of the office of compliance and enforcement at the U.S. Food and Drug Administration's Center for Tobacco Products, to Juul CEO Kevin Burns, dated September 9, 2019, https://www.fda.gov/inspections-compliance-enforcement-and-criminal-investigations/warning-letters/juul-labs-inc-590950-09092019.

232   Juul risked: Warning letter from Ann Simoneau.

232   On September 11: The White House, "Remarks by President Trump in Meeting on E-cigarettes," transcript, September 11, 2019, https://www.whitehouse.gov/briefings-statements/remarks-president-trump-meeting-e-cigarettes/.

233   Mango and Mint: Letter from Altria CEO Howard A. Willard III to Senators Richard J. Durbin et al.

233   Brands like Vuse: Angelica LaVito, "Juul's Momentum Slips as NJOY Woos Customers with Dollar E-Cigarettes," CNBC, August 20, 2019, https://www.cnbc.com/2019/08/20/juuls-momentum-slips-as-njoy-woos-customers-with-dollar-e-cigarettes.html.

233 On September 15: Jesse McKinley and Christina Goldbaum, "New York Moves to Ban Flavored E-cigarettes by Emergency Order," *New York Times*, September 15, 2019, https://www.nytimes.com/2019/09/15/nyregion/vaping-ban-ny.html.

233 On September 19: "Suozzi Introduces Bipartisan Legislation to Address the Vaping and Smoking Epidemic," news release, Office of U.S. Congressman Thomas Suozzi, September 19, 2019, https://suozzi.house.gov/media/press-releases/suozzi-introduces-bipartisan-legislation-address-vaping-and-smoking-epidemic.

233 Massachusetts came next: Office of the Governor of the Commonwealth of Massachusetts, "Governor's Declaration of Emergency," declaration, September 24, 2019, https://www.mass.gov/files/documents/2019/09/24/Governors-Declaration-of-Emergency.pdf.

233 Rhode Island, Montana, Washington: Jamie Ducharme, "As the Number of Vaping-Related Deaths Climbs, These States Have Implemented E-cigarette Bans," *Time*, September 25, 2019, https://time.com/5685936/state-vaping-bans/.

233 which relied on: Ali et al., "E-cigarette Unit Sales, by Product and Flavor Type."

233 from Montana: Renata Birkenbuel, "'We Vape, We Vote': Missoula Vape Shop Owners Sound Off on Trump, FDA," *Missoula Current*, September 13, 2019, https://missoulacurrent.com/business/2019/09/missoula-vape-shops/.

233 to Rhode Island: Kevin G. Andrade, "Store Owners, Employees Rally in Support of Vaping Products," *Providence Journal*, September 25, 2019, https://www.providencejournal.com/news/20190925/store-owners-employees-rally-in-support-of-vaping-products--poll.

235 almost a third: "Tobacco in China," Tobacco, Health Topics, the World Health Organization (website), last accessed January 2, 2021, https://www.who.int/china/health-topics/tobacco.

235 China National Tobacco Corporation: Tom Hancock, "China Tobacco Looks to Take on Global Cigarette Makers," *Financial Times*, April 3, 2019, https://www.ft.com/content/6c820eb0-51fc-11e9-b401-8d9ef1626294.

236 in some hospitals: Palko Karasz, "Two U.K. Hospitals Allow Vape Shops in Bid to Promote Smoking Ban," *New York Times*, July 10, 2019, https://www.nytimes.com/2019/07/10/world/europe/uk-hospitals-vaping-shops.html.

237 "I have worked": "Juul Labs Names New Leadership, Outlines Changes

to Policy and Marketing Efforts," news release, Juul Labs Inc., September 25, 2019, https://www.juullabs.com/juul-labs-names-new-leadership -outlines-changes-to-policy-and-marketing-efforts/.

238   It didn't hurt: Catherine Ho, "Juul New CEO Is from Big Tobacco. That May Help It Survive," *San Francisco Chronicle*, September 25, 2019, https://www.sfchronicle.com/business/article/Juul-s-new-CEO-is-from -Big-Tobacco-That-may-14468383.php.

239   Joe Murillo: Jennifer Maloney, "Juul Hires Another Top Altria Executive," *Wall Street Journal*, October 1, 2019, https://www.wsj.com/articles /juul-hires-another-top-altria-executive-11569971306.

240   First, he halted: Juul Labs, "Juul Labs Names New Leadership."

240   Next, he pulled: Catherine Ho, "Juul Ends Support for Prop. C, SF Measure to Overturn E-cigarette Sales Ban," *San Francisco Chronicle*, September 30, 2019, https://www.sfchronicle.com/business/article/Juul-to -end-support-for-Prop-C-SF-measure-to-14481579.php.

240   And in mid-October: Angelica LaVito, "E-cigarette Giant Juul Suspends Sales of All Fruity Flavors Ahead of Looming US Ban," CNBC, October 17, 2019, https://www.cnbc.com/2019/10/17/e-cigarette-giant-juul -suspends-sales-of-fruity-flavors-ahead-of-looming-ban.html.

240   Mango alone had: Letter from Altria CEO Howard A. Willard III to Senator Richard J. Durbin et al.

241   "Dust hasn't settled": Anonymous, "Company's Long Term Outlook Is Still Strong. Good Margins, Strong Brand Recognition Among Smokers, Clear Market Need for It, etc. . . . ," post on Blind [Anoymous Professional Network], October 18, 2019.

242   In October 2019: Angelica LaVito, "Juul Names New CFO Amid Management Shake-Up, Several Top Executives Are Out," CNBC, October 29, 2019, https://www.cnbc.com/2019/10/29/juul-ousts-executives-names -new-cfo-amid-shakeup-at-the-embattled-e-cigarette-company.html.

242   Other Juul executives: LaVito, "Juul Names New CFO Amid Management Shake-Up."

242   cut five hundred jobs: Jennifer Maloney, "Juul to Cut About 500 Jobs," *Wall Street Journal*, October 29, 2019, https://www.wsj.com/articles/juul -to-cut-about-500-jobs-11572301778.

243   In a lawsuit: Siddharth Breja v. Juul Labs, Inc., Case no. 3:19-CV-7148, Complaint for Damages and Injunctive Relief, filed October 29, 2019.

244   In December 2019: Siddharth Breja v. Juul Labs, Inc., Case no. 3:19-CV-7148-WHO, Declaration of Harmeet K. Dhillon in Support of Dhillon Law Group Inc.'s *Ex Parte* Motion to Withdraw as Counsel of Record for Plaintiff and for an Extension of the Hearing and Briefing Deadlines on Defendant Juul Labs, Inc.'s Motion to Compel Arbitration, filed December 10, 2019, https://www.documentcloud.org/documents/6585599-Declaration-in-Support-of-Dhillon-Law-Group-s-Ex.html.

244   by BuzzFeed.News: Stephanie M. Lee, "Leaked Juul Documents Cast Doubt on a Former Executive's Claim of 1 Million 'Contaminated' Pods," BuzzFeed.News, December 18, 2019, https://www.buzzfeednews.com/article/stephaniemlee/juul-report-contamination-lawsuit.

244   Only 143 customers: Juul Labs, Fielded Product Assessment Form, report number RPT-01333 Rev B, August 2019, https://www.documentcloud.org/documents/6580991-Juul-Report-BuzzFeed-News.html.

245   It was posted: Benjamin C. Blount et al., "Evaluation of Bronchoalveolar Lavage Fluid from Patients in an Outbreak of E-cigarette, or Vaping, Product Use-Associated Lung Injury—10 States, August–October 2019," *Morbidity and Mortality Weekly Report* 68, no. 45 (November 2019): 1040–41, https://www.cdc.gov/mmwr/volumes/68/wr/mm6845e2.htm.

245   both India: Lauren Frayer, "India Banned E-cigarettes—but Beedis and Chewing Tobacco Remain Widespread," NPR, October 9, 2019, https://www.npr.org/sections/goatsandsoda/2019/10/09/768397209/india-banned-e-cigarettes-but-beedis-and-chewing-tobacco-remain-widespread.

245   and China: Elsie Chen and Alexandra Stevenson, "China Effectively Bans Online Sales of E-cigarettes," *New York Times*, November 1, 2019, https://www.nytimes.com/2019/11/01/business/china-vaping-electronic-cigarettes.html.

246   Crosthwaite decided to: "Juul Pulls Its Mint-Flavored Pods from the Market," *Convenience Store News*, November 8, 2019, https://csnews.com/juul-pulls-its-mint-flavored-pods-market.

246   At the time: Angelica LaVito, "Juul Halts Sales of Its Popular Mint Flavor," CNBC, November 7, 2019, https://www.cnbc.com/2019/11/07/juul-halts-sales-of-its-popular-mint-flavor.html.

247 from California: "Attorney General Becerra and Los Angeles Leaders Announce Lawsuit Against JUUL for Deceptive Marketing Practices Targeting Underage Californians and Endangering Users of Its Vaping Products," news release, Office of Attorney General Xavier Becerra, November 18, 2019, https://oag.ca.gov/news/press-releases/attorney -general-becerra-and-los-angeles-leaders-announce-lawsuit-against-juul.

247 and New York: "Attorney General James Sues JUUL Labs," news release, Office of New York Attorney General Letitia James, November 19, 2019, https://ag.ny.gov/press-release/attorney-general-james-sues -juul-labs.

247 Several school districts: Alexa Lardieri, "Three School Districts Sue Juul Labs over E-cigarette Use," *U.S. News & World Report*, October 8, 2019, https://www.usnews.com/news/education-news/articles/2019-10-08 /three-school-districts-sue-juul-labs-over-e-cigarette-use-in-schools.

247 That fall, Altria: Angelica LaVito, "Altria Writes Down Investment in Troubled E-cigarette Maker Juul by $4.5 Billion," CNBC, October 31, 2019, https://www.cnbc.com/2019/10/31/altria-writes-down-juul -investment-by-4point5-billion.html.

247 It was a significant: Taylor Nicole Rogers, "Juul Is Cutting 500 Jobs by the End of the Year, and Its Cofounders Have Both Lost Their Billionaire Status After Less Than 10 Months in the 3-Comma Club," Business Insider, October 29, 2019, https://www.businessinsider.com /juul-cofounders-adam-bowen-james-monsees-no-longer-billionaires -2019-10.

249 another hearing: *The Federal Response to the Epidemic of E-cigarette Use, Especially Among Children, and the Food and Drug Administration's Compliance Policy, Hearings Before the Subcommittee on Economic and Consumer Policy*, 116th Cong. (testimony of Mitch Zeller, director of the U.S. Food and Drug Administration's Center for Tobacco Products).

249 raised the legal: "Newly Signed Legislation Raises Federal Minimum Age of Sale of Tobacco Products to 21," CTP Newsroom, Tobacco Products, U.S. Food and Drug Administration (website), January 15, 2020, https:// www.fda.gov/tobacco-products/ctp-newsroom/newly-signed-legislation -raises-federal-minimum-age-sale-tobacco-products-21.

249 It at least: Jamie Ducharme, "The Federal Legal Age to Buy Tobacco Prod-

ucts Has Been Raised to 21: Here's What That Could Do to the Vaping Industry," *Time*, December 20, 2019, https://time.com/5753106/tobacco-21 -vaping-industry/.

250 Shortly after the: "FDA Finalizes Enforcement Policy on Unauthorized Flavored Cartridge-Based E-cigarettes That Appeal to Children, Including Fruit and Mint," news release, U.S. Food and Drug Administration, January 2, 2020, https://www.fda.gov/news-events/press-announcements/fda -finalizes-enforcement-policy-unauthorized-flavored-cartridge-based-e -cigarettes-appeal-children.

250 Altria wrote down: Jennifer Maloney and Dave Michaels, "SEC Investigates Altria's Investment in Juul," *Wall Street Journal*, February 21, 2020, https://www.wsj.com/articles/sec-investigates-altrias-investment-in-juul -11582317475?mod=hp_lead_pos3.

250 "I'm highly disappointed": Jennifer Maloney, "Altria Takes $4.1 Billion Charge on Juul Investment," *Wall Street Journal*, January 30, 2020, https://www.wsj.com/articles/altria-takes-4-1-billion-writedown-on-juul -investment-11580386578.

250 The emergency brake: Jennifer Maloney, "Juul Scales Back Overseas Expansion," *Wall Street Journal*, January 15, 2020, https://www.wsj.com /articles/juul-scales-back-overseas-expansion-11579143865.

251 On a Thursday: Stephanie M. Lee, "Juul Cofounder James Monsees Is Stepping Down," BuzzFeed.News, March 12, 2020, https://www .buzzfeednews.com/article/stephaniemlee/juul-james-monsees-resigns.

253 Juul-funded research: Juul Labs, "New Research Continues to Provide Data."

254 A Cochrane analysis: Jamie Hartmann-Boyce et al., "Electronic Cigarettes for Smoking Cessation," Cochrane Database of Systematic Reviews 10 (October 2020), https://doi.org/10.1002/14651858.CD010216 .pub4.

254 34 million adult: "Smoking Cessation: A Report of the Surgeon General—Smoking Cessation by the Numbers," Tobacco, Reports & Publications, Surgeon General Home, U.S. Department of Health and Human Services (website), https://www.hhs.gov/surgeongeneral/reports -and-publications/tobacco/2020-cessation-sgr-infographic-by-the -numbers/index.html.

254 Recent CDC data: Maria A. Villarroel, Amy E. Cha, and Anjel Vahratian, "Electronic Cigarette Use Among U.S. Adults, 2018," National

Center for Health Statistics Data Brief, no. 365 (April 2020), https://www
.cdc.gov/nchs/products/databriefs/db365.htm.

254 DNA changes: Andrew W. Caliri et al., "Hypomethylation of LINE-1
Repeat Elements and Global Loss of DNA Hydroxymethylation in
Vapers and Smokers," *Epigenetics* 15, no. 8 (February 2020): 816–29,
https://doi.org/10.1080/15592294.2020.1724401.

254 most prominent papers: "Retraction to: Electronic Cigarette Use and
Myocardial Infarction Among Adults in the US Population Assessment of
Tobacco and Health," *Journal of the American Heart Association* 9, no. 4
(February 2020), https://www.ahajournals.org/doi/10.1161/JAHA.119.014519.

254 another 2019 study: Dharma N. Bhatta and Stanton A. Glantz, "Association of E-cigarette Use with Respiratory Disease Among Adults: A
Longitudinal Analysis," *American Journal of Preventive Medicine* 58,
no. 2 (February 2020): 182–90, https://doi.org/10.1016/j.amepre.2019
.07.028.

254 who retired: Email from Professor Pamela Ling to mailing list of Professor Stanton Glantz, subject line: "Stan Glantz has retired from UCSF,"
sent September 9, 2020.

255 thirty-nine state attorneys general: Chris Kirkham, "Juul Under Scrutiny by 39 State Attorneys General," Reuters, February 25, 2020, https://
www.reuters.com/article/us-juul-ecigarettes-investigation/juul-under
-scrutiny-by-39-state-attorneys-general-idUSKBN20J2JL.

255 one hundred school districts: Stephen Sawchuk and Denisa R. Superville,
"School Districts Are Suing JUUL over Youth Vaping: Do They Stand a
Chance?" *Education Week*, February 27, 2020 https://www.edweek.org
/policy-politics/school-districts-are-suing-juul-over-youth-vaping-do-they
-stand-a-chance/2020/02.

255 Hundreds of lawsuits: "Juul MDL Complaints Consolidate National
E-cigarette Cases," Law360, March 11, 2020, https://www.law360.com/articles
/1251860/juul-mdl-complaints-consolidate-national-e-cigarette-cases.

255 The Federal Trade Commission: In the Matter of Altria Group, Inc. and
Juul Labs, Inc., United States of America Before the Federal Trade Commission, docket no. 9393 public version, signed April 1, 2020.

255 Securities and Exchange Commission: Maloney and Michaels, "SEC
Investigates Altria's Investment in Juul."

255 Altria has repeatedly: Renata Geraldo, "Altria Cuts Juul Valuation to

Below $5 Billion," *Wall Street Journal*, October 30, 2020, https://www.wsj
.com/articles/altria-cuts-juul-valuation-to-below-5-billion-11604067336.

256 If that number: Letter from Altria CEO Howard A. Willard III to Senator Richard J. Durbin et al.

257 FDA had received: "Tobacco Product Marketing Orders," U.S. Food
and Drug Administration.

257 filed its long-awaited: "Juul Labs Submits Premarket Tobacco Product
Application to the U.S. Food and Drug Administration for the Juul
System," news release, Juul Labs Inc., July 30, 2020, https://www.juullabs
.com/juul-labs-submits-premarket-tobacco-product-application/.

257 There are signs: Teresa W. Wang et al., "E-cigarette Use Among Middle
and High School Students—United States, 2020," *Morbidity and Mortality Weekly Report* 69, no. 37 (September 2020): 1310–12, https://www.cdc
.gov/mmwr/volumes/69/wr/mm6937e1.htm.

258 disposable vaporizers: Allison Aubrey, "Parents: Teens Are Still Vaping,
Despite Flavor Ban. Here's What They're Using," NPR, February 17,
2020. https://www.npr.org/sections/health-shots/2020/02/17/805972087
/teens-are-still-vaping-flavors-thanks-to-new-disposable-vape-pens.

258 "Juul is almost": Aubrey, "Parents: Teens Are Still Vaping."

259 Richard Mumby: Richard Mumby (rpmumby), LinkedIn profile, https://
www.linkedin.com/in/rpmumby/.

259 Kevin Burns: Dan Primack, "Scoop: Ex-Juul CEO Has a New Job," Axios,
June 10, 2020, https://www.axios.com/juul-ceo-alto-7a816391-2b83-4a80
-8325-02a277b8c349.html.

259 Ashley Gould: Ashley Gould, LinkedIn profile.

259 Howard Willard: "Recovering from COVID-19, Altria CEO Howard
Willard Retires," Associated Press, April 17, 2020, https://apnews.com
/article/5b8c868a15afcaa05e7bbd708b0182fb.

259 Even Juul itself: Jennifer Maloney, "E-cigarette Maker Juul Is Moving
Base from San Francisco to Washington, D.C.," *Wall Street Journal*, May
5, 2020, https://www.wsj.com/articles/e-cigarette-maker-juul-is-leaving
-san-francisco-for-washington-d-c-11588640401.

259 pulled back from: Stephanie M. Lee, "Juul Will Stop Selling in Five European Countries, Including France and Spain," BuzzFeed.News, May 1,
2020, https://www.buzzfeednews.com/article/stephaniemlee/juul-europe
-leaving-france-spain.

259   plans to exit: Jennifer Maloney, "Juul to Cut More Than Half of Its Work-
      force," *Wall Street Journal*, September 3, 2020. https://www.wsj.com/articles
      /juul-to-cut-more-jobs-explore-exiting-europe-and-asia-11599091500.

259   "Popping anxiety pills": Anonymous, "Popping Anxiety Pills Like Tic Tacs,"
      post on Blind [Anonymous Professional Network], September 2, 2020.

259   Adam, at least: Ducharme, "How Juul Hooked Kids."

ACKNOWLEDGMENTS

First, I have to thank everyone who shared their time, energy, and expertise in interviews for this book. Your stories helped it come alive.

I owe so much to my incredibly sharp agent, Becky Sweren. Becky had a vision for this book from day one, and I could not have asked for a better shepherd through the process. Endless thanks to her and the whole team at Aevitas, including Allison Warren, Shenel Ekici-Moling, and Nan Thornton.

Among Becky's many contributions: landing this book at its best possible home, Henry Holt. Amy Einhorn and the whole Holt team showed this project so much enthusiasm right away, and I'm eternally grateful to Paul Golob for bringing me on board. Enormous thanks to James Melia, my editor/personal Kris Jenner, who made countless improvements to this book and edited with unflagging good humor and energy. Thank you also to Christopher O'Connell, Maggie Richards, Caitlin O'Shaughnessy, Marian Brown, Lori Kusatzky, and the many other people who worked on this book behind the scenes.

One of those people is Barbara Maddux, my talented fact-checker. I breathed many sighs of relief knowing I was working with someone so thorough and vigilant.

My colleagues at *Time* magazine also shaped this book. Thank you to

Mandy Oaklander, who was the first person to encourage me to write about vaping and who gave invaluable notes on my manuscript; Elijah Wolfson, who without hesitation gave me the time and support to do this project; Alice Park, Jeffrey Kluger, and Charlotte Alter, who were so generous in sharing their book-writing experiences; and Annabel Gutterman and Melissa Chan, who keep me entertained with countless Slack messages.

My friends also deserve deep thanks. Madeline Bilis's excitement in the Meredith cafeteria made me think I might actually be able to write this book, and her smart notes on the manuscript made it so much stronger. Kristen Gray, Nicole Chenelle, and Molly Donahue—New Hampshire's finest— continue to make me glad I had such good taste in friends as a teenager. Tom Minieri scouted Williamsburg's most scenic stoops in ninety-degree weather. And Emily, Jordan, Matt, Chris, Andrew, Kev, and Owen deserve medals for talking about vaping on so many Zoom calls.

My parents taught me to love reading and writing as soon as I could, and in so doing changed the course of my entire life. Nothing I have ever accomplished would be possible without their love, support, and encouragement, this book included. Sorry for being a pain when you tried to give me edits. Dustin, thanks for being the best possible example of rising above stress and staying cool. I love you guys.

Finally, my thanks aren't enough for Arthur, who talked me off so many ledges but encouraged me to take the plunge on this project when it mattered most. Thank you for always believing in me and this book, for letting me talk through every last anxiety and idea, and, most of all, for not leaving when I was absolutely certain I was the victim of an email hacking scheme. I'd be one foot short of a pair without you.

ABOUT THE AUTHOR

Jamie Ducharme is a staff writer at *Time* magazine, where she covers health and science. Her work has won awards from the Deadline Club, the New York Press Club, and the Newswomen's Club of New York. Originally from New Hampshire, Jamie now lives in Brooklyn. *Big Vape* is her first book.